Triumph
Of
Surrender

A Walk of Intimacy With Jesus

"Deep calls to deep ..."
~Psalm 42:7

Celeste Li, M.D.

Illustrated by John Li, M.D. and Joshua Rivaldo

PLUM
TREE
MINISTRIES

Triumph Series

Book I:
Triumph Over Suffering
A Spiritual Guide to Conquering Adversity

Book II:
Triumph Of Surrender
A Walk of Intimacy With Jesus

Book III:
Triumph in Warfare
Coming Soon!

Triumph Over Suffering Devotional
Hope in the Pain. Healing in His Presence.
By Cristina Williams,
with photography by Donna Briley

No profits are ever made from the sale of these books. All proceeds are given directly to the church or used to minister to the Body of Christ at large. Thank you for your love, prayers and support. May God bless you and your family with hope and healing.

-The Plum Tree Ministries Team

*Dedicated to those
who seek His face.*

*May you come to see Him as He truly is,
and to see yourself through His eyes.*

*Lord Jesus, my Rock and my Fortress,
You are my Hiding Place and my Shield,
my Strength and my Song.
In You I take refuge;
You surround me with songs of deliverance.
I have no words to express
the honor of being Your pen.
Please give to each one
who dives into this book
sweet and intense revelations of Your glory.
Amen.*

Jupiter, Florida
plumtreeministries@gmail.com
"The surviving remnant of the house of Judah will again take root downward and bear fruit upward." Isaiah 37:31

Cover photography and design by Alec Li.
Book design and layout by Donna Briley and Alec Li.

*If you find anything in this book helpful for your ministry –
whether your ministry is a formal teaching or
reaching out to a friend – you are welcome to teach it, reprint it,
copy it, quote it, or reproduce it in any format, including written,
visual, audio, or electronic, without my express permission.
I hope the Lord blesses you and others with it.
If you are using something that is footnoted,
please acknowledge the original author.*

Contents

Foreword by Julie Mullins   iii
Introduction   v

Part I: Intimacy Through Stillness   1

Chapter 1: "My Sheep Hear My Voice"   3
Chapter 2: Heaven Touches Earth   27
Chapter 3: Toppling Barriers to Intimacy   71

Part II: Intimacy Through Surrender   121

Chapter 4: Surrendering to His Sovereignty   123
Chapter 5: Demolishing Idols that Thwart
          Our Fellowship   161
Chapter 6: To Forgive As Jesus Forgives   197

Part III: Intimacy Through Sanctification   239

Chapter 7: The Life of the Heart   241
Chapter 8: A Walk of Repentance   277
Chapter 9: From Roots to Fruit   321

Appendix 1: Soaking in His Love   351
Appendix 2: Greek and Hebrew Words   356
Appendix 3: Resources   357

Endnotes   360
Acknowledgments   366
Contributors   369
Index: Detailed Table of Contents   370
About the Author   375

Foreword

Surrender ... I don't know about you, but this one word alone brings less than positive images to my mind. White flags that represent lost battles. Memories of childhood games played with my older brother, being forced to "give up," to surrender, because I had been out-smarted, outscored and outplayed ... again! (I am a bit competitive so this one stings!)

But there's another picture of surrender that was deeply embedded in my mind and heart a number of years ago. When my son, Jefferson, was just a toddler, his favorite time of day was when his father, Todd, would arrive home from work. Jefferson would stop everything he was doing and run as fast as he could into his dad's arms. Todd would pick him up, lock eyes, tell him how much he loved him and throw him in the air. At that point, Todd would then put him down, but Jefferson would raise his arms to be picked up again, and again, and again. There was so much joy wrapped up in those simple moments of a child in his father's arms! So much confidence and trust that those arms were strong enough to pick him up time and time again.

As the years went on, those same arms carried Jefferson when he was too tired to carry himself, comforted him in times of fear, and embraced him after times of correction. This is a picture of what our Heavenly Father does for us.

Surrender is about a relationship between a loving, strong, caring Father and His trusting children – children who have an intimate knowledge of who they are and *whose they are.*

When we come to Him as children who are confident in the strength and abilities of their Father, we begin to understand surrender. The more we get to know Him, the more we will trust Him.

This same picture of surrender is found throughout the pages of this book. This book is an invitation to a journey that will lead to a lifestyle of intimacy and complete trust in the One that can be completely trusted. This invitation is deeply personal. Celeste's writings could be compared to that of a passionate tour guide, taking you to the deep places that she has experienced and sharing the secrets that can only come from someone who has taken this journey herself and experienced true transformation. This book is an outflow of the life that she has lived and the people that she has brought along with her over the last several years. Her passion to guide others to a place of complete trust and confidence in their Heavenly Father has inspired me and so many others in our church family.

But be prepared ... a lifestyle of surrender may or may not change your *circumstances*, but it will undoubtedly change *you*. Remember, surrender isn't the finish line, it's the starting line. So get ready to jump into your Father's arms and experience the joy of surrender!

Julie Mullins
Christ Fellowship Church

Introduction
Deep Calls to Deep

As much as we all desire to hear the Lord's voice, I sense that the even deeper cry of our hearts is to truly *know* Him. We long to be able to trust the unfathomable depth of His love for us, and to depend upon Him for our every move. Jesus calls this total reliance upon Him *abiding*.

"Abide in Me, and I in you. As the branch cannot bear fruit of itself unless it abides in the vine, so neither can you unless you abide in Me. I am the vine, you are the branches; he who abides in Me and I in him, he bears much fruit, for apart from Me you can do nothing ... If you keep My commandments, you will abide in My love; just as I have kept My Father's commandments and abide in His love."

John 15:4-5, 10

Francis Frangipane writes, "We are called to abide in Him, not just visit with Him."[1] Indeed. Abiding is not merely visiting – abiding is *taking up residence*. It is waiting, not running ahead. Abiding is not merely obedience, but *utter dependence*, as a branch is attached to the Vine. **Apart from Me you can do nothing.**

Abiding is intimacy. A closeness, a deep penetrating understanding of what is important to Him, of where His priorities lie, of the goals He is pursuing. Intimacy is making our home in His Presence – and Him making His home in ours. It is our hearts beating in rhythm with His: slow measured beats in times of rest in Him, and pounding racing beats when He is moving. It is rejoicing with what pleases Him – and being broken with what grieves Him. Intimacy is us baring our heart to Him – and Him sharing a piece of His heart with us. When we abide, we ache to understand His ways – not to predict or control Him, but simply to *know* Him. Abiding will require that we spend much time alone with Him to give Him time to teach us the desires of His heart. Abiding demands that we take our focus off our problems and put it on our relationship with Jesus, and in this sequel to *Triumph Over Suffering*, we will do just that.

Deeper levels of surrender lead to more intimate abiding. As you read the title of this book, you may have found it difficult to fathom that surrender is *triumph*. Yet, as we journey through this book of intimacy with Jesus, I think that we will find that the more we are able to release to His control, the more He will fill us with Himself. The more we decrease, the more He will increase. And coming to these new levels of surrender means that Jesus is victorious in our hearts – and we, of course, share in His victory.

David describes intimacy this way:

**Deep calls to deep
in the roar of your waterfalls;
all your waves and breakers
have swept over me.
By day the LORD directs his love,
at night his song is with me –
a prayer to the God of my life.**
Psalm 42:7-8 NIV

The Depth of His Spirit is calling to the depth of our spirits, inviting us, enticing us, captivating us, drawing us to drown in His overwhelming Presence. He is calling us to a place of such deep abiding that He directs us with His love by day, and sings over us at night. He is offering us hearing with heightened clarity, knowing His will with deeper certainty, obeying Him with greater surety. He is drawing us to a place where the waves of His love crash over us and take our breath away. Don't try to resist. Come with me on a journey of sweet intimacy with Jesus.

And realize, that as *we* chase after Jesus with all our heart, *He* truly is chasing after us with all of His.

Part I

Intimacy
Through Stillness

John Li

Chapter 1
"My Sheep Hear My Voice"

*I*saiah commissioned in the throne room. Elijah hiding in the cave. Peter seeing visions on the rooftop. Jochebed hiding Moses in the reeds. Elizabeth recognizing the unborn Messiah. Daniel fasting at the Tigris. Paul caught up into the third heaven. Mary certain that Jesus would turn the water into wine. These are definitely sheep who heard His voice. I want to hear Him in this way too; I desire to know Him this deeply. I wonder what journey these mighty men and women traveled in order to reach this place of intimacy with the Lord.

I like how David expresses His passion to know the Lord so deeply:

O God, You are my God; I shall seek You earnestly;
My soul thirsts for You, my flesh yearns for You,
In a dry and weary land where there is no water.
Psalm 63:1

Like David, we desire greater intimacy, but we may
be thwarted from that desire because we are entangled
in Satan's lies. We may be thinking, "What if I call out
to Him, and He doesn't answer me? What if God doesn't
really want *me?*"

If you are struggling in this place of confusion, thirsting
and yearning for Him yet fearful that He may not respond,
you may be encouraged to discover that He is yearning for
you, too.

"Is Ephraim My dear son?
Is he a delightful child?
Indeed, as often as I have spoken against him,
I certainly still remember him;
Therefore My heart yearns for him;
I will surely have mercy on him,"
declares the LORD.

Jeremiah 31:20

I want to assure you that God wants you, and wants
you *desperately.* He is seeking you passionately. He has
orchestrated your emptiness to bring you to recognize
your deep need for Him. As St. Augustine writes, "Our
hearts are forever restless until they find rest in You."[1]
God is pursuing you incessantly, and He promises to make
Himself findable when you seek Him with all your heart.

Before we explore any further, let's pray.

Heavenly Father, thank You for Your
pursuit of us. We come before You with great
humility, to give You ourselves, and to ask that
You would give us more of Yours. Please give
us the courage to go wherever You are leading,
to persevere and not turn back, even when the
road is rocky. Amen.

Is His Deep Calling to Your Deep?

My family and those closest to me will chuckle a bit when they hear that I am writing about hearing God's voice. Oh, the number of times I have had to return to them and humbly (or not so humbly) say, "I think I've heard from God wrong." This book is designed to be a tool to enable us to hear Him more clearly, and to guide us right into the heart of God – but please don't look to me for all the answers. If you do, you will miss what God has *just for you.*

My husband John reminded me that it is crucial to avoid comparisons while pressing on in our spiritual growth. I've asked him to put his thoughts into words.

Some people are blessed with hearing His voice, or receiving visions and dreams, but that isn't me. I seem to get little nudges – strange, unlikely coincidences, nothing earth shattering. I spent a lot of time being jealous of other people who seemed to get daily downloads or heard audible voices, but of course jealousy didn't help.

What we must realize is that everyone hears from the Lord differently. We are all on different journeys, and others' journeys can inspire us but should not drive us to guilt, shame, jealousy, or competition.

I like to think of it as a radio transmission. The radio transmission is out there, but I need to tune my receiver to God's frequency. I may have become distracted by CNN and ESPN and have been drawn away from God's channel. But just because I am hearing nothing doesn't mean He isn't transmitting!

Don't feel badly if daily downloads don't come rolling in right away – it took my wife years to write this book. It just means that it will take daily practice to tune ourselves into His transmissions. If you cannot implement everything today, focus on what you can. Sometimes it may help to work through this book a bit at a time, and in a few weeks or months return to the book to take the next step.

What is important is that we don't remain stagnant in our relationship with Jesus, but we press on to know Him more and learn to receive more of His radio transmissions. And when we persist in seeking Him, moving at our own pace, we will indeed find that Jesus will match that pace.

John Li, M.D.
Jupiter, Florida

Indeed, God is infinite in His uniqueness and will develop His relationship with us in individual and special ways. And yet, there are some common denominators that I hear from those who are close to Him. As we journey together through this book, let's work through Biblical truths to draw closer to the One we love.

Hearing Is Expected, But Not Automatic

Well, we just might as well admit it. It's hard to have a conversation with Someone when we can't hear what they are saying. It gets a bit one-sided. So in order to be able to have a conversation with God, we will need to be able to *hear* Him.

I've heard that bank tellers go through a rigorous program to train them to recognize counterfeit bills. I was fascinated to learn that the bulk of the training involves examining and touching *genuine* bills, not counterfeit ones. The banks want the genuine bills to be so cemented in the tellers' minds that they will immediately recognize the counterfeit bills, because the counterfeit ones appear so foreign to them.

If we are having difficulty hearing from the Lord, if we are struggling to recognize His voice from the counterfeits of Satan, ourselves, and the world, maybe it's time to spend more time with the Genuine. In my walk, I have certainly found that I needed to go the route of the bank teller.

As we read Jesus' teachings on hearing God's voice, realize that His audience was very familiar with shepherding and could easily relate.

"... the sheep hear his voice, and he calls his own sheep by name and leads them out. When he puts forth all his own, he goes on ahead of them, and the sheep follow him because they know his voice. A stranger they will simply not follow, but will flee from him, because they do not know the voice of strangers ... My sheep hear My voice, and I know them, and they follow Me; I give eternal life to them, and they will never perish; and no one will snatch them out of My hand."

John 10:3-5, 27-28

Author Phillip Keller, both shepherd and pastor, provides a unique perspective on this passage. In his book, *A Shepherd Looks at the Good Shepherd and His Sheep,* he writes,

> Sheep quickly become accustomed to their owner's particular voice ... They can distinguish it from that of any other person.
>
> If stranger should come among them, they would not recognize nor respond to his voice in the same way they would to that of the shepherd. Even if the visitor should use the same words and phrases as that of their rightful owner they would not react in the same way ... [They are] actually conditioned to the familiar nuances and personal accent of their shepherd's call.

... The instant sheep hear and recognize their shepherd's voice, they lift their heads, turn in the direction from which the sound comes, and cock their ears to catch every syllable ... their owner's call ... commands their full and undivided attention.[2]

Even more fascinating to me is that sheep are named! Phillip Keller goes on to write about sheep cared for by shepherds in the Middle East and Africa. He expounds,

> ... each one is known by name. These names are not simple common names such as we might choose. Rather, they are complex and unique because they have some bearing on the history of the individual beast. For example, an ewe might be called: "The one born in the dry river bed," or "The beautiful lamb for which I traded two pots of honey."[3]

Wow! Do I crave to live like those sheep! To hear Jesus call me *by name,* to give Him my full and undivided attention, to come when called! Let's go back to the passage from John 10 and see what we can learn about how our Shepherd wants us to hear.

- We hear Him so unmistakably that we **follow** His leading.

- We hear Him with an ability to distinguish His voice

from a cacophony of other voices (the world, the culture, the dark, our own voice).

- We hear Him with such certainty that we will **simply not follow** any voice that is not His; indeed, we will **flee from** the call of the world, from the dark, from our own flesh.

Do you struggle to hear Him this clearly? I certainly do. Somehow, the "simply not following" doesn't always seem that simple.

Discerning His Voice Is a Gift

Distinguishing His voice from the cacophony is a gift from the Lord. First Corinthians includes this in the gifts of the Holy Spirit: **the ability to discern whether a message is from the Spirit of God or from another spirit** (1Cor 12:10 NLT). NKJV calls this gift the **discerning of spirits**; NASB the **distinguishing of spirits.**

As with all gifts from God, we can't earn them or deserve them, they are simply His blessing upon us.

Every good thing given and every perfect gift is from above, coming down from the Father of lights, with whom there is no variation or shifting shadow.
James 1:17

However, God does tell us that we can *request* His gifts.

"Ask, and it will be given to you; seek, and you will find; knock, and it will be opened to you. For everyone who asks receives, and he who seeks finds, and to him who knocks it will be opened. Or what man is there among you who, when his son asks for a loaf, will give him a stone? Or if he asks for a fish, he

will not give him a snake, will he? If you then, being
evil, know how to give good gifts to your children,
how much more will your Father who is in heaven
give what is good to those who ask Him!"

Matthew 7:7-11

When we seek Him, knocking and asking for a gift such
as hearing Him more clearly, He assures us that He will
give this good gift to His children.

The Importance of Developing Discernment

Although discerning His voice is a gift given by the
Holy Spirit, we are also responsible to *develop* that gift.
In the passage above from John 10, Jesus declares, "My
sheep hear My voice." *Sheep*. Not lambs. Although we will
begin to hear Him when we first become His lambs, we are
not automatically experienced hearers. Recognizing and
responding to the Shepherd's voice comes with maturity.
For their own welfare and protection, lambs must develop
into mature sheep who have learned to recognize their
Shepherd's voice.

David certainly was a mature sheep who often heard
the Lord's voice. His acute sensitivity was pivotal in many
battle victories. As we study one of those battles, let's
watch how David heard from the Lord.

Now the Philistines came up once again and
spread themselves out in the valley of Rephaim.
When David inquired of the LORD, He said, "You shall
not go directly up; circle around behind them and
come at them in front of the balsam trees. It shall
be, when you hear the sound of marching in the tops
of the balsam trees, then you shall act promptly, for
then the LORD will have gone out before you to strike
the army of the Philistines." Then David did so, just

as the LORD had commanded him, and struck down the Philistines from Geba as far as Gezer.

2 Samuel 5:22-25

When David inquired of the Lord, God gave him the game plan for victory. Clarity. Certainty. Unique and specific hearing for his particular situation. David heard those commands clearly and unquestionably.

But the game plan would have failed if David had been insensitive to the Presence of the Lord at that crucial moment on the battlefield. If David had been unable to perceive God's movement, if he was deaf to the sound of the Lord's army marching in the tops of the balsam trees, if he was not discerning enough to recognize the sound of the Lord — he would have missed God's perfect timing.

Training to Hear His Voice

Hebrews tells us that the way to develop discernment is through constant practice:

But solid food is for the mature, for those who have their powers of discernment trained by constant practice to distinguish good from evil.

Hebrews 5:14 ESV

If "constant practice" causes you to think of athletes in training or soldiers preparing for battle, you are on the right track. How necessary is this training? *Imperative* if we desire to obey God's voice and His alone. Let's read an example of what happened when a very Godly man listened to a voice other than God's.

Now Sarai, Abram's wife had borne him no children, and she had an Egyptian maid whose name was Hagar. So Sarai said to Abram, "Now behold,

the LORD has prevented me from bearing children.
Please go in to my maid; perhaps I will obtain
children through her." And Abram listened to the
voice of Sarai.

Genesis 16:1-2

Why did Abram listen to the voice of Sarai? Perhaps
because her voice tickled his ears and told him what he
wanted to hear (2Tim 4:3).

Basic Training

Before we proceed in our search for clearer hearing and
greater intimacy, we are going to visit briefly the most
basic of training grounds. Constantly practicing these
four elementary teachings are paramount to develop our
relationship with the Lord. Be sure your foundation here
is solid before diving deep into the rest of this book.

Become Steeped in Scriptures

Continue to pour over your Bible, meditate on it,
memorize it. Knowing His Word will make it easier to
identify His voice when He speaks, because it will sound
just like Him. I've invited Libby, one of my Triumph
Servant Leaders, to share how the Lord spoke to her when
she persisted in immersing in His Word.

*For me, the key to hearing God through the Scriptures is
desire. I need to want to hear from Him, and to be actively
seeking His will and direction in my life.*

*Many years ago, as I was reading the Bible once again
beginning to end, I picked up right where my bookmark
was, in Ezra. As I was reading, I was thinking, "Why am
I reading this book? This has nothing to do with me right
now." Then suddenly I read, "**For Ezra had set his heart***

to study the law of the LORD and to practice it, and to teach His statutes and ordinances in Israel" *(Ezra 7:10). And as this verse leapt off the page and into my heart, I realized that this is exactly the mission God was calling me to: to study the Word and apply it and teach it to others. It was one of many defining moments in my life as the Lord revealed His calling on my life.*

Libby Hammond
Triumph Servant Leader
Scipio, Indiana

Choose Your Church – and Your Companions – Wisely

As your spirit comes to recognize the Holy Spirit's movement during worship in church, you may then begin to more easily recognize Him at other times also. But it's not merely about attending church; it's about an opportunity to serve, and the genuine honest open relationships you develop with other abiding Christians, knowing that **he who walks with wise men will be wise** (Pr 13:20) and **bad company corrupts good morals** (1Cor 15:33).

A lamb will probably need to be trained by others who know how to recognize the Shepherd's voice. Mature sheep, such as a natural or spiritual parent. It most likely won't be very helpful for a lamb to try to learn the Shepherd's voice from the other inexperienced lambs, because the other young lambs don't know the Shepherd's voice themselves so well, either. Experienced sheep who are able to train lambs will be mature sheep who are led by the Holy Spirit and clearly recognize the Shepherd's voice themselves.

Change Your Expectations

Let's remind each other to be open to any way that the Lord may choose to communicate. As Peter tells us, **in the last days ... your young men shall see visions, and your old men shall dream dreams** (Acts 2:17). Our infinitely creative and passionately loving God may also

speak to us with poems or songs, for **He will rejoice over
you with singing** (Zeph 3:17). And after all, if God can
speak through a donkey, He can speak through anyone
(Num 22:28-30).

Quit Feeding Your Flesh

**For the mind set on the flesh is death, but the
mind set on the Spirit is life and peace.**
Romans 8:6

This is a deep spiritual battle; Satan does not want
our spirits to connect with the Spirit of Christ. He will be
relentless in his efforts to draw us to focus our mind and
our life on things of the flesh instead of on things of the
Spirit.

**"No one can serve two masters; for either he will
hate the one and love the other, or else he will be
loyal to the one and despise the other. You cannot
serve God and mammon."**
Matthew 6:24 NKJV

Have we chosen to **set no worthless thing before my
eyes** (Ps 101:3)? Or are we spending our time watching
TV, talking on our cell phones, glued to our computers?
Engaged in other media, or immersed in secular movies
and music and books? Spending long hours at work, in our
extensive social lives, or with worldly friends? Jesus warns
against even idle words,

**"But I tell you, on the day of judgment men will
have to give account for every idle (inoperative,
nonworking) word they speak."**
Matthew 12:36 AMP

As we spend more time with God, we are positioning
ourselves to hear God. When we spend more time in the
world, we are positioning ourselves to hear the world and
the forces of darkness in the world. As Susie Larson writes,

"Someone once said that both God and the devil have a plan for our lives. And we are the ones who cast the deciding vote."[4]

We have come to a fork in the road. God has a plan for your life. Satan has a plan for your life. You choose.

Positioning Our Spirit Through Exposure

I call this exposure *quality time in great quantity.* Listening more than we talk. Running around with the other little lambs is not quality time because it will probably be too noisy and filled with too many distractions. Quality time is long periods in the shepherd's arms as He cleans off burrs, and takes care of hoofs and eyes. This is the time when the lambs can learn not only the sound of His voice, but also His heart, His character, and His ways of love and compassion. In His arms, His lambs can learn to *trust* Him.

Sometimes, when we are learning something new, a season of full immersion can lift us up to a new level. Right now, I am challenging *you* to a season of complete absorption. Don't simply read this book and put it aside, but apply what God is teaching you here, every step of the way. Just as a student desiring fluency in a language or an athlete seeking to hone his skills may enter into a full immersion experience, I invite you to use this book to enter into a time of full immersion. I pray that as you submerge, you will indeed learn the language of God and will come to know Him in greater measure.

The bottom line is that if we desire, like those bank tellers, to recognize the Genuine, we've got to immerse in Him. To flood ourselves with Him. To bask in Him, drown in Him, marinate in Him. To saturate ourselves with Him, soak in Him, steep in Him.

Are you beginning to grasp the time and energy commitment necessary to grow in sensitivity to His Spirit? To develop a deep rich relationship with your Shepherd? Ah, you're still with me, so I trust you've chosen the path of intimacy back at the fork. Let's travel on ...

Spending Quality Time in Great Quantity

God didn't sacrifice His one and only Son for us so that He could have a couple of minutes with us here and there! He gave *everything* to secure a relationship with us. He yearns for our complete and undivided attention. Jesus emptied Himself, took on human form, *and suffered and died* in order to enter deeply into relationship with us. To open the doors of communication as nothing else could. Likewise, we are commanded to **put on the Lord Jesus Christ, to clothe yourselves with the Lord Jesus Christ** (Rom 13:14 NASB, NIV). How do we "put on" Jesus?

I believe that one of the ways that we can enter into deeper relationship with Jesus, to hear His voice, to clothe ourselves with Him, is by learning to move from the physical to the spiritual. We are spiritual beings in a physical body. Often, the physical overwhelms the spiritual, and we walk in the flesh instead of in the spirit. Yet God is Spirit, and if we want to hear from Him, we must learn how our spirit connects with His Spirit.

God wants our spirits to know how to connect with His Spirit, how to hear from Him through church, through His creation, through His Word, through Godly men and women. God wants us to hear from Him constantly!

Most importantly, He craves one-on-one time with us. He desires us to be alone with Him: **"Be still and know that I am God"** (Ps 46:10 NIV). These are treasured times that He trains our spirits to know His Spirit.

What will this time alone with Jesus be like? Quality time in great quantity. By quality time I mean completely alone, sacred time set aside in a special place, nothing scheduled, no distractions, no to-do lists, no cell phones, no doorbells, no kids or friends or other people. I don't mean simply alone. I mean *alone* alone. I mean *solitude*.

And by quantity time I mean *quantity*. It seems that quality only comes out of quantity. Think of top athletes. Yes, they are undoubtedly gifted in their athletic ability, but additionally, they spend copious amounts of time honing their skills.

Draw the parallel. Think of the most Godly men and women you know, who seem to have a direct hotline to God. Do you think they learned to hear Him this clearly just by spending a couple of minutes reading their Bible each day? No way! In her book *Jesus Calling*, Sarah Young writes, "An hour or two alone with Him seemed too brief."[5]

God is the same yesterday, today, and forever. Just because we can now break the sound barrier doesn't mean that God grows our relationship with Him in sound-barrier-breaking speeds. God is still growing people at seed-speed. Think about how many years God took to develop His relationship with some of His precious ones. To teach them to hear His voice. To equip them and strengthen them for the work He had assigned for them. David ... hid in caves for years between his anointing and his crowning. Moses ... shepherded for 40 years before he extended his staff over the Red Sea. Paul ... 10 years in Tarsus before being launched into his missionary work. Joshua ... wandered in the desert for 40 years with the Israelites before even beginning to conquer the Promised Land. Abraham ... decades waiting for Isaac. Even Jesus did not begin His public ministry until He was 30. What makes us think that *we* will grow up overnight?

Satan's Attack on Our Relationship With God: Busyness

I believe that one of the most powerful weapons Satan wields against our relationship with God is busyness. I think this little story will help us to realize the gravity of this.[6]

> *Satan called a worldwide convention of demons. In his opening address he said, "We can't keep Christians from going to church, reading their Bible, and knowing the truth. We can't even keep them from forming an intimate relationship with Jesus ... So we'll let them ... but we will steal their time so they don't have time to develop a relationship with Jesus ..."*
>
> *"How shall we do this?" his demons shouted.*
>
> *"Keep them busy in the nonessentials of life and invent innumerable schemes to occupy their minds. Tempt them to spend, spend, spend, and borrow, borrow, borrow. Persuade their wives to go to work for long hours and the husbands to work 6-7 days each week, 10-12 hours a day, so they can afford their empty*

lifestyles. Keep them from spending time with their children. As their families fragment, soon their homes will offer no escape from the pressures of work!

"Overstimulate their minds so that they cannot hear that still, small voice. Entice them to play the radio whenever they drive and to keep the TV and computers going constantly. See to it that every store and restaurant plays secular nonbiblical music constantly. This will jam their minds and break that union with Christ . . .

"Pound their minds with the news 24 hours a day. Invade their driving moments with billboards. Flood their mailboxes with junk mail, mail-order catalogues, sweepstakes, and every kind of newsletter and promotional offering free products, services, and false hopes.

"Keep skinny, beautiful models on the magazines and TV so the husbands will believe that outward beauty is what's important, and they'll become dissatisfied with their wives. Keep

John Li

the wives too tired to love their husbands at night ...

"Give them Santa Claus to distract them from teaching their children the real meaning of Christmas ...

"Even in their recreation, let them be excessive. Have them return from their recreation exhausted. Keep them too busy to go out in nature and reflect on God's creation. Send them to amusement parks, sporting events, plays, concerts, and movies instead. Keep them busy, busy, busy!

"When they meet for spiritual fellowship, involve them in gossip and small talk so that they leave with troubled consciences. Crowd their lives with so many good causes they have no time to seek power from Jesus. Soon they will be working in their own strength, sacrificing their health and family for the good of the cause."

Convicted? Me too. Realize that some of these activities aren't themselves evil or wrong, but in excess can draw us away from God. To illustrate, I'd like to introduce you to Gary, one of my Triumph Servant Leaders. I've invited him to share the tragic consequences of the overwhelming busyness that had pushed God out of his life.

My relationship with God was at a stalemate for thirty years. I was a believer, but I was simply not practicing my faith. In the busyness of running two businesses, I had no time to read my Bible, go to church, or spend any time alone with God.

My wife packed up and left one Saturday when I was out fishing. She left nothing in the house but a few chairs – and a book she had never read, Triumph Over Suffering. I picked it up and only had to read the introduction to realize that God had put this book there for me. I couldn't get through the book fast enough. This book prepared me to recognize God's will for my life. Since that first read, God's plan has come alive in me.

For the first time in my life, I started my mornings with God. The more I dove into God's Word, the more I craved it. Like a compass, it steered me back onto His path. I began to understand that my problems were not a punishment, but an experience designed to draw me back to Him.

As painful as my divorce has been, I realize that if my wife had not left me, I may never have turned back to God. I am wiser, more rested, and more peaceful. Together, God and I have conquered busyness, and I am able to enjoy, appreciate, and rest in God.

Gary McDaniel
Triumph Servant Leader
West Palm Beach, Florida

It took tragedy to open Gary's eyes to the busyness that was strangulating him. Now, with Jesus in the center of his life, Gary has indeed brought balance to his life and is immersed in his relationship with God and work for the Lord's Kingdom.

Many interests can keep us busy. For Gary, it was handling two businesses along with recreational activities that tore him away from God and from his wife. For others, it may be hobbies or social life – or even ministry work. If we don't recognize and deal with busyness in our lives, it can progress to an even greater hindrance to our relationship with God: burnout.

Satan's Attack on Our Relationship With God: Burnout

Busyness can lead to burnout in a very insidious fashion. The stress of busyness becomes burnout when physical, mental, emotional, or spiritual resources are depleted.

Burnout is characterized by an "exhaustion of physical or emotional strength or motivation, usually as a result of prolonged stress or frustration."[7]

Those who suffer from burnout feel "exhausted, empty ... and unable to cope ... drained and exhausted, overloaded, tired and low, and do not have enough energy." The medical community states that "Self-sacrifice ... and extreme commitment ... may be at the root."[8]

Other symptoms may include isolation, lack of motivation, emotional blunting, and even physical symptoms such as headaches and digestive problems. People with burnout may struggle with concentration and creativity, and often feel ineffective and frustrated.

Webster's gives us a striking word picture here. "Burnout is the time when a jet or rocket engine stops working because there is no more fuel available."[9]

How can we avoid running out of fuel? How can we prevent our rocket ship from plummeting? Here are some concrete strategies that I use to help prevent burnout:

- Maintaining God's priorities.

- Healthy diet, regular exercise, proper sleep, and Godly boundaries.

- Recharging batteries by keeping a healthy rhythm of Sabbath rests.

- Sacred time alone with Him daily, not merely in prayer and the Word, but also imperatively in solitude and listening, in order to give Him ample time to fill us with His love.

Scripture indicates that God is to be forever number one in priority (Ex 20:2-3, Dt 4:24, Heb 12:29). What follows next will be different for each one of us, as God uniquely tailors His call on our lives. We will need to seek God for *His* order – which may even change from day to day.

Note that "God" being in first place does not equal ministry work being in first place. "God" means our *relationship* with God. When we are abiding in Him, He will orchestrate His perfect priorities. When we are working for the Lord and not for men, everything in our lives *is* indeed Kingdom work (spouse, children, work, school, ministry, household chores, etc). But don't confuse God's assigned work with *relationship*. If relationship with God is not our first priority, we are opening the door to burnout.

When Jesus had sent out the seventy in Luke 10 to heal the sick, they returned amazed and excited that the Lord had worked through them so powerfully. **"Lord, even the demons are subject to us in Your name,"** they report to Jesus (Lk 10:17).

I have read that Luke Chapter 10 and Matthew Chapters 10 and 11 are parallel passages.[10] Cross-examining them, I do agree. Moving to Matthew's version, we can see how Jesus responds to His disciple's ministry work:

"Come to Me, all who are weary and heavy-laden, and I will give you rest. Take My yoke upon you and learn from Me, for I am gentle and humble in heart, and you will find rest for your souls. For My yoke is easy and My burden is light."

Matthew 11:28-30

Powerful ministry followed by a warning to rest and to rely on Jesus. In Mark's version, Jesus took them to secluded place to rest (Mk 6:31). As I ponder these verses, I realize that, for me, it seems just a few short steps from pride, to bearing burdens God did not assign, to burnout. When I begin to think that I had anything to do with the victory, I am next assigning myself more work to do in order to "accomplish" more and more Kingdom work. The result of this will eventually be burnout. If I forget that Jesus is doing all the work, using me as His imperfect vessel, His hands, His feet, His mouth, His pen, then I may fall into that trap of striving, earning, and pridefully accomplishing – in the flesh. I will soon run myself to exhaustion.

All of us, in our walk with the Lord, are called to periodically assess our path. For just because we *can* do something doesn't necessarily mean that we *should*.

All things are lawful, but not all things are profitable. All things are lawful, but not all things edify.

1 Corinthians 10:23

When it comes to helping people, we are to be careful that we are not carrying others, but are helping others to find their strength in God (1Sam 23:16 NIV). We want to be pointing them *to God* for answers to their problems. We will want to ask the Lord for a heart of deep humility, recognizing that only Jesus saves and heals; only Jesus delivers and rescues.

It is our deep connection with the Lord that will enable us to hear Him clearly, and to avoid the pitfalls of assigning ourselves work. I have heard this self-assignment of work to be called false burden bearing. Let's listen to how Paul addresses this issue in Philippians:

And this I pray, that your love may abound still more and more in real knowledge and all discernment, so that you may approve the things that are excellent ...

Philippians 1:9-10

I think these verses are saying that the more we really **know** God, the more our love will abound. The greater our **discernment**, our ability to sense God's Spirit and to hear and understand God's voice, the more we will be able to receive His love and allow that same love to flow through us to others.

Paul prays for real knowledge and all discernment **"so that."** So that we **may approve the things that are excellent.** Excellent, *diaphero* in the Greek, means something that "makes a difference,"[11] something that "matters," something that is "of more value."[12] As we grow in true deep revelation of who He is, and are able to sense His Spirit and hear His voice, we will be able to test and approve **what really matters** (NLT).

Are you hungry for more? As we move into the next chapters in this journey of intimacy, we'll continue utilizing the bank teller approach. We will explore some details on finding and maintaining that deep connection with the Lord in order to discover *the things that really matter.*

At the end of each chapter – and peppered throughout the upcoming chapters – you'll find questions designed to challenge you to examine your heart and encourage you to apply the teachings to your own life. Many people find that when they write down their answers, the teachings become clearer and more deeply implanted in their hearts. Journaling can invite the Holy Spirit to move through our minds and hearts in a more penetrating fashion. So grab your journal and a pen and let's go!

Questions Chapter 1: *"My Sheep Hear My Voice"*

Memory Verse:

"Abide in Me, and I in you. As the branch cannot bear fruit of itself unless it abides in the vine, so neither can you unless you abide in Me. I am the

**vine, you are the branches; he who abides in Me and
I in him, he bears much fruit, for apart from Me you
can do nothing."**

John 15:4-5

1) Read John 15:1-11. (Try the NASB or NKJV to
find "abide." NIV and NLT use "remain.") Write down
everything you learn about abiding from this passage. Use
the exact wording of Scripture to invite Him to implant
His Word deeply into your heart. Look up abide in your
English dictionary, or, if you have one, in your *Greek Word
Study*, and record what you learn. Then, define abiding in
your own words.

2) Read Romans 8:1-14, then re-read the section *Quit
Feeding Your Flesh*. Take some time to prayerfully evaluate
your activities. Are you feeding your flesh, or your spirit?

3) Honestly evaluate where you are spending your
time. Write down what a typical week looks like for you,
and determine if you are overwhelmed with busyness.
Busyness could be an attack from Satan working to prevent
you from growing up in the Lord. Read Romans 12:1-2.
Based on these verses, how can we discern the way that
God wants us to spend our time?

4) Re-read the section *Spending Quality Time in Great
Quantity*. God has a plan for your life. Satan has a plan
for your life. The choice is yours. If you are interested in
a season of immersion in Jesus, what will you change to
give yourself more time to spend with the Genuine? Write
down the details. Then write down your commitment to
the Lord.

5) Write a prayer to the Lord, thanking Him for the
revelation He has given you during this time with Him,
confessing as necessary, reiterating your commitment, and
asking the Holy Spirit to give you the desire, wisdom, and
strength to walk out that commitment.

Chapter 2
Heaven Touches Earth

Where can I go from your Spirit?
Where can I flee from your
presence?
If I go up to the heavens,
you are there;
If I make my bed in the depths,
you are there.
If I rise on the wings of the dawn,
If I settle on the far side of the sea,
Even there your hand will guide me,
Your right hand will hold me fast.

Psalm 139:7-8

Of course we know that He is always with us and will never leave us or forsake us. We can never escape His Presence. By faith, we know all this.

But I think that what we may be seeking is an *awareness* of His Presence. A deep *connection* to that Presence. A sense that He is truly speaking to us, leading us, guiding us. A reassurance that we *are* abiding in Him, and He is abiding in us. Times when heaven touches earth.

Heaven Meets Earth in Corporate Worship

Much of this chapter is dedicated to connecting to the Lord in our alone time with Him. But before we explore this area, I want to emphasize that our connecting to the Lord with the Body of Christ is equally paramount. God commands us to be deeply rooted into the Body of Christ, involved in corporate worship, in serving, in accountability and connection (Heb 10:24-25). He promises to be with us in a special way when we are gathered together with other believers (Mt 18:20). When we station ourselves in a place where the Holy Spirit comes down in a powerful way, such as when we worship in church with other believers, we may begin to sense the flow of His Presence. And, as we begin to recognize Him in church, when He is here *in force*, it may help us to recognize His Presence at other times when He is here more gently, also.

Of course we realize that all churches are imperfect because they are composed of imperfect people. Nevertheless, God wants us to be positioned in a place where we can be instructed and led by the pastor that He has anointed to shepherd His flock. If we deny that we are part of the Body, it doesn't make us any less a part of the Body (1Cor 12:15), but it *does* mean that we are missing out on the tremendous blessings God has for us when we are connected into the Body.

Seeking Him in Our Time Alone With Him

God does indeed want to be real to us. He wants us to remain acutely aware of His Presence, to sense Him leading us and hear Him speaking to us. Of course God doesn't need us to do *a single thing* in order to communicate with us. He is infinitely powerful and can make His voice heard to any person at any time and in any place. Somehow, though, I think He wants us to partner with Him in the communication experience. Not as King and slave, but as *friends*. He seems to crave the development of *relationship*.

Yes, there are certainly times when He will speak to us seemingly uninvited, when we are not even in a place of listening. But the journey through this book is about learning how to connect to Him when we are alone with Him, so we will increasingly be able to remain connected when we step out of that secret place of His Presence and into our everyday lives.

We talked in the last chapter about positioning ourselves to hear from Him. Let's take it a little deeper. God is Spirit, and learning *to transition from the physical to the spiritual* will facilitate our connection with Him. He is so tender; He has provided some ways for us to achieve this challenging transition. He wants so passionately to meet with us that He has furnished some doorways for us to enter His Presence. Let's look at a few.

Thanking and Praising

Enter His gates with thanksgiving and His courts with praise.

Psalm 100:4

I have heard it said that this Psalm is talking about the temple, and symbolically about His Presence. Studying diagrams of Solomon's temple, I see that entering the *gates* brought people into the outer plaza of the temple area. Entering the *courts* brought people in deeper, in towards the temple itself.

Praying with deep heartfelt gratitude can draw us into the first level of His Presence. Worshipping with praise, giving Him homage, glory, and devotion, can bring us into an even more intimate level of His Presence.

Our Daily Bread declares, "God does not need our praise, but we need to praise God."[1] Yes, praise is indeed for *our* benefit, not His. God is infinite in His glory and majesty, and our praise cannot add anything to Him. Yet it *pleases* Him when we praise Him. He blesses us when we praise Him by reminding us of Who He is, and of who we are in Him. Praise fixes our minds on Him and feeds our spirit, bringing us to a place of humility, joy, and peace.

Before we go on, let's take a moment to thank God. What are three things you can thank God for today? Write them in your journal or in the margin here, then pause and let your deep gratitude flow to Him.

Now if we really want to thrive in His Presence, we must not merely enter, we must be *planted*. Listen to how Psalm 92 expresses it:

**Planted in the house of the LORD,
They will flourish in the courts of our God.**
Psalm 92:13

In order to flourish, we must be planted first. Flourishing in our relationship with Him is bearing fruit. Let's explore some ways to plant ourselves.

Meditating on God

God instructs us throughout the Psalms to **meditate on His works, His precepts, His wonders,** and **His Word** (Ps 77:12, 119:15,27,148). When we suppress the distractions and focus our heart on who He is, on His character and His ways, we welcome His Spirit to connect with our spirit and to speak to us with great clarity.

Appreciating His Creation

God teaches us that He speaks to us through His glorious creation:

The heavens declare the glory of God;
The skies proclaim the work of his hands.
Day after day they pour forth speech;
Night after night they reveal knowledge.
They have no speech, they use no words;
No sound is heard from them.
Yet their voice goes out into all the earth,
Their words to the ends of the world.

Psalm 19:1-4 NIV

Standing in awe of His creation can sweep us into the Presence of God. When our hearts race in appreciation of a sunrise or a sunset, or our souls exclaim with pleasure when a wild animal or a delicate butterfly crosses our path, we can be hurtled right into His Presence. Simply stopping to contemplate His beauty in a flower can do the same. We can behold His artistry in the ocean, the mountains, forests, gardens, or streams, or in the dark night sky bejeweled with stars. When we deliberately seek places where His majesty will overwhelm us, we may find that He just *loves* to visit with us.

Establishing a Secret Place of His Presence

Psalm 31 talks about God hiding us in **the secret place of His Presence** (Ps 31:20). The environment we choose to seek out God can be a crucial part in transitioning from the physical to the spiritual.

But thou art holy, O thou that inhabitest the praises of Israel.

Psalm 22:3 KJV

But You are holy, O You who dwell in the holy place where the praises of Israel are offered.

Psalm 22:3 AMP

I think Psalm 22 is indicating that when we repeatedly come to a place where we worship and praise Him, He considers that a special invitation to come and inhabit that place! Recognize how He loves to show up in church, when a body of believers worships together. Yet we can also worship at home or out in nature or wherever He may lead. As you go to that secret place to worship and praise Him day after day, He begins to inhabit that place. Your spirit may become attuned to receiving from His Spirit right there, so that merely entering this secret place may draw your expectant spirit to leap to attention to more easily hear from Him.

I am reminded of the many hours Moses spent in the tent of meeting. Psalm 103 tells us that God **made known His *ways* to Moses, His *acts* to the sons of Israel** (Ps 103:7, emphasis added). God demonstrated His *acts*, His deeds accomplished by His mighty arm, to the Israelites. But He reserved the revelation of His *ways*, His character, His nature, the why behind His actions, for Moses, who spent so much time in His Presence in the tent of meeting. Might it be similar for us today?

Understand that it's more than His inhabiting a physical place. It's Him inhabiting *us*. Of course at the moment of our salvation, the Holy Spirit, comes to live inside of us. Yet, as we grow in Him, He fills us with Himself in greater and greater measure. Psalm 22 seems to say that as we praise Him, He is pleased to make us His resting place, His dwelling place. He tarries with us, simply enjoying being inside of us as we praise Him.

His Word

Plunge into His Word, that He may pour His love into you. I like how Psalm 119 explains how the Holy Spirit communicates with our spirit through the Word. First, the psalmist describes his immersion in Scriptures: he **delights** in the Word, he **sets his heart** on it, and he is **consumed with longing** for it. He has **hidden it in his heart** and he **holds fast** to it. He **trusts** it, **obeys** it, and **puts his hope** in it. This is no casual reading of the Bible!

Next, listen to how God speaks to him: the Word **comforts** him and nourishes him with God's **unfailing love**. The Bible is his **counselor**, giving him **understanding, knowledge, and good judgment,** and even **makes him wiser than his enemies.** The Word **sustains** him, **strengthens** him, and teaches him **fear and awe** of God. It is the **joy of his heart** and a **lamp unto his feet**, and it **sets his heart free.**

Is this really *God* speaking to him? The psalmist declares, **"For You Yourself have taught me."** *God Himself* is speaking through His Word! And not only is **the word of God ... living and active** (Heb 4:12), but additionally,

All Scripture is God-breathed and is useful for teaching, rebuking, correcting and training in righteousness, so that the man of God may be thoroughly equipped for every good work.
2 Timothy 3:16-17 NIV

The *Navigator Series* explains that Scripture shows us God's path, where we've gotten off it, and how to get back on it and *stay* on it.[2] The Holy Spirit uses Scripture to fully *equip* us so that we will be ready for the destiny that God has prepared for us. Sometimes the Scripture's conviction will be gentle; other times,

"Is not My word like fire?" declares the LORD, "and like a hammer which shatters a rock?"
Jeremiah 23:29

Yes, at times we need that fire and that hammer. It is imperative that we be prepared and furnished with everything necessary to fulfill His purposes, and we can count on the Word of God to do just that:

… the word of God, which also performs its work in you who believe.
1 Thessalonians 2:13

Just what will God sound like when He speaks through Scriptures? As Libby described in the last chapter, the words may leap off the page and into your heart as you realize that this verse or passage is just for you right now. Or your worries and burdens may be lifted as you take your focus off yourself and put it on Jesus. Or He may give you a message for someone that you don't even yet know that you will be encountering today, or provide a solution to a problem or an answer to a question that you have been mulling over. Or He may give you no solutions or answers at all, but simply an overwhelming sense of His peace and His Presence.

Journaling

Prayerfully journaling can help to sort through confusion and chaos, and bring us into His clarity. For me, the Holy Spirit uses the act of honestly transferring my thoughts onto paper to expose hidden areas of my heart, and to teach me the truth of His ways. When I pray for Him to speak to me through journaling, it seems that He has just been waiting to be invited to move me out of denial and deception. He is indeed able to work in an honest and willing heart, to conform me to the image of Christ.

⚹ *Expectant Listening*

Let's observe one of Habakkuk's encounters with God. He is so certain that the Lord will speak to him, he intends to wait until He comes.

> **I will stand on my guard post**
> **And station myself on the rampart;**
> **And I will keep watch**
> **To see what He will speak to me,**
> **And how I may reply when I am reproved.**
> **Then the LORD answered me and said,**
> **"Record the vision**
> **And inscribe it on tablets,**
> **That the one who reads it may run."**
>
> Habakkuk 2:1-2

Habakkuk seems to know that if he wants to hear from the Lord, it will require quantity time (standing and stationing). Note he is listening with quality time also — he is not distracted; he is keeping watch. He is also expectant: he will see what God will speak to him. My guess is that he wasn't budging until He heard from the Lord.

How did God speak to him? He heard His voice, and saw His vision. God Himself commanded Habakkuk to journal **that the one who reads it may run.** I suspect that he must have spent much time alone with God to be able to recognize when it was God speaking after the long waiting.

If we could only know how desperately He wants us to hear Him! We must listen with great expectation!

I would like to invite my friend Cathy to share one of her journaling experiences. As you read, realize that the first time you are still before Him, expectantly listening, you may not hear quite so much and with such detail as Cathy has. This woman is a very mature Christian who has spent countless hours over many decades listening to the Lord's voice and developing her discernment.

I was teaching the class Heart of Healing. We sat still before the Lord, asking Him a question, and writing down His answer. Rarely having approached God in this way, I was a bit hesitant. Skeptically, I posed my question to God, "What time of the day is it best for me to journal?" As I watched and waited, pen in hand, God spoke to my heart:

> *"As the day breaks and the shadows flee away,*
> *I will be with you.*
> *The stillness is in the air*
> *And I am there.*
> *We will meet together*
> *And have sweet fellowship.*
> *No noise, no disturbance,*
> *Just peace will come over you.*
> *Streams of living water will flow from your being.*
> *I am in those streams.*
> *Time will stand still.*
> *This is the time you will get to know Me most.*
> *I am waiting to meet with you.*
> *Open your heart to Me.*
> *This will be a new experience,*
> *So jump in."*

Cathy Moesel
Inner Healing and Deliverance Ministry
Covenant Centre International
Palm Beach Gardens, Florida

Stillness

God instructs us, **"Be still and know that I am God"** (Ps 46:10 NIV). To me, this is so critical – yet so difficult. Being physically still, emotionally still, and mentally still in order to know that *He is God* can be challenging, and may require much training by constant practice! To first learn how to use this door to enter the spiritual from the physical, it might be helpful to create a place of complete silence and solitude. When I first began this practice of stillness, in order not to interrupt the flow of the Holy Spirit, I would turn off every single phone, computer, and electronic device, and I would get as far away as possible from work stressors, to-do lists, piles of unfinished paperwork – and the doorbell. Your secret place of His Presence is a good place to practice physical, mental, and emotional stillness.

- *Physical stillness* to me means no moving. No talking. Just listening. Getting into a comfortable position helps.

- To reach *emotional stillness*, I find that I must come to a place of such deep surrender to Him that He has quieted my racing emotions and brought me to a place of great peace. A place where I trust my life to His control. A place where I am able to rest in His peace because I am relying on *Him* to run the universe – and also to run the intimate details of my life. If I am having difficulty achieving emotional stillness, I find it helpful to sing worship songs first.

- To me, *mental stillness* means coming to a place of complete focus on God. It is quieting my racing thoughts and putting aside to-do lists. It means disciplining my mind so that it does not wander aimlessly, but is focused on knowing, recognizing, and acknowledging that *He is God*. If I simply clear my mind without focusing on the Lord, I can open my mind up to voices other than God's. I like to concentrate on one of God's attributes, or focus on one of His names, or thank Him for His Presence or His mighty works, or meditate on a Scripture verse.

Don't be afraid of the silence. Often, we will not hear God until we hear the silence first. And when God speaks in the silence, it may well be the roaring of waterfalls as His waves and breakers wash over you.

The NASB translates Psalm 46:10, **Cease striving and know that I am God.** One trap that I seem to fall into repeatedly is the lie that I need to earn His love and approval. I find stillness to be an incomparable antidote to that striving. Here I am, doing nothing to earn His love, not even praying or worshipping or reading my Bible, and He *still* pours His love and acceptance and approval into me. His love given in this way whispers deeply into my spirit, "My love is unconditional." It drives out the lie and etches the truth of His unconditional love on my heart as few other encounters with Him can.

Music

I believe that God invented music, and I find music to be a key spiritual connection for my spirit to transcend the physical and to find His Spirit. We're going to spend a bit of time on this particular doorway, not only because it is important, but also because it can be tricky to navigate.

Many passages emphasize the importance of music. When David was designing the temple and giving assignments to the priests, he commanded,

"Four thousand are to praise the LORD with the musical instruments I have provided for that purpose."

1 Chronicles 23:5 NIV

Four thousand people praising the Lord! Four thousand!
Enter His courts with praise (Ps 100:4).

How can we walk through this doorway? I have some
suggestions:

- Sing praise and worship alone with Him – at home,
  in the car, out for a walk, at the beach, in the
  mountains, in the woods.

- Let song burst out spontaneously when we are
  overwhelmed with gratitude for what He has done
  or when we appreciate His creation. Or even more
  powerfully, when we are in the darkest valley of
  pain and despair.

- Raise our voices and hands in church with a body of
  believers. This can propel us into a deeper connection,
  for He promises to be in our midst when even two or
  three are gathered in His name (Mt 18:20).

- And also sing praise and worship in your secret place
  of His Presence.

The Deep Spiritual Power of Music

I am not sure that I can really explain this, but
somehow music seems to be deeply spiritual. It seems to
reach into the depth of my being and grip my soul, easily
catapulting me to realms I would otherwise struggle to
reach. Music seems to have a powerful influence upon
my emotions, effortlessly lifting me up, motivating me,
energizing me, inspiring me. It seems to activate in me
joy, hope, excitement, determination – or depression,
brooding, hopelessness, frustration, anger. It seems to rile

my emotions, stir my spirit, and entice my physical body to follow the direction that the pull of the music is leading.

Music also imprints thoughts, words, and ideas into my mind. Advertising agencies capitalize on this — think of how many jingles we have memorized without an ounce of effort.

To further explore the power of music, I'd like to introduce you to my friend Goldie. A life coach, professional musician, and author, Goldie first learned about the power of music as a young child working with her father, a psychiatrist in a mental health institution. She witnessed severely ill and even catatonic patients as they were transported by music to earlier times in their lives when they were not trapped in mental illnesses. As the music touched them, stoic expressions changed to smiles, and dull eyes gleamed with a hint of hope. It was then that Goldie knew that music would be part of her life calling.

Music did indeed become her focus, and upon graduation from college she worked as a music therapist in both open and locked psychiatric units, and also performed as a professional musician. So it will probably come as no surprise to hear that the Lord used music to eventually draw Goldie to Himself. I'll let her share her story.

My husband Dave was brought up Catholic, and my family practiced Conservative Judaism, so when our friends invited us to their prayer meeting, we thought that we were in a whole different world. The people seemed to have so much joy as they raised their hands and sang like angels. This was quite a contrast to our experience as professional musicians, singing in bars and supper clubs to people who were only interested in drinking. The people at the prayer meeting warmly greeted us and seemed genuinely happy that we were there. There was such a sense of acceptance, unity, and love. At one point, Dave and I were both moved to tears as the music penetrated our hearts. We both felt that perhaps it was God who was missing from our lives all these years, and perhaps it was time to open our hearts to the possibility that He really does exist. It was the power in the music that touched us deeply and opened our hearts to the love of God. We left that evening with a sense of awe and wonder.

At a subsequent prayer meeting, when the priest asked if we would like to receive Jesus as our Lord and Savior, Dave and I got on our knees and invited the Lord into our lives and hearts. I began crying tears of joy. I felt like I was instantly being changed, and Second Corinthians 5:17 became a reality: **"Therefore, if anyone is in Christ [Yeshua], he is a new creation. The old has gone, the new has come!"**

There is a Scripture that says that the Jew requires a sign, and what happened next was surely the sign that confirmed that my salvation was real. I did not know one word of Hebrew, however, the moment I received Jesus as Lord and Savior, I suddenly began speaking in Hebrew. There was a nun present who understood Hebrew and translated what I was saying. I was praising the Lord and thanking Him for revealing Himself to me as the long-awaited Messiah!

A man who was present at the prayer meeting had a special word for me, "Goldie, your gift will be the gift of joy." Immediately I felt a rush of joy, and intuitively recognized that it was a supernatural gift from the Lord. It was particularly special since I had been so depressed throughout most of my childhood.

Jane "Goldie" Winn, MSS
Excerpt from <u>*Rainbow in the Night:*</u>
<u>*A Journey of Redemption*</u>

Before her salvation, Goldie had already been using music to reach deeply into the souls of her clients, but now with Jesus in her life, her work took on an eternal dimension. Let's listen in to a time God utilized music to reach a woman trapped in the bondage of mental illness.

Working in a locked unit, I was especially drawn to an African American woman who had been admitted with a history of psychotic episodes, depression, and suicide attempts. I learned that she loved music, and as her psychotropic medicines began to take effect, I requested that she be brought down to my clinic for private music therapy. She had a guitar, and I asked her to play some songs she had written. The lyrics were very dark, but she sang with so much passion. The goal as a music therapist is to start where the client is and bring her to a more positive place. I began slowly introducing music with more positive lyrics, and eventually she began singing songs that were more hopeful. Our sessions were very productive, and slowly the real person emerged; she was allowed onto the unlocked unit and could join all of my music therapy sessions.

Before she was discharged, I got special permission to take her to my church for a service. I was a brand new believer and was very excited to introduce her to The Lord. That night, during the worship service, she gave her life to The Lord. We prayed for a miraculous healing, and this precious woman was totally healed of all mental illness! The psychiatrist was totally amazed that she was able to get off all her psychotropic medicines. She eventually became a worship leader and a missionary. She recently wrote to me, 42 years later, thanking me for reaching out to her in the hospital and making a way for her accept The Lord!

Once again I witnessed the power of music. Just as God used David's music to minister to Saul when he was tormented, it was through music that Jesus set this captive woman free. I am so grateful that The Lord used me as an instrument of His love and grace.

Jane "Goldie" Winn, MSS
Delray Beach, Florida

Notice how Goldie started right where her patient was. She did not force different musical choices upon her, but simply connected with her, earned her trust, and gently led her to a new place. Just as God used David to set Saul free, God continues to use Goldie to minister to tormented people and set them free. Goldie provides an opportunity for God's music to draw them unto Himself, so that He can touch their hearts and bring freedom. In her own words,

As worship leaders, my husband and I have witnessed the power of music. Worship prepares hearts to receive the Word of God and provides a direct line to connect with The Lord in a personal way. We have watched people receive supernatural healing and deliverance from past hurts that were preventing the Holy Spirit from freely moving in their lives. It has been an awesome experience to witness The Lord's love reaching down and touching His people as we freely worship Him and make a way for others to enter into the Holy of Holies.

Jane "Goldie" Winn, MSS
Delray Beach, Florida

Now let's make it a bit more personal.

Our *Own* Music Can Usher Us Into the Holy of Holies

I'd like to introduce you to Michael Richter. Michael is a tax partner in a CPA firm, and also advises clients in using the wealth they have been gifted with to advance God's Kingdom. Additionally, Michael and his wife, as leaders in the powerful ministries of *JH Ranch* and *Outback America*, are focused on investing in families to strengthen, restore, and heal relationships. I have asked Michael to share how music played a part in his journey to reach deep abiding in Christ.

Business success was the center of my life and I had dedicated my ambitions to making that happen, with an ultimate goal of retiring by the age of 50. My relationship with my wife moved into second place. Even though I spent time first thing in the morning with the Lord, and regularly prayed and asked God for wisdom and discernment in life as well as guidance relating to business decisions, my quiet time was in essence a distant third place. Nevertheless, the Lord was very gracious to me and my family, and was blessing me in those areas beyond my expectations.

Little did I realize that the blessings would continue to fuel the behavior and thinking that created a spiral that drove me into a depressive state of mind. I had never experienced this before in my life. I was 27 years of age and had all the business success that I had asked for, yet I began to despair of life.

I began to physically work my body to create a flow of endorphins to boost my mental state, but it was not enough to shake this feeling of despair in my life. It became difficult to lead a company and make business decisions that were important. I decided to take a weekend off, and headed to a farm property that we owned to just work the land. I thought maybe that would shake the depression.

That weekend turned out to be catastrophic for me. The chain saw that I was using threw a cedar splinter into my left pupil, right into dead center. I immediately lost sight in that eye, and my brother and pregnant wife rushed me 100 miles to a hospital in Houston. Needless to say that this excursion did not turn out like I had hoped, and the loss of vision drove me deeper still into the depression that I wanted so intensely to overcome.

The beauty of that accident was that it pushed me into making my relationship with the Lord the priority of my life. The ensuing year was a difficult one. I did not know whether I would ever see through that eye again, and I continued to struggle with depression. The depression was my little secret that only God and I knew about, and since I was a hard-headed German, it remained that way for a number of years.

As I was driving to the office, I began to sing aloud in the car the hymns that I had learned over the years of my life. I sang those great hymns of faith over and over, day after day. After about three months of singing hymns in the car, I began to realize that my heart was lifted up in a way that actually allowed me to function fairly well at the office and at home. The process of singing back to the Lord the truths of His Word continued to heal me mentally, physically and spiritually, until the depression left me. Little did I realize that the Lord was singing His words over me just as He declares,

> **"The LORD is in your midst,**
> **A mighty one who will save;**
> **He will rejoice over you with gladness;**
> **He will quiet you by His love;**
> **He will exult over you with loud singing."**
> *Zephaniah 3:17 ESV*

The Lord did exactly that in my life. He was in my midst, He was mighty to save me from depression, and He gave me back most of my sight – with a slight scar on my cornea to remind me of His faithfulness. He rejoiced over me with gladness, He quieted me with His love, and He continues to exult over me with loud singing. Thank you, Lord, for reaching out to me through Scripture in the hymns of faith.

Michael Richter
Houston, Texas

Did you know that God sings? God loves music so much that He rejoices over us with singing! As Michael sang those hymns, I think *God* sang over him, and walked him through that doorway into a place of peace, joy, and rest in Him. As Michael worshipped the Lord through music, God delivered him, setting him free from the bondage of depression.

Selecting Our Music to Enter His Presence

In my experience, there are particular musical compositions that draw me towards God. This kind of music brings me to think about God; it causes gratefulness to well up inside of me; it brings me to spontaneously praise Him. It reminds me of all that He has done for me, of all His many blessings. This type of music opens me up to hear from Him. It attunes my spirit to His and prepares me to receive His touch. It draws my focus onto Him and enables me to hear from Him with greater clarity. This music also comforts me and lifts up my spirit when I am down. Even when life is fraught with pain and hardships, it brings me into places of joy and great peace. I walk away from these musical sessions buoyed up and strengthened, full of hope and prepared for the challenges that I am facing that day.

It seems to me that some music will more powerfully connect me to the Holy Spirit than others. Some of that is personal taste. But I believe a greater factor is whether the Holy Spirit's anointing is on the music and the musician. Let's go to the Word to study David, the writer of over seventy psalms, and a man whom God anointed powerfully as a minister of music.

Then Samuel took the horn of oil and anointed him [David] **in the midst of his brothers; and the Spirit of the LORD came mightily upon David from that day forward . . .**

1 Samuel 16:13

David grew closer to the Lord; in contrast, King Saul fell away, choosing a path of disobedience.

Now the Spirit of the LORD departed from Saul, and an evil spirit from the LORD terrorized him.

1 Samuel 16:14

Saul's servants, recognizing Saul's torment, offered to...

"... seek a man who is a skillful player on the harp; and it shall come about when the evil spirit from God is on you, that he shall play the harp with his hand, and you will be well."

So Saul said to his servants, "Provide for me now a man who can play well and bring him to me." Then one of the young men said, "Behold, I have seen a son of Jesse the Bethlehemite who is a skillful musician, a mighty man of valor, a warrior, one prudent in speech, and a handsome man; and the LORD is with him."

1 Samuel 16:16-17

David was brought into Saul's palace, and ...

... it came about whenever the evil spirit from God came to Saul, David would take the harp and play it with his hand; and Saul would be refreshed and be well, and the evil spirit would depart from him.

1 Samuel 16:23

David's harp playing drove away the evil spirit and brought the Lord's peace to a troubled king. What kind of man was David, that he was chosen to be such a vessel for the Lord? From the above verses we read ...

- The Spirit of the Lord **was mightily upon** him and **the LORD is with him.**

- He was a **skillful musician.**

- He was a **mighty man of valor** – noble, courageous, and virtuous.

- He was **prudent in speech** – discerning, wise, and understanding.

- He was a **warrior**. Indeed he was a warrior in the physical sense of the word. But he was also a spiritual warrior. Again and again God worked through David's music to deliver the king.

If we are really serious about hearing from God, if we really desire to deepen our relationship with Him, if we are seeking ways to marinate in Him, to steep in Him, to drown in Him, to enter His Holy of Holies, I believe that we will find it helpful to tune in to God's music. I sense that we will find it invaluable to seek out music performed by musicians who, like David, have the Spirit of the Lord mightily upon them. We may want to ask, What is the musician's walk with the Lord? Is the Spirit of the Lord upon this musician or this group? Are they people of courage, virtue, and integrity? When we are selecting a musician to usher us into the Presence of the Lord, I think that it is critical to choose with the same discernment that we use to choose the pastor to preach to us, the Bible study teacher to instruct us, the mentor to guide us, or the author of a book to challenge us. Since we are steeping, let's steep in music heavily anointed by the Holy Spirit.

Music's Potential to <u>Draw</u> Us To God

In her testimony above, Goldie shared how she led the tormented woman from dark music to God's music, and ushered her into the Holy of Holies. Goldie is truly a modern-day David. Likewise, we can make the same musical choices for ourselves, as Michael did, utilizing carefully chosen music and musicians to usher us into the Holy of Holies.

God loves music so much that He rejoices over us *with singing*. God, in His bountifulness, designed this beautiful doorway as a means for us to transition from the physical to the spiritual. He created music to touch us in the most inner parts of our being.

Yes, God invented music, but I think that Satan works to pervert it. Just as Satan attempts to twist God's Word to try to drive us away from God and to lure us into sin (Mt 4:1-11), I think that Satan may attempt to twist music in an effort to erect barriers between God and us, to churn up sinful thoughts and emotions, and to tempt us into sin. Fasten your seatbelts; we're going to look at the other side: music's ability to *interfere* with our relationship with God.

Music's Potential to <u>Lure</u> Us Away From God

Some types of music do not seem to have any deep spiritual effect drawing us towards or driving us away from God. For this type of music, what we choose to listen to may simply be a matter of feeding the flesh or feeding the spirit, of choosing where we want our focus to be. As with any activity, even if it's a good activity, too much time immersed here can leave us with little time for God. This type of seemingly neutral music has the potential to *lure* us away from God by keeping our minds occupied with things other than God.

I am not saying to legalistically shun all secular music. But when it comes to selecting what I will *fill* my mind with, I put it to the Philippians 4:8 test:

Finally, brothers, whatever is true, whatever is noble, whatever is right, whatever is pure, whatever is lovely, whatever is admirable--if anything is excellent or praiseworthy--think about such things.
Philippians 4:8 NIV

And Philippians 4:9 reminds me why I would want to make 4:8 decisions: **And the God of peace will be with you.** I do so crave God's peace — not flimsy worldly peace that is dependent upon my circumstances, but *God's peace* that passes all understanding, peace that is unshakable even in the darkest of valleys and the most challenging of trials. I find that deep immersion in worship music throughout each day helps to keep me connected to God. And in difficult times, I need that immersion even more so.

Music's Potential to <u>Drive</u> Us Away From God

Other types of music seem to do more than simply distract us and lure us away from God. This type of music seems to have the potential to *drive* us away from God. Joni Eareckson Tada describes music that she had listened to when she had become quadriplegic and fell into depression, and how it still can affect her today. Her words stand in sharp contrast to Michael and Goldie's testimonies that we read earlier. Joni Eareckson Tada writes,

> Those weird, crazy sounds were background music to my suicidal despair, when I would wrench my head back and forth on my pillow, hoping to break my neck at a higher level. Now I turn the dial whenever I hear screeching guitars or a hard, angry beat. I cannot listen. I'm not living in denial or refusing to face up to reality; I merely have a healthy respect for the powerful effect of music — I am as paralyzed now as I was then, and I'm asking for trouble if I expose my mind to music that conjures dark thoughts.[3]

Indeed, we cannot live in a bubble and expect that we will never be exposed to music that drives us from God.

And we don't want to avoid all music that isn't "spiritual," for this may be a trap of legalism that will simply isolate us from the world that we are called to impact, love, and serve. We can, however, choose what we will *meditate* on, what we will *flood* ourselves with, what we will *marinate* in and *focus* upon. We can be sober in spirit and on the alert to three different ways our spirits can be affected by music: our spirits can be lifted up to the Lord, or driven to drift aimlessly and fruitlessly, or sucked down into mental and emotional darkness.

> **Who among us can live with the consuming fire?**
> **... He who walks righteously**
> **and speaks with sincerity**
> **... He who stops his ears**
> **from hearing about bloodshed**
> **And shuts his eyes from looking upon evil ...**
>
> Isaiah 33:14-15

We want to live with that Consuming Fire, and Isaiah seems to point the way. Choosing anointed music to reverberate through our hearts and souls can help to keep our minds focused on Him. When I bathe myself with music that is *infused* with His Holy Spirit, even when that music has finished playing, my heart continues to sing. I am making melody in my heart to the Lord (Eph 5:19), which keeps me focused on Jesus and connected to Him.

Combining Avenues of Connection: Stillness in Solitude With Music

As we seek the Lord's face with greater intensity, I think that we can also facilitate our spirit's receptivity to His Spirit by combining music, solitude, and stillness before Him. Yes, there are times to dance and sing and praise and worship, but there are also times when God calls us to stillness. There are times when we will need utter silence to hear from Him, and also times when Godly music will facilitate the hearing. These are times to **be still** as He commands, allowing quiet worshipful music to simply wash over us. Some of my friends call this "soaking." My friend Gail calls it "liquid prayer." Recognizing that Jesus is our Living Water (Jn 4:10), she describes how the Holy Spirit pours His liquid love into our dry souls when we are open to hear from Him.

When Gail has witnessed a powerful move of the Lord, she runs off to soak. When Gail feels the Lord is giving her a new direction or convicting her of sin, she runs off to soak. When Gail hits a time of trial, she runs to Him to soak. When Gail wants a deeper understanding of a spiritual reality, she races home to soak. As Jesus by His Holy Spirit pours His love into her during these times, she emerges strengthened, and with His path clear in her mind and her obedience settled in her heart.

Hmmm ... sounds a bit like Daniel to me. In Daniel Chapter 6, King Darius had signed a law forbidding anyone to worship any god or man except King Darius himself. The law declared that the punishment would be the lion's den.

Now when Daniel knew that the document was signed, he entered his house ... and he continued kneeling on his knees three times a day, praying and giving thanks before his God ...

Daniel 6:10

I am thinking that these times of prayer so refreshed and strengthened him that when the moment of the lion's den arrived, he endured the trial with courage and peace.

Just as my friend Gail soaks in worship music, my friend Bobbie soaks in Scripture. She takes a verse and repeats it out loud a few times, then rests in silence. As she meditates on that verse, allowing it to richly dwell within her, the Holy Spirit pours His liquid love into her heart.

As we practice stillness and encounter His Presence, I think we will find that we will want to come to Him this way every day, even, as Daniel did, multiple times a day. As we seclude ourselves from the busyness of the world, this can become the deepest of prayer times as we move closer to Him. As His Spirit connects with our spirit, it may be a precious time of basking in the love that He pours out. The Holy Spirit may use this time to captivate us with His love, to fill us with His wisdom, to replenish our spirit with His strength, to convict and transform us, and to teach our spirit to recognize His voice.

Clearer Hearing: But I Want To Be Certain!

Yes, me too. I think, though, that when I say that I want to be certain, what I am really saying is that I don't want to mess up. Because I fear failure, I want to get it right; I want to hear perfectly; I want to be certain before I obey. Do you hear the focus on me? My motive is wrong. I'm not concerned about grieving His Spirit or losing connection with Him; I'm not troubled about those who may be hurt by my mishearing. I'm worried about *how I'm going to look* if I get it wrong. I want to be perfect. I am in need of humility, right motives, and a focus on glorifying Him.

Sometimes God does not give me the certainty in the way I want it. Perhaps because my motives are skewed. Perhaps because if I heard every detail with great clarity, I would glorify myself instead of glorifying Him. And certainly because He wants me in a place of dependence upon Him the whole way through.

When I don't hear with the clarity I desire, I am encouraged by this passage from Exodus. Moses is having his burning bush encounter with the Lord. I think you will agree with me that this is one of the most obvious, explicit, powerful, dramatic, and very clear God-talks-to-man passages in the Bible. And yet, Moses, nervous, fearful, doubt-ridden, wants to know if he really is hearing clearly from God. So God gives him a sign:

And He said, "Certainly I will be with you, and this will be the sign to you that it is I who have sent you: when you have brought the people out of Egypt, you shall worship God at this mountain."

Exodus 3:12

The *sign* that it is truly God's call to lead the Israelites out of Egypt is that they will arrive safely to worship at Mt. Sinai?! I sort of think Moses was looking for a right-now kind of sign. But that is not what God was giving him at that moment. No certain proof. Nothing tangible to lay his hands on. Although as if to quell Moses' doubts God did eventually give him the signs of the staff and the leprous hand, Moses would not know *for sure* that he had heard correctly from God until the deliverance was complete and they were all worshipping at Mt. Sinai.

I think it is this way for us often, too. As frustrating as this may be, we may not know *for certain* that we have heard correctly until we have obeyed the best we know how, and have arrived. So what can we do if we are riddled with doubt?

To start, we can do our best to seek Him with all our heart. Surrender fully to Him and ask Him to purify our motives. We must also check to be sure that what we are hearing lines up with Scripture. Additionally, it can be helpful to seek wise counsel, especially for heavy decisions – decisions that will have long-term impact, or decisions that mean large course corrections in our lives, or decisions that will affect people other than ourselves. At times we may put out the fleece and ask God for confirmation – and He *may* give us additional confirmation – but in the end, we must simply *step out in faith*. We must trust that what we have heard *is* from Him, and respond in obedience.

And as we step out, we must recognize that we will sometimes be wrong. We must be teachable and open to correction. It is not a sin to be imperfect. *Imperfection* is called being human. *Rebellion against God* is called sin.

We must obey as best we understand, and trust God to cover us and to guide us back onto His path if we have not heard correctly. Just as God redirected Paul from Asia Minor and to Macedonia by a vision (Acts 16:6-10), God can steer us back onto His path if we have not heard correctly. And we must trust that He will work through, and make up for, all our mistakes and mishearings. His plan takes all our failures into account! He is omniscient, He knows the end from the beginning, and nothing surprises Him!

I would like to share with you a very personal story about what it meant for me to step out in faith.

God was leading me to write this book that you have in your hands. His voice was loud and clear, and He confirmed it again and again. But for years something was holding me back. I was tortured with these thoughts: What if I don't hear Him well enough, and then write what I want instead of what He wants? What if I am not spiritually mature enough, and write something that is not Biblically sound? What if I fall into pride, and write to glorify myself instead of glorifying Him? What if my motives are not completely pure, so that I write in the flesh and not in the Spirit? I am more than ten years old in the Lord – I should know how to hear clearly by now – what if I don't get it right?

Do you hear all the "I" questions? For me, this is a tip-off to pride, self-idolatry, and idolatry of people. Yet there was even more going on in my heart.

In a state of utter fear, completely stymied from obeying His call, I felt I could not hear from Him at all. I didn't know where to start or what to write. As I sought Him and sought Him, I finally heard Him say ever so gently, "You won't always get it right." I realized that I was frozen in perfectionism and fear of failure.

The Holy Spirit led me to understand that it is my job to write, using the gifts that He has given me. It is His job to move. He will be the One to transform hearts, to heal, to restore.

His words rang in my mind, "You won't always get it right." I can't do it flawlessly. I can't hear from Him perfectly. All He desires is my heart to be right with Him, hearing Him and obeying Him the best I can. And He will take care of the rest. It is His plan, His book – not mine – and He will accomplish what He intends no matter where I fail. He does not need me in order to fulfill His plans. Indeed, He merely invites me to flow with Him. His plan takes into account all my failures, because He knows them all ahead of time. His grace is sufficient for me, and His power is perfected in my weakness (2Cor 12:9).

Celeste Li
Jupiter, Florida

Truly, I think that often we won't know for certain that we have heard Him correctly until we are worshipping on Mount Sinai. Until we see how His hand has worked His plan through to completion. Then, with great confidence, we can look back and say as Moses must have said, "Yes, I did hear from God!"

Achieving Balance in Our Time With God

Regarding our time with the Lord, I have heard it said,

- Too much Bible dries up
- Too much Holy Spirit puffs up
- Perfect balance grows up

Please understand that the problem is not "too much Bible study," or "too much time alone with the Holy Spirit," but *imbalance*. Let's explore.

Too Much Bible Dries Up

It seems that we can become "dry" if all of our time with the Lord is study of the Bible. Perhaps that is something Paul had in mind when he wrote, **for the letter kills, but the Spirit gives life** (2Cor 3:6). If we are studying the Word without the consistent in-pouring of the Holy Spirit, without constantly receiving His unconditional love and tenderness and compassion, we become at risk for falling into such traps as legalism, rigidity, judgment, or impatience. We can become so concerned with research and details and minutia that we forget the depth of His love and the infiniteness of His grace. The Word may no longer be living and active, but dry, or even dead. Remember that we do not need *human* wisdom, but *the Holy Spirit's* teaching of the deep mysteries and truth of the Word:

But when He, the Spirit of truth, comes, He will guide you into all the truth.

John 16:13

Too Much Holy Spirit Puffs Up

On the other hand, spending all our time with the Lord in stillness and listening without the grounding of the truth of the Word can bring us to a prideful place. Colossians warns us about people who are ...

... not holding fast to the head, from whom the entire body ... grows with a growth which is from God.

Colossians 2:19

Verse 18 of Colossians describes these people as **inflated** and **vainly puffed up** (NASB, NKJV), obsessed with visions of angels that they may or may not have seen. We need to hold fast to our Head, to Jesus Christ, the Word of God. The Word is Truth, and we come face to face with the truth when we read the Word. Truth will convict us and correct us, and if we are **careful to do according to all that is written in it** (Josh 1:8), it will also mature us.

For the word of God is living and active and sharper than any two-edged sword, and piercing as far as the division of soul and spirit, of both joints and marrow, and able to judge the thoughts and intentions of the heart.

Hebrews 4:12

We need to encounter Truth in the Word, we need His Spirit to guide us into that Truth, *and* we need to do it.

Perfect Balance Grows Up

Bible study is indeed critical to our spiritual maturity. We need the deep truths and convictions that come with studying the Word. Additionally, singing, worshipping, journaling, praying, repenting, and serving are all critical disciplines. But if all our time with the Lord entails "doing," we can fall into an insidious trap. We may find ourselves doing these activities to "earn" His attention and affection.

Our hearts and spirits desperately need sweet times with the Holy Spirit, times of listening, solitude, stillness, and soaking. During these precious times of stillness He pours His liquid love into us and showers us with His grace.

Only God can keep us in balance:

A just balance and scales belong to the LORD; All the weights of the bag are His concern.

Proverbs 16:11

Pause to be still before the Lord, asking Him to reveal if you are slipping to one extreme or the other. Write what He has spoken to you in your journal or in the margin here, and ask Him to teach you how to maintain your balance.

Clarifying "Balance"

I'd like to take this idea of balance to another level, but first I'd like to clarify that what we are seeking is not what the world calls "balance," *but what God calls balance.* In the world's eyes, we are way off-balance, a people of extremes following a God of extremes: grace provided for the most egregious of sins; loving our enemies; considering a simple lustful look as adultery.

However, when we are so not-of-this-world that we meet the world with complete love, without even a hint of judgment, hypocrisy, haughtiness, or spiritual pride, this ridiculously off-balanced love of Christ is poised to touch the world's hearts.

Of course we will be criticized, slandered, attacked and even murdered (Mt 5:11-12, 2Tim 3:12). Sometimes, this will be because we are imperfect in our love, and it is tinged with judgment or pride, and so has rightly drawn criticism. Other times, the persecution will come because no servant is greater than his master (Jn 15:20). But as we seek to live like Jesus in a perfectly balanced off-balanced life, we can trust God to work through our shortcomings and sins as He draws people to Himself.

Achieving a Godly Balance
Between Work and Rest

I admit that figuring out a Godly balance between serving the Lord and resting in Him has been an interesting struggling point for me. It is natural for me to be doing, and a number of years ago the Lord told me that I needed to slow down and spend more time with Him. I listened and obeyed as best I understood, and spent more time praying, studying the Word, soaking, and listening in solitude. I spent more time with the Genuine, and did indeed grow to know Him with greater intimacy.

But at one point I began to think, if time with God is good, more time with God must be even better. My husband was concerned that I might be becoming so heavenly minded that I would have trouble relating to others. He was concerned that I may become stymied in my ability to connect, reach, and minister to people. I thought of the saying, "You're so heavenly minded that you're no earthly good." At first I really didn't believe my husband, but it turns out he was right. The Holy Spirit took me here:

For God is not the author of confusion, but of peace.
1 Corinthians 14:33 NKJV

Much to my surprise, confusion is *akatastasia*, which Strong's says is "instability."[4] Instability. What would make someone unstable? Being *off-balance*. I had to chew on that for a while.

And if God is not the author of imbalance, I suspected that Satan was. The Holy Spirit really had my attention now. I began to understand that not only could I become off balance in my time alone with Him (attaining the right mix of Bible and Holy Spirit time), but I could also become off-kilter trying to balance serving and spending time with Him.

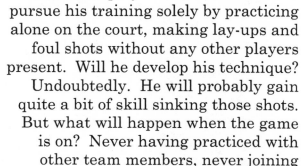

Think of a basketball player who has decided to pursue his training solely by practicing alone on the court, making lay-ups and foul shots without any other players present. Will he develop his technique? Undoubtedly. He will probably gain quite a bit of skill sinking those shots. But what will happen when the game is on? Never having practiced with other team members, never joining in pick-up games or one-on-ones, never learning how to score when the opposition is interfering with his aim, the skills he honed while alone will probably fall short of the proficiency necessary to be victorious when it really counts.

Yes, we need time alone with the Lord. Yes, many of us probably need much more time with the Lord, immersing in the things of God more, removing distractions, feeding our spirits and not our flesh. But to become mature in our hearing, our powers of discernment must be trained by constant practice, and that training will happen as we live out our daily lives in the world. To grow up in Him, our faith will need to be challenged and tested, and that will happen as we live out our everyday lives abiding in Him.

So what is that perfect balance between work and rest? I suspect that it will be different for each person, and also different in each season of our lives. It seems that each of us will need to seek the Lord to guide us into His perfect balance for each season of our life. For me, when He wanted to develop my sensitivity to His Spirit, He first took me to a lengthy season of spending much more time with the Genuine – not always reading the Bible or praying, but resting in Him. As He attuned me to His Spirit, He then began to send me out into the cacophony to train my powers of discernment and to grow my faith.

This continues to be a challenging battle for me. It seems that I can slip out of balance pretty easily. I find that I most easily fall into striving, earning, doing. One of the hints that I have fallen out of balance and need more time alone with Him is when I find myself in a place of confusion or uncertainty, or when I am wreaking a lot of havoc in relationships. It then becomes clear to me that I need to be spending more time alone with Him.

Yet at times I can also fall out of balance in the other direction, wanting to spend time with Him instead of doing His assigned work, trapped in perfectionism and fear of failure. I can be as Peter at the transfiguration, desiring to set up a tent on the mountain just to camp out when Jesus is heading down the mountain to work (Mt 17).

This struggle feels like standing in the center of a seesaw. Too much weight on the "doing" side will cause me to crash down into striving and earning. But I can easily overcompensate and throw my weight too far to the "camping-out-with-Him" side. I sure can at times get off-balance here, and become so "heavenly minded" that I cannot relate well to people. I think that figuring out this balance with the Lord will be a lifelong journey for me.

"When Jesus Shows Up"

As I puzzled through all of this, I began to think of a time when Jesus visited the home of Mary and Martha. Let's read it together.

As Jesus and his disciples were on their way, he came to a village where a woman named Martha opened her home to him. She had a sister called Mary, who sat at the Lord's feet listening to what he said. But Martha was distracted by all the preparations that had to be made. She came to him and asked, "Lord, don't you care that my sister has left me to do the work by myself? Tell her to help me!"

"Martha, Martha," the Lord answered, "you are worried and upset about many things, but only one thing is needed. Mary has chosen what is better, and it will not be taken away from her."

Luke 10:38-42 NIV

Mary has chosen what is better. So, if sitting and connecting with Jesus is better than good works, why, I wondered, don't we simply always sit? I gained some insight into this question from John C. Maxwell's book *Wisdom from Women in the Bible.*

Dr. Maxwell clarified that of course Jesus is always with us, but there are unique times when Jesus *really* shows up. It seems that there is a time for good works, and a time for solitude. These two we must learn to balance. But additionally, there are the unpredictable times "when Jesus shows up." Listen to how Dr. Maxwell describes this.

In *Wisdom from Women in the Bible*, Dr. Maxwell imagines what it would be like to visit heaven for a day and learn from some people of the Bible. He "meets" with Martha, who "described" what she learned that day Jesus came to visit her and Mary:

> "Jesus entered the room, and I left the room to go into the kitchen. It's sometimes easier to serve Jesus than to stay with Jesus...
>
> [Martha continued,] "It doesn't matter where you are or what you're doing: when Jesus is in the house, focus on Him ... When Jesus shows up, don't go do something else. Don't go into the kitchen or workroom. Don't get busy. Stop and hang with Jesus ...
>
> "When Jesus is in the house, it's not about what I'm doing for Him. It's about what He's doing – no matter what that may be. We don't know when He will show up. We don't know what His agenda will be ... We just need to be willing to stop and be with Him."[5]

I understand. In Mary's time, Jesus showed up in flesh and blood. Now, He shows up in the Person of His Spirit. Those moments "when Jesus shows up" are the times to sit at His feet. To bask in His Presence. To enjoy Him for *Him*. These are powerful opportunities for Him to build His relationship with us. On these occasions He wants us to just be with Him. To stop everything and focus on Him. To enjoy *Him*. As we sit at His feet, He will pour into us whatever *He knows* that we need right now. That could be love, hope, forgiveness, mercy, encouragement, faith, joy, peace, strength, or any number of outpourings of His

Spirit. He shows up to fill us with *Himself*.

When Jesus shows up, we won't know His agenda. At the moment of His appearance, whether we are serving or studying our Bible or doing anything else, this is the time to do as Mary did: to stop whatever we are doing, to sit at His feet, to listen for His voice, and wait until we hear. This is the time to sit and listen *until* He shows us what His agenda is. To *wait* until He directs us. It's possible that He may want us to speak, to serve, to move. It's possible that He may want us to read His Word, to worship, or to intercede in prayer. It's possible that He may want us to be still and listen and learn. Or, He may want us just to rest in His Presence as He showers us with His love and fills us with Himself. We will not know His agenda until we stop, sit, listen, and wait.

When Jesus shows up, we do not want to run off to work as Martha did. Martha missed the opportunity of His Presence because she didn't stop and sit. She was off-balance. But Mary had better balance. She knew when to sit.

Like Martha, we, too, can miss Jesus if we continue to work when His Holy Spirit arrives and calls us to sit. We, too, can miss Jesus if we are too busy and distracted. And we can even miss an intense encounter with Him if we are so immersed in studying our Bible when He arrives that we miss *Him*.

When Jesus shows up, we do not want to be as preoccupied as Peter at the transfiguration, busy planning to build tents to memorialize the experience.

Peter said to Jesus, "Master, it is good for us to be here; let us make three tabernacles: one for You, and one for Moses, and one for Elijah" — not realizing what he was saying. While he was saying this, a cloud formed and began to overshadow them; and they were afraid as they entered the cloud. Then a

voice came out of the cloud, saying, "This is My Son, My Chosen One; listen to Him!"

Luke 9:33-35

Additionally, Peter was talking so much about how wonderful the experience was that he *missed what Jesus was saying.* God interrupted him and commanded him to be quiet and listen. Likewise, we, too, can be so busy talking instead of remaining still and listening that we miss entirely what the Holy Spirit is saying.

Peter wanted to camp out, but Jesus knew that there was work to be done, for at the base of the mountain a demonized boy awaited His healing power. Likewise, if we are not listening, we may remain sitting when it is time to head down the mountain to work.

When Jesus shows up, we must stop, sit at His feet, and listen and wait. He may want to speak mysteries to us; He may want to give us a deeper revelation of Himself.

Or He may want to equip and guide us, because He knows what warfare we will encounter at the foot of the mountain.

As we sit and listen, we can become attuned to His voice, able to hear Him when He whispers to us that it is time to head off down the mountain to destroy the works of the devil. Jesus knows how desperately we want to be with Him, whether that means sitting at His feet or moving when He moves. We want to know when to sit, and when to work. We don't want to bustle about working when it is time to sit. But neither do we want to remain sitting when He has moved, because in order to continue to abide in Him, when He moves, we must move with Him. If we remain sitting when He has moved, we will no longer be at His feet, because His feet are no longer there.

"She Has Kept This for the Day of My Burial"

Let's move forward in our Bibles to a time one week before Jesus' death, when we again encounter this woman who so wisely had sat at His feet.

Then, six days before the Passover, Jesus came to Bethany, where Lazarus was who had been dead, whom He had raised from the dead. There they made Him a supper; and Martha served, but Lazarus was one of those who sat at the table with Him. Then Mary took a pound of very costly oil of spikenard, anointed the feet of Jesus, and wiped His feet with her hair. And the house was filled with the fragrance of the oil. But one of His disciples, Judas Iscariot, Simon's son, who would betray Him, said, "Why was this fragrant oil not sold for three hundred denarii and given to the poor?" This he said, not that he cared for the poor, but because he was a thief, and had the money box; and he used to take what was put in it. But Jesus said, "Let her alone; she has kept this for the day of My burial."

John 12:1-7 NKJV

One week before He died, Mary anointed Jesus. The fragrance of even one drop of that powerful nard would last a very long time. So what about an entire pound? I have heard that some theologians believe that even a week later, while Jesus was being tortured to death, the sweet fragrance of that jarful of very concentrated perfume would still cling to Him. Mary had anointed Jesus *for His burial.*

How did Mary know that this was the time to anoint? Did she know that in a week Jesus would be laid in the tomb? The disciples themselves had spent much time with the Lord, and they themselves didn't even know. When Jesus told them that He would be killed ...

... the disciples understood none of these things, and the meaning of this statement was hidden from them, and they did not comprehend the things that were said.

Luke 18:34

Peter, James, and John fell asleep when the time was most critical to pray. Thomas didn't have any idea where Jesus was going. When the greatest spiritual battle was raging, Peter wielded his sword and waged a physical battle. The meaning of Jesus' words were hidden from them. But Mary seems to have grasped something that none of His disciples had understood: she knew when to anoint. She may not have fully known that she was anointing for His burial, but she did know what to do and when to do it. How did she know?

I think that the reason she knew what to do and when to do it, was because *when Jesus showed up* ...

- She chose what was better. **"Mary has chosen what is better, and it will not be taken away from her"** (Lk 10:42 NIV).

- She stopped everything and sat at His feet, because she maintained Godly balance.

- She gave Him her full attention, basking in His Presence.

As Mary focused on Jesus, He poured Himself into her. Perhaps she even received revelations from the Lord as she sat at His feet.

Although Martha's serving may have been important, Jesus described her state as **troubled**, a word that means "a tumult ... noise, uproar ... to disturb in the mind, trouble, make anxious."[6] Her serving in this manner must surely have hindered her joyous connection with the Lord.

In contrast, Jesus says that **"Mary has chosen what is better."** The word **better** is *agathos* in the Greek. *Agathos* does not necessarily mean "better" in terms of more righteous, but "better" meaning yielding the most bang for the buck.[7] When Jesus showed up, Mary stopped and put all her focus on Him. As He poured Himself into her, I think the result was a deep knowing of her Savior. Because she sat, listened, and waited, she then knew when to keep sitting, and she knew when to anoint.

When Jesus shows up, only one pursuit is necessary: basking in His Presence. Opening our hearts so that He can fill us with Himself. Sitting at His feet is **to our advantage.** Sitting at His feet is **the good part, the better part, the only thing worth being concerned about** (AMP, NASB, NIV, NLT). And Mary *chose* to do just that.

Questions Chapter 2: Heaven Touches Earth

Memory Verse:

"But only one thing is needed. Mary has chosen what is better, and it will not be taken away from her."
Luke 10:42 NIV

1) Luke 10:38-42 is a familiar passage. Read it *in light of* John 12:1-7. Imagine what it would be like to be Mary in both of these scenarios. Feel the agony in her heart as she comprehends that her Lord's death is imminent.

Sometimes we may think, "Well, if Jesus was here like He was in Mary's time, I'd sit at His feet, too." Pause to let the reality hit that Jesus *is* indeed here. Journal your thoughts.

2) Spend some time alone with the Lord, asking the Holy Spirit to show you any imbalance. Ask Him not only about balance between serving and resting in Him, but also about Scripture and Holy Spirit time.

3) Create a secret place of His Presence where you will immerse in His Word, where you will praise and worship Him, where you will journal, soak, and be still in silence. Come here expectantly, realizing, as Clint Brown sings in *Secret Place,*

> *There are no secrets in the secret place*
> *I've been told that in Your Presence*
> *I don't have to be ashamed*
> *With trembling hands*
> *I'll remove the mask that's on my face*
> *There are no secrets in the secret place.*[8]

4) Of all the doorways that we discussed in this chapter, it seems that many find soaking to be the most helpful doorway to transition from the physical to the spiritual. This "liquid prayer," the combination of being still in solitude with music, seems to help many to open their hearts to hear from the Holy Spirit. If you have never tried this before, now is a good time to start. And if this is already familiar territory for you, now is a good time to increase your time with the Genuine.

Realize that, like any of these disciplines and doorways, it may take much time and practice to receive from Him. When I first tried to be still before Him, I could barely sit for one song! Now, I sit still before Him nearly every day. Don't be discouraged; listen expectantly! The Holy Spirit cannot wait to pour His liquid love into your dry soul.

5) Use the Word to praise Him in your secret place. Stand up and read out loud from the depth of your soul a passage of praise, such as Psalm 145, Psalm 103, or Isaiah 40:12-31.

6) Spend time in the beauty of His creation appreciating Him and the works of His hands. Sit in stillness and let the awe of who He is and the depth of His love for you burrow into your heart and soul.

John Li

Chapter 3
Toppling Barriers to Intimacy

earing His voice, developing a sensitivity to His Spirit, and becoming discerning have been our focus in the first two chapters. All critical in a relationship with God. But there is something here that we may not recognize yet. I believe that the true cry of our hearts is *intimacy*. Pause for a moment and let the Holy Spirit speak to you on this point.

In comparison to genuine intimacy, hearing His voice is a bit superficial. If we were honest here, I think we may admit that hearing His voice is all about *us*. About knowing what He wants *so that* we can partner with Him, obey Him, and not miss what He has for our lives. Noble, certainly. But genuine intimacy is vastly deeper: a penetrating closeness with our Creator and Savior, a relationship in which we know Him as fully as He knows us.

When I was a child, I talked like a child, I thought like a child, I reasoned like a child. When I became a man, I put childish ways behind me. Now we see but a poor reflection as in a mirror; then we shall see

face to face. Now I know in part; then I shall know fully, even as I am fully known.

1 Corinthians 13:11-12 NIV

He already knows *us* fully, yet we see *Him* only as a poor reflection as in a mirror. There will be a day when we see Him face to Face, and know Him as fully as He knows us. We indeed were built for eternity, and our hearts ache and long for that day. But what about now? We can indeed come to know Him more fully, day by day, as we put childish ways aside and mature in our walk with Him.

If we want to grow in intimacy with Him, I believe that we must resolve some nagging questions deep down in our hearts, questions about who He is, and about who He says we are. There are three critical questions that we are going to tackle in this chapter:

1) If **God is for us** (Rom 8:31), then why does it sometimes feel like He is *against me?*

2) Does God *really* want to spend time with me?

3) If God loves me so much, why can't I *feel* that love?

I think that grasping God's truths here and settling these issues will topple some seemingly insurmountable barricades to true intimacy.

Question #1: If God Is For Us, Why Does It Sometimes Feel Like He Is Against Me?

When we are hurting, we may feel rejected by God. We may begin to believe that God has abandoned us, that He doesn't care enough about us to intervene. We may begin to feel that God has conceded the battle to Satan, that He just gave up, that somehow we weren't worth fighting for. But that is simply not who God is!

God's cherished plan for mankind is a world without sin, Adam and Eve in the Garden of Eden before the fall. Deep fellowship with our Creator, perfect communion with Him, walking with Him, connecting with Him, the Father's love and grace flowing in us and through us, and that same love flowing right back to Him and then to others.

But Adam and Eve, having been given free will, rejected God's cherished plan, and rejected God. They chose rebellion and disobedience, they chose pride and control, they chose idolatry of themselves. They chose to eat of the tree, seeking to be like God, and they severed their connection to God. And even more was lost, for Adam and Eve's sin will continue to affect the entire world until the end of time.

But that is not the end of the story! God's plan of restoration sent Jesus to die in our place. We are right now in the middle of His plan, as He is continuously working to fully restore mankind to Himself. He describes what the end of His plan will look like in Revelation Chapters 21 and 22, the perfect fellowship untainted by sin that we will once more have with Him.

If we could just see with God's eyes, see how our sins and the sins of our ancestors have given Satan an engraved invitation to brutally tromp all over our lives... And, even more importantly, if we could just see God's hand of protection holding the dark back, as God says to Satan, *"No, I won't let you go that far"* (Lk 22:31, Job 1:1;12).

Satan craves to run rampant in our lives — and indeed the sin we were born into and our own personal sins have invited him in. God does not invent evil — Satan and his dark forces, wicked men under Satan's control, and even we regular old sinners are the inventors of evil. But God in His sovereignty prevails. He chooses. With great love and care, with complete omniscience, God *hand-picks* our sufferings – for our good, and His glory. Pause and meditate on the verses below, and jot in the margin or write in your journal what the Holy Spirit is speaking to you.

And we know that God causes all things to work together for good to those who love God, to those who are called according to His purpose. For those whom He foreknew, He also predestined to become conformed to the image of His Son.

Romans 8:28-29

The LORD has made everything for its own purpose, even the wicked for the day of evil.

Proverbs 16:4

In this you greatly rejoice, even though now for a little while, if necessary, you have been distressed by various trials, so that the proof of your faith, being more precious than gold which is perishable, even though tested by fire, may be found to result in praise and glory and honor at the revelation of Jesus Christ.

1 Peter 1:6-7

We also exult in our tribulations, knowing that tribulation brings about perseverance; and perseverance, proven character; and proven character, hope; and hope does not disappoint, because the love of God has been poured out within our hearts through the Holy Spirit who was given to us.

Romans 5:3-5

Why Doesn't God Shield Us
From <u>All</u> the Works of the Devil?

Yes, I have asked that question many times myself. I believe that the answer lies in His infinite love. His infinite love gives us the gift of free will – even though it means that His heart will bear enormous pain as His creation rejects Him every day. Even though it means that as men destroy men, His heart is ripped to shreds. Even though it means that He suffers with us, because He lives *inside* of us. He chooses not to rescind that gift of free will, the tremendous gift of love and dignity that He has bestowed upon us. Only free will allows us to freely love – and He treasures our freely given love in a way that is beyond our comprehension.

I posed this question to Pastor Julie Mullins of Christ Fellowship. She explained,

> God is all-powerful and *can* do anything. However, When God gave us the freedom to choose or reject Him, He in essence put limitations on His own power. It is not His lack of concern or desire to hurt us that causes us pain or affliction. It is the free choice of man to do wrong. The impact of sin spills out on the guilty and the innocent. God longs for us to invite Him into our deepest points of pain so that He can bring hope and healing.

Pain does not mean that God has abandoned us. Pain does not mean failure. Pain simply means that, for reasons that may remain a mystery to us, God has chosen to restrain Himself, to restrict His movements within the confines of this broken world.

We live in a fallen world, and God takes full responsibility for His decision to give men and angels free will. If we are angry about anything, we can take it up with God. Don't blame other people, don't blame the world, don't blame Satan. Pain and suffering is not God's cherished plan. Yet He is in control, and His plan in His timing will come to pass.

God is not the cause of our pain, but He sees it and takes full responsibility. I think He wants us to trust that although Satan meant evil against us, God meant it for good (Gen 50:20). We may not see His hand at work, but we can trust that He is working for our good – and His glory. When we go to Him in full honesty, pounding our fists on His chest, He can handle it. He is bigger than our anger and pain, and He will touch us. He may or may not remove the pain. He may or may not give us understanding. He may or may not open our eyes. But when we trust in His perfect plan and seek Him in our pain, He promises to comfort us, pour His love into us, and give us *Himself*.

The Evil One Cannot Touch Us

When mankind chose rebellion, God did not promise us a life without pain. When we committed our lives to Jesus, God *still* did not promise us a life without pain. Instead, Jesus promises, **"In this world you will have trouble,"** and goes on to say, **"But take heart! I have overcome the world. I have deprived it of power to harm you and have conquered it for you"** (Jn 16:33 NIV, AMP).

I think that the word **harm** means more than simply to injure, or to cause pain or suffering. I think **harm** connotes damage and destruction, with long-lasting, even eternal consequences. We are living in a world that *will* cause pain and suffering, a world that is full of trials and heartache and frustrations, a world that will bring us tribulation, persecution, and distress (Rom 8:35) – but nothing in this world can permanently destroy us. Because we belong to Jesus and our eternal life with Him is secure, nothing can take away His love for us. Nothing can remove our security in Him. Our bodies may be ravaged by disease, our finances may be in shambles, our homes may be demolished by wars or tornadoes, our loved ones may be lost, our marriages and our families may be in chaos – but none of this can touch our relationship with Jesus. God does not promise us that we will not suffer, but He *does* promise us that Jesus' comfort will always be greater than our suffering. Trusting in Him protects us from harm.

We know that anyone born of God does not continue to sin; the one who was born of God keeps him safe, and the evil one cannot harm him.
1 John 5:18 NIV

Jesus protects us, watches over us, and keeps us safe, so that the evil one cannot **harm** us, **touch** us, **lay hold of or get a grip on** us (NIV, NASB, AMP). This word in the Greek is *haptomai*, "to connect, to bind ... to touch. Refers to such handling of an object as to exert a modifying influence upon it ... touching for the purpose of manipulating." *Haptomai* differs from another Greek word which means only "to touch the surface."[1] To me, this means ...

- Satan can grope around for us, but he cannot **get a grip on** us, for we belong to Jesus, His gift of life is *eternal*, and no one can snatch us from His hands (Jn 10:28).

- Satan can brush us, but he cannot **lay hold of** us, because God has sealed us with His Spirit, guaranteeing that we will be saved on the day of redemption (Eph 1:13-14, 4:30).

- Satan can threaten our eternal inheritance, but he cannot **touch** it, because it is imperishable and shielded by the power of God (1Pt 1:4-5).

Satan can nudge us, shoot flaming arrows at us, even collide with us. He can try – and he surely will try – to control us and to customize us for his plans. And that may hurt. But if we are abiding in Christ, he cannot integrate us into his designs. Can he harass us? Sure. Tempt us? Certainly. Sift us like wheat? When God gives him permission. But he cannot *touch* us. He can temporarily manipulate us, but he cannot reshape us eternally for his purposes, *for God has the last word.*

Additionally, if we are growing in Christ, abiding in Him, repenting and submitting to the process of being conformed to His image and we **do not continue to sin,** when Satan handles us, he cannot exert a modifying influence on us. If we are abiding in the Vine, he cannot bind us to his darkness.

Belonging to Jesus does not guarantee a life without pain. It does not guarantee that we will not be affected by the wickedness of the world. It does not guarantee that our lives and the lives of our loved ones will be untainted by trouble. It does not guarantee that we will not make sinful choices with horrendous consequences. But when we return to Him, He will bandage our wounds, and He will heal us (Hos 6:1, 14:1). Although some of His healing may not be completed until eternity, as we draw nearer to Him, His healing comes forth in greater measure.

Come meet Mark and Diane. Their story puts skin on the verses that we have been discussing. Mark, a high-powered engineer, had lost his job over two years ago ...

As the jobless months wore into jobless years, we realized that we had a choice. We could remain in our shallow relationships with God, praying simple prayers with a touch of self-pity, or we could repent of our lukewarmness and idolatry of our own plans, and learn what it meant to have a deep spiritual relationship with the Lord.

God wanted us to grow more intimate with Him in that

time of need, and He made that very clear to us. We chose to surrender our agenda to His, and to seek Him with all our hearts. As we encountered God, what we discovered was a deep sense of tranquility.

Knowing that God was walking <u>with</u> <u>us</u> through this trial gave us a feeling of peacefulness, strength, power, and freedom. We had never felt so confident in every situation; we completely surrendered all of our worries and concerns. We began to hear Him speak to us; we felt His presence; we never felt alone. The more we asked Him to come into our lives, the deeper He developed our relationship. The deeper our relationship, the less we were engulfed by fear. The less our fear, the greater was our ability to trust His every move, even when we thought the situation was grim.

In His perfect timing, God did more than bless Mark with any old job. He gave him <u>a perfect job</u>, a job that fits his personality and abilities. A challenging job with lots of room for growth, coupled with benefits and a salary that we didn't even pray for. Two years was a long time to wait, but we know now that this job hadn't even been created yet, and God wanted us to wait for it. He was with us when other jobs were tempting. Many times we heard God's words, "Not this one." He taught us wisdom, perseverance, patience, endurance, and strength.

We as a couple have been taught by the greatest Teacher of all, a Teacher who has the best plans for us and who knows our deepest needs and wants. A Teacher who unconditionally loves us. A Teacher who never failed us and never left us.

We pray that everyone receives God's grace the way we have and grows in the spiritual way we did. There is nothing more satisfying in life than knowing who you have on your side: God and each other.

Mark and Diane
Tallahassee, Florida

Faith, tested by fire, proven genuine. Trials resulting in perseverance, proven character, and hope. Trials hand-picked by the One who loves them infinitely. Trials resulting in a depth of intimacy that would have never happened without that lengthy season.

Belonging to Jesus means that God is always working for our good. He has ordained each trial, each battle. Why does He shield us from some attacks and not from others? Sometimes, that remains a mystery. But even if we have no answers, He calls us to fix our eyes on Him:

Therefore we do not lose heart. Though outwardly we are wasting away, yet inwardly we are being renewed day by day. For our light and momentary troubles are achieving for us an eternal glory that far outweighs them all. So we fix our eyes not on what is seen, but on what is unseen. For what is seen is temporary, but what is unseen is eternal.

2 Corinthians 4:16-18 NIV

Looking with eyes of the flesh, we may begin to believe the lies that God is not protecting us, that He has abandoned us. But looking with the eyes of God, He will show us the eternal weight of glory.

God does not promise to remove our trials, but to *walk with us* through them, bringing forth good – for His Kingdom, and for us. He may give us revelation, or He may not. We can torment ourselves with questions: Why me? What is God trying to tell me? How can I stop this physical, mental, emotional, or spiritual pain? Or … we can seek God. His ways are simply higher than our ways, as He fulfills the purposes that only He knows in their entirety. Creatively unpredictable, faithfully steadfast, and lovingly kind, what He really wants to know is, *Will you trust Me?*

Struggling with these concepts and verses? I agree they are challenging. Reading (or re-reading) *Triumph Over Suffering* may deepen your understanding.

Question #2:
Does God <u>Really</u> Want to Spend Time With Me?

Am I *really* important to Him? Does this Almighty, All-Holy, Completely Perfect Creator of the Universe *really* want to spend time with miniscule, sinful, pretty-useless-and-clearly-imperfect me? We may feel unworthy and undeserving of His time. Not good enough, righteous enough, or valuable enough to merit His attention. Perhaps God wants to be in relationship with pastors and leaders and super-spiritual prayer warriors, but not little insignificant me. We may believe that our sins – be they sins of action or deep heart sins that no one would even guess – disqualify us from anything more than but a "passing glance."

I would like to introduce you to my friend Cristina. She is a brilliant speaker and writer, so anointed by the Lord that she literally glows with His Light. Few would guess that this private war rages in her heart and soul.

I often confuse my relationship with the Lord as that of the many dysfunctional relationships I've been in with earthly men. There are seasons when I feel like nothing I do (or don't do) is ever enough. I begin to wonder if my suffering is a punishment for not walking in complete obedience.

I fall into a trap of believing that I have to fight for and really prove to God how much I love Him and, in return, deserve His love. I realize I seek to accomplish that in much the same way I have with my father, ex-boyfriends, bosses, and my husband. Certainly, I must have to earn it.

There are moments when I get the sense God is like a man who tests a woman over and over again to see how much she will endure and if she will stick around. Meanwhile, the woman continues to fight for her man, exhausted, wondering how much longer this game will last. She questions if her love and loyalty for him is really strong enough to keep it up.

As many women do in those types of relationships, there are moments when I'm ready to hang it all up. I start to believe the lies, soon contemplating, in some ways practicing, the best way to go through the awkward and painful break up. While that may be necessary for certain earthly situations, I remember how pure and unconditional God's love is for me.

I know there are holes and cracks that the enemy uses to creep inside of me. Even when Satan can't seem to get in all of the way, my love for the Lord is still threatened by the devil's secret (sometimes not-so-secret) admiration for me. The evil one stalks me, hoping I'll be drawn in by the fake jewels he dangles.

Just as precious metals go through the refining process, I want to let the real jeweler complete His work in me. As an outsider, peering over God's shoulder, it might seem hard to understand why I had to experience abandonment, financial loss, broken relationships, chronic illness, addiction, morbid obesity, severe anxiety, rejection, failed careers and businesses, sexual immorality, and more.

It's through the fire, through the trials, that my eyes have been opened to Christ's brilliance and His strength for my perseverance. He's creating a masterpiece, one so magnificent that not even the finest showcases carry anything like it. I remember as a child, my mom used to make my sister and I walk back into the house to put on our jewelry, if we forgot (or didn't want to wear it). Whether it was pure gold or gold plated, later in life, I often found myself thinking that what I had wasn't good enough. My material items didn't seem to measure up, and neither did I.

Jewelry is one of those things I discovered men sometimes used in my life to lure me into sinful behavior or into their grip. I discovered their gift was conditional and came at a high price. It sparkled with lies.

Although Satan may offer me jewels from the world, I must remember the real ones God gave me. Too many times I fell for the devil's tricks, almost like the "buy now, pay later" approach at retailers. I could not afford the cost required to clean up the mess of Satan's pearls (my hurts) now broken off the string and scattered on the floor. I needed help.

I was presented with the best gift of all, Jesus. He gave me a beautiful tribute for my new role as His chosen princess, jewelry made of the purest gems. The earrings my Father gave me are a reminder that He listens to my cries for help. The necklace is His gentle touch over my heart to let me know that His love is real and unconditional.

They are not physical pieces. Rather, a spiritual reminder that, with each time I gently push the back of any earring close to my ear lobe and delicately join the clasp of any necklace to the chain, I am His daughter and I've been set free from chains of darkness.

Best of all, I didn't have to buy or do anything to get them. The price has already been paid. I simply had to say yes and receive the gift of salvation and sanctification, the victory and intimacy, which is only possible with Jesus.

Like many women, I love jewelry, but the entire spiritual set I wear (an accessory to my full armor of God) is a symbol that nothing here on earth shines the way the light of Christ does. The impostor will not fool me.

Cristina Williams
Bible Teacher, Speaker, and Writer
Fort Lauderdale, Florida

What about you? Can you relate to Cristina's story? Do thoughts of unworthiness resonate with you? Let's take a moment to pause and let the Holy Spirit search our hearts. Let's pray and wait, still before Him, asking Him to reveal any lies entrenched in our hearts. Jot a few notes in the margin or in your journal as He reveals.

"I'm Not Valuable Enough for His Attention"

I believe that this deception of worthlessness, self-hatred, self-condemnation, is one of the most insidious, deep-rooted lies that the enemy has implanted in the core of the hearts of many. I also believe that exposing and demolishing this lie is paramount to developing true intimacy with Him.

I think that this lie is particularly difficult to uproot because Satan seems to start with the truth, and then wrap his lie around that core truth. The truth he starts with is that we are not worthy of God's love and attention. The lie he then intertwines into it is that we need to *earn* God's love and attention.

Indeed, we could never be worthy enough, good enough, righteous enough, or holy enough to deserve His attention. We cannot earn or deserve His love and affection. These truths requires deep humility to accept.

But – He *still* wants to give us His attention anyway! He knows every word before we speak it, every thought before we think it, every nook and cranny of our hearts, the good and the bad – and He *still* calls us valuable, precious and honored in His sight! He still *chooses* to pursue us, and He is passionate about spending time with us! His heart *yearns* to be with us! And it seems that these truths require an equal dose of humility to accept.

Think in these terms: What if a gentleman, at huge personal cost and sacrifice to himself, offered to his beloved a ring, asking her to enter into a covenant of marriage with him ... and she, recognizing her imperfections, said, "I cannot accept this because I am so unworthy." Or maybe, "I am so undeserving; let me contribute a bit of money for this gift, because then I won't feel quite so guilty." Imagine the pain of rejection inflicted on that gentleman's heart! God gave us free will, risking rejection ...

Let's go to the Word to begin the work of demolishing this unworthiness stronghold.

"Where Are You?"

Why did God create us? Face it, He is omniscient and knew completely that we humans would turn away from Him. Yet He *still* spoke the universe into existence, He *still* formed the earth in His hands, He *still* breathed life into man. Why? In Genesis we'll search out some answers together.

After Adam and Eve rebelled, they made clothes out of fig leaves and tried to hide from God — let's pick up the story right there.

They heard the sound of the LORD God walking in the garden in the cool of the day, and the man and his wife hid themselves from the presence of the LORD God among the trees of the garden. Then the LORD God called to the man, and said to him, "Where are you?"

Genesis 3:8-9

"Where are you?" Where are you??? Those three little words stop me in my tracks. The greatest sin has just been committed. The sin that will touch every single person who will ever walk the earth, from that moment 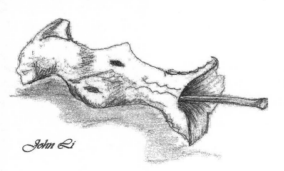 until the end of time. Every single person. The sin that set the consequences of the curse into motion. The sin that ushered into the world hatred, pain, suffering, shame, anguish, heartache, illness, divorce, abuse, war, murder, death. The sin that tore mankind away from God, that drove a wedge between God and man, that erected a barrier between God and man that is infinity miles high and infinity miles wide and infinity miles deep.

The sin that wrested us from the perfect peaceful rule of God and threw us under the horrendous bone-crushing reign of Satan. And God says, *"Where are you?"*

When I read this passage, my first thought is, "What have you done?" Even though I know deep inside that I am equally as sinful and rebellious, in horror and shock and anger and furor I would demand, *"What have you done?"*

But not God. God says, *"Where are you?"* Of course God knows where they are. But hear His heart. God, the Infinite Almighty One, the One who holds the waters in the hollow of His hand, the One who marks off the heavens by the span, the One who calculates the dust of the earth by the measure, says to His sinfully rebellious creation, **"Where are you?"** His heart seems to cry out, *"Please don't hide from Me. Come to Me. Only I can help you."*

God has indeed put Himself in a very vulnerable place. He has left His heart completely unprotected. There He stands, utterly defenseless against the pain of rejection. He gave man the free will to accept or reject Him, and Adam and Eve have just driven a stake into His heart.

Can you see the anguish in His face, feel the tremble of His hands, witness the tears coursing down His cheeks? *"Where are you?"* God gave them His heart, and they stomped on it, ripped it to shreds, and handed it back to Him. Listen to His heart's cry: *"Where are you?"* It's all God wants. It's why He created us. Relationship. Connection. Fellowship. Communion. A deep penetrating closeness with the most treasured of His creation, mankind. *Do you know this God?*

We may not be able to truly comprehend the passion of His desire for relationship *with us.* I think many of us have such a distorted view of God, a caricature really. We may visualize Him rejecting us for messing up, withholding His love from us if we don't spend time with Him, holding the bar impossibly high and casting lightning bolts down upon us when we blow it. We are diagnosed with cancer and may think God is abandoning us because we had walked away from Him. Our kids are not right with God and we may think God is letting us have it because we made one too many wrong decisions in our parenting. We are in financial ruin and may think that God is trying to "teach us a lesson."

But this is not the heart character of God! He is not rejecting us, withholding His love from us, or casting lightning bolts down upon us. He is not abandoning us or trying to teach us a lesson. We may have chosen life without God, but He didn't choose life without us. Everything, *everything*, He is working is because He is pursuing us.

God wants us to see Him with new eyes. He wants us to believe deeply and unshakably in our hearts and souls that His greatest desire is for *relationship* with us. Quit trying to understand it, to make sense of it, or to justify it. Quit trying to earn His attention or to become worthy of it. We could *never* deserve His attention! The Infinite wanting a relationship with a mere human makes no sense. It's not *supposed* to make sense. It's not our job to understand. It is our job to *choose* to believe that what He says is true. Bowing our hearts to these two truths, admitting that we could never be deserving enough of any of His grace, goodness, or love – *and* accepting that He knows us fully *and wants us anyway* – will require face-down humility.

- You cannot earn His love –
  because you've already got it.

- You cannot grab His attention –
  because you've already got it.

- You cannot deserve His acceptance –
  because you've already got it.

- You cannot win His desire to spend time with you –
  because you've already got it.

- And you cannot entice Him to pursue you –
  *because He has already been seeking you
  your entire life.*

Go back and read those bullet points again. And then
once more. Now be still in His Presence, and let the power
of those truths permeate your heart.

Being Pursued By God

My friend Mike is a man who has only recently come to
recognize that he has been protected and pursued by God
his entire life. But hold on; I'm getting ahead of the story.
Let me back up and introduce you to him.

Mike grew up in a severely abusive household. By age
14, he was homeless, living on the streets of New York City
without family ties and with only an eighth grade education.
Fearing for his life, he joined a gang, and seemed destined
for a life of destruction. But at age 18, in an amazing turn
of events, he stumbled into a John 3:16 Fellowship Hall
and turned his life over to Christ. I'll let Mike pick up the
story here.

*I knew immediately that God was calling me to leave the
gang. Please understand that no one <u>ever</u> leaves a gang.
Gang membership is for life. Anyone trying to leave a gang
would simply be ... wiped off the face of the earth.*

*But I had said yes to God, and I knew that meant that
I must say yes to His call to leave the gang. He wanted
me to trust Him to be my only source of protection. In
demonstration of my commitment to Him, I threw my gun
into the river.*

*What happened next was truly miraculous. Suddenly,
my <u>entire</u> <u>gang</u> just disappeared. Some were put in jail;*

some moved out of state; some died. Almost overnight, the gang no longer existed.

I had obeyed God's call and stepped out in faith, throwing my gun into the river. God answered that step of obedience by setting me free.

Mike
Stuart, Florida

Mike has shared this testimony to offer hope. "If God did it for me, He will do it for you," he declares.

Miraculously, Mike went on to become a disciple of faith and a soldier of the Lord; miraculously, he obtained further education, married, and raised a close-knit family. Miraculously, he reunited with his family of origin and brought the gospel message to them. To the outside observer, God's hand was so clearly on his life, but Mike himself did not recognize this until much later. Let's let him explain.

There were some things going on at work that I am not at liberty to discuss; let's just say it was not right with God. I took it to God in prayer. Although I had no job prospects in sight, God told me to resign my position immediately, and I obeyed. As I resigned, a great weight was lifted off me, so I knew that I had done the right thing.

As if three weeks of fruitless job searching weren't trial enough, I found myself with new medical problems. I developed severe blood clots in my legs and lungs, and a pool of blood on the top of my heart. I was admitted to the ICU, one step from death. At the same time, my brother was dying from cancer. My 86 year-old mother, who is not in good health, intended to fly in from Puerto Rico to see my brother, but she missed her flight and did not see him before he died. I told my family not to tell my mother that I was in the hospital; I didn't think she could handle the news. A few weeks after I was discharged from the hospital I started to bleed internally and externally – blood was pouring out.

I had a very painful infection in my side – on a scale of 1 to 10, the pain was a 20.

As I laid there in the ICU, I thought, this can't be happening: no job, no insurance, running out of money, my brother just died, my mother missed the opportunity to see him before he died, and she doesn't know I'm near death myself ... I asked God, "Is there anything else?" I was beginning to feel like Job – persecuted.

All this happened during a time when I was in a men's Bible study of Triumph Over Suffering. Because I was learning that God has been with me all my life, I didn't blame God. I didn't cry or get upset or get angry. I suddenly realized that if I had remained in my old job, I would have certainly died as the job was physically demanding, and also because an ambulance would not have arrived on time.

Suddenly, I realized that God has indeed been with me all of my life. In the heart pain and the anger and the hate and the beatings and the cries of unhappiness, He has always been there. This Bible study and the men who I now call my brothers have helped me to see so much that I didn't see or understand. I have had many battles spiritually as well as physically and mentally, and I have learned that fear and regret is a cruel prison we build for ourselves. Once we get past that and understand that every passing minute is a chance to turn our life around – WOW! There is so much wonder of God to experience.

In a surprising set of circumstances, my resume landed on the desk of a friend of long ago, a brother in Christ from a previous church. God provided me with a wonderful job, minutes away from my home, with terrific pay, benefits, and working conditions – and a Christian boss.

I know now that God has always been there for Job, as well as for me, since the day I was born. The love of God is endless and He is never far from me. I know what it is like to be hated, beaten, called names, and ridiculed even by people who said they loved me. But I also know that God has been with me from the day I was born. He was with me when I was going through my years in the gang. He was with me when I was one step from death in the ICU. And He lives inside of me.

God has blessed me with health, money, and a job – a wonderful place to work just ten minutes from my home. My mom is doing well; my brother is with God and we will meet again. Now is God good or what? I still feel like Job – but this time loved!

Mike
Stuart, Florida

Mike walks in such humility; he will be the first to tell you that he doesn't deserve all the Lord has done for him. He recognizes that God does not stick with us because we are deserving or worthy or good or righteous or holy. The reason that He does not forsake us is because of His great Name.

"For the LORD will not abandon His people *on account of His great name*, because the LORD has been pleased to make you a people for Himself."
1 Samuel 12:22, emphasis added

God does not abandon us because of His Name, and His Name is Love. Even if we are faithless, God remains faithful to us because that is who He is (2Tim 2:13). Although we fall short of being deserving enough of His faithful Presence, He will not fail us or forsake us, and He is with us wherever we go (Josh 1:5,9).

How God Defines Himself

Then Moses said to God, "Behold, I am going to the sons of Israel, and I will say to them, 'The God of your fathers has sent me to you.' Now they may say to me, 'What is His name?' What shall I say to them?"

God said to Moses, "I AM WHO I AM;" and He said, "Thus you shall say to the sons of Israel, 'I AM has sent me to you.'"

God, furthermore, said to Moses, "Thus you shall say to the sons of Israel, 'The LORD the God of your fathers, the God of Abraham, the God of Isaac, and the God of Jacob, has sent me to you.' This is My name forever, and this is My memorial-name to all generations."

Exodus 3:13-15

What intrigues me here is that when Moses specifically asked God His name, God didn't choose a name that spoke of His omnipotence, omnipresence, sovereignty, or glory. He gave His name as Yahweh, "I AM," which says to me that God wanted to emphasize not His *doing*, but His *being*. Yahweh, He Who Always Was And Always Will Be, simply and forever, *exists*. The Amplified Bible translates it, **I AM WHO I AM and WHAT I AM, and I WILL BE WHAT I WILL BE.** Somehow, it seems to me that He is saying to us that *doing* is not the only thing – not for Him, nor for us. What He wants most is for us to *be* with Him.

Even more fascinating to me is the **furthermore.** God gave Moses a second name for Himself, "the God of your fathers, the God of Abraham, the God of Isaac, and the God of Jacob." This name says to me, "Relationship." After establishing His sheer existence, He seems to say to us, "And furthermore, I am all about *relationship*." Abraham, Isaac, and Jacob did nothing – in fact could do nothing – to earn this relationship. He simply *chose* them as His children.

"Existence, and furthermore, relationship." I think this is a new perspective for me.

Why God Forgives Sins

We know that God forgives our sins in Jesus and removes them as far as the east is from the west in order to restore our relationship with Him. I had always thought that He did that for *our* good. But then I read ....

"I, even I, am he who blots out your transgressions, *for my own sake,* **and remembers your sins no more."**
Isaiah 43:25 NIV. emphasis added

He blots out our sins *for His own sake.* Not for *our* sake, but for *His* sake.[2] This God, who owns *everything*, what could He possibly want?

I think that God wants the *only* thing that He gave us complete ownership of: Our heart. Our love. Our relationship. He stands at the door and knocks – indeed, He is *pounding* on the door. He so desperately wants us to let Him in, because He *craves* relationship with us. Deep penetrating closeness. His heart aches for relationship with us so fiercely that He went to His death to make a way. Not a way to *force* relationship on us. But a way to create a door. And when we choose to open that door, He cannot wait to come racing in.

I want you to really comprehend the passion with which He seeks us. **We were dead in our trespasses and sins,** hideous in our sinfulness, **objects of wrath** (Eph 2:1,3). When we were that repulsive, He wanted us so much that He left eternity, emptied Himself of His powers and glory, and went to His death to rescue us and to win us to Himself. Pause and ponder this, and use the margins or your journal to write what is in your heart.

Adopted by God

He predestined us to be adopted as his sons through Jesus Christ, in accordance with his pleasure and will.

Ephesians 1:5 NIV

God chose us for adoption. Hear the tenderness in the names that He assigned: He calls us "children," He calls Himself "Father."

I have some friends who have adopted children, and their frankness about the adoption process gave me a whole new perspective on this word "adoption." They spoke about the tremendous personal cost, and also the heartache of years and years of waiting. Listening to their stories opened my eyes to the parallel of God's adoption of us. God's heart ached as He waited, sometimes many years, to adopt us. Waiting for us to stop running from Him; waiting for us to allow Him to enfold us in His arms. With a jolt I also realized how much it cost Him to adopt us: His Son's life; His own life.

I feel there is something very unique about being adopted. I mean, from a parent's perspective, a naturally born child isn't really quite the same kind of choice. Adoption specifically says, *I want you.* Yes, you – the one with the crooked smile, the financial mess, the body ravaged by disease – *I want you.* The abandoned one, the betrayed one, the divorced one – *I want you.* The angry one, the depressed one, the suicidal one, the one with the hard heart – *I want you.* The arrogant one, the control freak, the anxious one, the one overwhelmed by fear – *I want you.* The one with the dark past, the one who is running from Me, the one who thinks your sins are unforgivable – *I want you.* The one who thinks you blew it too badly, that it is too late, that there is no hope – yes, you also, *I want you.* I want to adopt you as My child, to redeem you and make you holy and blameless in My sight, to clothe you in My righteousness, *I want you.*

He who did not spare his own Son, but gave him up for us all--how will he not also, along with him, graciously give us all things?

Romans 8:32 NIV

This verse emphasizes how much *more* He wants to be with us now that He has adopted us!

God is *for* us, He is not *against* us! He is orchestrating everything for our good! He is rooting for us, fighting for us; He is on our side! We have the Almighty God of all the Universe in our corner! He has put our sins as far away from us as the east is from the west, and He *chooses* to remember our sins no more:

**As far as the east is from the west,
So far has He removed our transgressions from us ...
"For I will forgive their iniquity,
And their sin I will remember no more."**

Psalm 103:12, Jeremiah 31:34

I don't think we will be able to move forward in intimacy if our hearts do not believe that no matter what has happened to us or how badly we've messed up, *God is for us.*

*Question #3:
If God Loves Me So Much,
Why Can't I <u>Feel</u> That Love?*

This is love: not that we loved God, but that he loved us and sent his Son as an atoning sacrifice for our sins.

1 John 4:10 NIV

Jesus' death for us defines God's love for us. If God loves us *that* much, if He is love and His love flows constantly and freely from Him, if He wants our company that much, then why do many of us find it so hard to *feel* that love?

There certainly could be many reasons. I've asked my husband to share what was blocking him from feeling God's deep love.

Sitting under an olive tree in the Garden of Gethsemane on a recent trip to Israel, I pondered why I could not feel the full depth of God's love. Like any good Christian, I have always understood that Jesus sacrificed himself for my sins, that He died on the cross and rose again three days later. I believe that this is true. I believe that He is my personal Lord and Savior. My head knowledge told me that Jesus loves me, but somehow, I wasn't totally feeling it. I could not figure out why not.

As I sat in the stillness of the Garden, I began to realize that the reason that I wasn't feeling His love was that for some reason the crucifixion story did not seem impressive enough. As sacrilegious and ungrateful as this might sound, there has always been a little annoying voice inside of me that argued, "So what?" An all-powerful all-knowing immortal being gets whipped, stabbed, and crucified and then POPS back ALIVE in three days without batting an eyelash! How great a feat is it for an <u>indestructible</u> Being to come back from the dead? It just didn't seem very impressive.

I backed up to look at this thought process with some perspective. If I was golfing and able to hit a hole-in-one three times in a row, people would be very impressed. Yes! In fact, it would make a cover story in the news.

But if <u>Jesus</u> did that, many people would probably not be impressed. Why? Because we <u>expect</u> Jesus to be able to do that. We will only be impressed if Jesus does something that the "average" omnipotent being cannot do. Hmm ... isn't that ludicrous? At this rate, <u>nothing</u> God does would be impressive! God cannot outperform God.

In reality, we really <u>should</u> be impressed with things for what they actually are. A hole-in-one three times in a row is indeed an impressive feat. The problem here is that we are trying to compare the finite to the Infinite. We see ourselves as so outclassed and outdone by Jesus that we cannot compete. And because we cannot compete, we may denigrate and minimize, saying things like, "So what? I am not impressed."

As I was squeezing an olive that had fallen off a tree, and the oil of the olive oozed out of its body, God's truth began to hit me. I thought about the life of Jesus being squeezed out of His body, and I was struck by the fact that I was not thinking about this in the right way. I began to realize that my thoughts were wrong in so many different ways.

If I was a hostage, and someone showed up to free me, would it matter if he did it bare handedly, or if he was armed with a gun, or if he drove a tank? If I made it back to safety, would the level of my gratitude depend upon whether my liberator suffered terribly or got by unscathed? The bottom line was that if someone saved my life, how could I not be grateful?

If someone paid two mites to bail me out of a bad financial situation, should it matter if it was the widow or Bill Gates? If that person bailed me out, shouldn't I be grateful no matter who it was?

Who is more impressive? The widow or Bill Gates? Some might say that since the widow gave all she had, she is more impressive. Some might argue that I didn't need to be grateful to Bill Gates because since he has so much money, the two mites meant nothing to him. Others would be overwhelmingly impressed with all Bill Gates has accomplished. Who is the greater? The answer is this: they <u>both</u> are impressive. They both deserve gratitude. It is not fair to hold Bill Gate's near infinite resources against him and dismiss his philanthropy.

Who is more impressive? The guy who died trying to save my life, or the guy who is agile enough and strong enough to survive while he completes the rescue mission? Hard to say ... but I did not want my gratitude to be dependent upon a subjective sense of impressiveness. Either way, my <u>gratitude</u>

should not be diminished. I realized that I needed to give gratitude where gratitude is due. I no longer wanted to let Satan dilute my gratitude with subjective junk.

I believe that is how Satan subtly directs us off course. He tempts our human nature to compare and judge, even if we have no right to judge. Satan wants us to think that God is not so extraordinary. He wants us to think that we can compare ourselves to God. When the comparison is peer-group-adjusted, we think that we are so cool when we do something above human average, yet we think that rising from the dead is ho-hum for the Lord that created the universe. Isn't Satan sneaky?

As the Lord worked in my heart to expose and uproot the lie that "God is not great," I found myself unknowingly trying to clean sticky olive oil off my fingers. I realized that I could not get rid of the tackiness with what I had nearby. I needed a detergent to wash away my problem. I needed some spiritual cleaning as well. God had certainly been working in my heart as I sat in the Garden, and I wanted to be grateful, but why then I was still not deeply feeling the love of the One who washed away my sins??

I realized that the battle in my heart wasn't over yet. That little annoying voice reminded me, "He died for lots of people, not just you."

Jesus came and died for so, so many people. How could it be personal? I wondered. It was like getting a valentine from a Special Someone ... and then finding out that the Special Someone gave the same card to a million other people. That made it seem not so special ...

... until I read the contents. You see, the <u>contents</u> were indeed very individual, specific, and meaningful. A valentine exclusively for me.

Right then the Holy Spirit revealed to me the reason that I was not feeling God's love was because of the selfishness of someone who thinks he is an only child. Although our Heavenly Father sent His only begotten Son to die on the cross for His <u>many</u> earthly sons and daughters, it is not diluted love. Infinite love cannot be diluted. Each person who accepts that love, who accepts that valentine, receives a *completely unique and personal relationship with the One who created him.*

In Gethsemane, I found that I needed to give gratitude for what I <u>actually</u> got, which is salvation and everlasting life, and that my gratitude should not be predicated on my subjective perception of the "impressiveness" of the sacrifice. Nor should I feel slighted that He gave it to so many people. In fact, I should be impressed that we serve a God who can do this not only for me, but for so many people. I am grateful that this incredible God is on our side! Can you imagine if He were not? I think I am starting to "feel the love ..."

John Li, M.D.
Jupiter, Florida

Multiple barriers had prevented John from experiencing the Lord's love. Not only ungratefulness and selfishness, but a deeply entrenched lie that "God is not great." It sounds pretty similar to the lie that Satan used to beguile Eve: *"God is not so great. Look how He is depriving you of something so wonderful. You can be like God, you know."*

But it was God's healing touch as He led John to open up His valentine that finally drove out that lie as well as the ungratefulness and selfishness. As God replaced the lie with His truth, John was able to begin to receive that love that had been crashing up against his barriers and yearning to come in.

Realize that receiving God's love is not passive; it is an active process requiring us to accept it and *take it in.* I had a similar inability to receive God's love, but for different reasons. My head knew that His love was unconditional, infinite, forevermore. But it was my hardened heart that prevented me from receiving that love. I simply was not capable of taking it in. How did I fall into this dark place?

I was 40 years old when Jesus saved me, and from the beginning, I really grasped His love. Somehow, I knew that

I had been chosen, I knew that He had waited just for me and that He had unique plans for me. I felt His forgiveness so complete and His grace so immense that I was drowning in it. I knew His unconditional love.

But somehow, over time, I lost that deep deep heart understanding of His unconditional love and grace. It wasn't that I fell away from Christ – I was running after Him with all my heart. But my heart had forgotten who I really was. I did not realize that my true identity rests only in what <u>God</u> says about me: that I am a child of God, chosen and dearly loved, accepted unconditionally and pursued unrelentingly.

How did that happen? In retrospect, I see that the dark employed a three-pronged attack. The first foothold the darkness used was my unforgiveness. I didn't consider myself an unforgiving person, but I was deceived. The Holy Spirit eventually revealed to me that when I came to Christ, I had forgiven as completely as I was able, but He had grown me in Him and was now calling me to deeper layers of forgiveness. My resistance had caused my unforgiveness to fester into bitterness, which had led to hardness of heart.

The second foothold the dark used was my unhealthy response to my pain. I had never worked with Jesus to process through the suffering of my life; I had never received His comfort and healing. I had simply locked all my pain up in a room of my heart, never intending to open it again. Since I didn't want to experience any further pain, I chose to barricade my heart. I shut out people, I closed down to love, and I developed nothing but the most superficial of relationships – with people, and with God.

Although God's love never stopped flowing to me, my heart of stone barricaded Him out. It wasn't that He <u>couldn't</u> break through, but He <u>chose</u> not to. He had invited me to partner with Him in dismantling the barricade, but I hadn't accepted or even recognized His invitation just yet.

Being unable to experience His love led to fear – fear of rejection, and fear of failure. I fell into the trap of striving to earn His love – the third prong of the attack. I was frantically chasing the wind. Like a hamster hopelessly running on a wheel, I tried to earn what was already mine but I didn't know I had. And because I was so afraid, I was working to control every moment of my life to orchestrate it just right to please God and to avoid rejection and failure. Yet another exhaustingly futile exercise.

I couldn't bear to think that I was failing in my relationship with God, so I barricaded my heart to deflect the rejection I was expecting. I was afraid to open up to Him in case He wasn't there. I couldn't bear any more pain. I did not have the faintest idea of what intimacy was or what abiding meant. I had no idea what God thought of me, so I could not experience His unconditional love. I had no idea how He defined me. All I knew was how I saw myself, and it wasn't pretty. I had lost my identity.

Celeste Li
Jupiter, Florida

There are quite a few issues covered in this testimony; we're going to discuss some of them now, and some later on in the book. Please understand that the level of suffering in the world's eyes is irrelevant. What is relevant is our *response* to the pain. Instead of choosing forgiveness, humility, trust in God and dependence upon His love and mercy, I had chosen unforgiveness, pride, independence, and striving to prove myself. A treacherous downward spiral.

Trusting God's Unconditional Acceptance

It is hopeless to seek acceptance for *what we do*, for His acceptance is only given because of *who He says we are*: His precious child. As we uselessly and pridefully strive to earn His love, we may eventually come to the realization that all our efforts are coming up short. We may then redouble our work, but to no avail. We simply cannot earn it. Suspended between the knowledge that we cannot earn His love and the lack of knowledge that we already have it, we may fall into a place of unworthiness or self-hatred. Great fear may fill our hearts. And the barrier to true intimacy with Him becomes fortified, block by block.

God already embraces us fully. He knows us fully, accepts us fully, and loves us fully. Sins and all. Listen to how Pastor Drew McClure at Grace Midtown Church in Atlanta puts it:

> Do you want cleanliness, or do you want life? Most of us think God would choose cleanliness over life. So we choose to sterilize our life. Bleach it. But here's the problem with sterile. It's actually the opposite of living. You have to kill the living organism because living organisms just make a mess. The mess is not a problem, it's what you do with it ... the mess becomes the vessel that great things grow out of.
>   ... if you are human ... you have an innate need to be fully known, fully accepted, and fully loved ... that you be seen, *as you are*, not as you *should* be. And having been seen, that you would be accepted. And having been accepted, that you'd feel loved. But our biggest fear is that we'd be fully seen, fully judged, and fully rejected ... That's the challenge of the gospel: to accept that you are accepted ... as you are, not as you should be. Loved, *as you are*, not as you should be ...
>   We know God is holy and we think that means God can't be around sin ... Are you really telling me that God's holiness is that fragile? ... His holiness is actually so strong that when He walks into a mess, it doesn't make *Him* dirty, it makes *us* clean ...
>   [The thought process of] "when God sees me, He doesn't see me, He sees Jesus" is just not true. If it was true, that means that you

can camouflage yourself in the blood of Jesus and Trojan Horse yourself into the Kingdom of God ... The Bible *does* say you're covered by the blood of Jesus, but it doesn't mean *camouflaged*; it means *embraced*.

God says, "I put Christ in you. I put the uniqueness of Him uniquely in you and I see you. I see your mess. I see your beauty. I see all of it. And I have a place for you."[3]

That is a powerful message. Don't try to Trojan Horse your way into the Kingdom of God. Your Creator fully knows you. Receive His unconditional acceptance and His nonjudgmental love. Then walk by the Spirit, and He will mature you.

Falling Into Satan's Identity Trap

If we are struggling to receive God's unconditional acceptance, if our minds are mired in thoughts of unworthiness, it may be an indication that we have fallen into Satan's identity trap. "I am not worthy enough of His love. My sin is too great to forgive. God would not really want to spend time with me, I am so sinful. I am not good enough. I need to earn God's love and acceptance. If I don't get it right, God will abandoned me, just like everyone else has."

For me, I didn't recognize these as specific "thoughts" or "beliefs." They were in the milieu of who I thought I was, such a part of my character and life for so many decades, that I had no idea that they were foreign beliefs. I didn't know that they were not *originally* my thoughts, that they were lies implanted by the darkness, probably when I was quite young. In my ignorance, I had taken on these thoughts as my own. I had come to believe that they *were* my thoughts, and so my heart believed that they were true.

These thoughts of rejection, self-hatred, self-condemnation, and unworthiness reflect a heart that does not believe some truths of His Word. Living in the lie that we must perform, produce, achieve, accomplish, or succeed in order to win His love and attention will erect a barrier to receiving it. Like a hamster on a wheel, we will exhaust ourselves trying to seize what we could *never earn*, what we *already have* and can *never lose*. The anxiety and fear will block us from receiving the love and acceptance that is *already ours!* Yes, we are completely unworthy and undeserving – but He gives us worth. He made us in His image and likeness, He chose us for Himself, and *He* declares our worth and value. He *becomes* our worth.

As I grew in the Lord, I eventually learned that these thoughts were lies that the enemy had embedded in my heart and mind and soul. I realized that I had nurtured them until I had come to believe that this was who I really was. Freedom from these tormenting thoughts would only come when I rejected the lies and chose to believe the truth in His Word.

A Heart of Stone

If you are having difficulty with intimacy with Christ, if you feel as if you can't hear Him very well or even at all, you may be dealing with a partially petrified heart. Satan seems to fight tenaciously against the destruction of this stony barricade, perhaps because he knows that when our hearts are full of love, we reveal Jesus so undeniably:

"By this all men will know that you are my disciples, if you love one another."
John 13:35 NIV

You can see from my testimony that in order to begin demolishing the barricade of stone around my heart, some things that God would deal with would include ...

- My unforgiveness.

- My locking Jesus out of the pain in my heart.

- My fear of rejection and fear of failure that fueled my striving to earn His love, acceptance, and attention.

You can see that I had serious trust issues. Satan had used a multi-pronged attack to drive me to erect this heart of stone, and God used a multi-pronged attack to start to dismantle it. I'll share some things with you.

Soaking in His Love

God's first step in the softening process was to teach me soaking: to seclude myself from busyness and play quiet worshipful music while remaining still before Him. He taught me to select my music carefully – this was not the time for music that convicted me of sin, but for music that flooded me in His love. For me, this soaking required hours and hours over many months for the tiniest crack to open up and a smidgeon of His love to work its way in.

My fear of being rejected by God was so great that I did not want to give Him a chance. It was safer holding Him at arm's length; that way, if I sensed what I thought was even the tiniest bit of rejection, I could quickly barricade my heart even more strongly before the "rejection" that I perceived would come barreling in. The Lord knew that I needed to learn to trust Him, and He was very patient with me. Day after day He poured His love into me as I did absolutely *nothing* to earn or deserve it. Slowly, my heart began to thaw, and I began to let Him in, to trust that He was true to His promises and would never forsake me, no matter how greatly I failed. He began this process over five years ago; today, I need even more the continued in-pouring of His love and His Spirit to sustain me.

Regaining My Identity

Another method God used to deal with my fear of rejection and fear of failure was to establish my identity in Him. Our identity is who we really are, with no masks or facades. The way I see it, in order to completely establish identity, there are three truths that God calls us to fully accept. I have listed them below. The first of these truths is generic for all believers and is easily found in His Word. The second two truths are personal to each one of us, and are revealed by the Holy Spirit.

- **The truth of who we are, defined by God in His Word:** God calls us His child, and has bestowed on us all the blessings that accompany sonship. Accepting this part of our identity will require immersion in His Word, and then a decision of obedience to accept what the Word says – whether we want to or not, whether we feel like it is true or not, whether the circumstances of our lives seem to confirm it or not.

- **The truth about the state of our hearts:** I have heard it said this way: He is honest with me, and I am honest with Him, about the state of my heart. In other words,

He is honest with me
and
I am honest with Him

about my deep heart sins and about my pain.

This transparency will require a humble willingness to agree with what He exposes, and a choice to repent and change. This will also require a humble willingness to pour out our soul to Him, to express difficult emotions such as anger and fear.

- **The truth about our uniqueness:** The Holy Spirit reveals to each of us who we are, with the specific gifting, calling, and purpose that He has designed *just for us.* Purposes that no one else can fulfill.

Let's look at these truths in greater detail.

Truth #1: Who God Says We Are

My friend Sandra, when she was in high school, fell off a roof and hit her head. When she regained consciousness, she had no idea who she was. She did not know her last name. She did not know her home. She did not recognize her parents, her brother, or her friends. She had completely lost her identity.

Imagine what a dangerous place this young teenager was in. Anybody could tell her anything – that she lived in a certain place, or attended a particular school. They could claim that they were her sibling, her relative, her teacher ... or her boyfriend. She was in a dangerous place, a weak place, a vulnerable place. Unguarded, unprotected, defenseless.

Similarly, Satan is after our identity. He has **come to steal, kill, and destroy** our identity. Because if Satan can wreak such havoc in our lives that we begin to believe that we don't have God's unconditional love, that we need to earn God's love and acceptance, that at any moment or for any reason God could reject us, then Satan has successfully destroyed our identity. Like Sandra, who had no idea who she really was, we will be wide open to attack by the dark. If the events of our lives seem to prove Satan's lies, and we have no foundation of truth to demolish Satan's lies, we will soon believe that his very persuasive lies *are* the truth. And from there, he can move to destroy our ministry, our calling, our families and relationships, our entire lives. Satan's is a very subtle, well-calculated attack.

Sandra had a teenage brother who fought for her. For the week that she had amnesia, her older brother did not leave her side. He knew what a vulnerable place she was in, and he protected her and guarded her.

We also have a Brother who is fighting for us. He will not leave our side. He lives to intercede for us, and when we are in the midst of a trial, He is praying for us. He is right now fighting to extricate us from this snare of identity loss, and He will not stop until His victory is secure.

I like how Tenth Avenue North clarifies our identity in their song, *You Are More:*

You are more than the choices that you've made,
You are more than the sum of your past mistakes,
You are more than the problems you create,
You've been remade. [4]

Our choices don't define us! Our past mistakes don't define us! Our sins and the messes we have made do not define us! All the consequences of our mistakes and how they have hurt others do not determine who we are!

But nor do our accomplishments and achievements define us. "The son of a king is a prince, not because he killed a dragon, but because his dad is already royalty."[5]

In all honesty, we don't have nearly enough authority to define ourselves. Other people do not have the authority to define us either. And certainly Satan does not have the authority to define us. It is *God* who defines us. His *choice* of us is what gives us our identity.

"You did not choose Me but I chose you, and appointed you that you would go and bear fruit, and that your fruit would remain."

John 15:16

You did not choose Me, *but I chose you.* Jesus gives us our identity. And just because we fell off a roof and *forgot* who we are, that does not change *who we are!* Just because my friend did not know what family she was in, just because she didn't know her last name, just because she didn't recognize her real home – all that didn't change the truth that she was a member of that family and belonged in that home!

Knowing that we know that we know *who He says we are,* setting our minds and hearts and wills to believe these things and choosing not to doubt or question them, can begin to cement our feet into the Rock of Jesus. Our identity will become unshakable because we have not been defined by ourselves, our works, our failures, the world, the darkness, or other people's opinions. We have been defined by the Lord our God, the Alpha and Omega, the Creator of all the Universe, and He never changes. When the torrents slam against us, we will not fall, because we have been built on a Rock.

Making that decision to choose to believe what God says about us, even if we cannot feel it at this moment, may be one of the keys to cracking open a heart of stone. This may enable us to receive from the Lord the intimate and deeply personal love that we so desire. Are you ready to make that choice? I am. Let's stop and pray right now.

God Gives Us Our Identity

As much as we may like to be defined by our accomplishments on earth, the truth of the matter is, we are not. God does not see us as teachers, plumbers, doctors, lawyers, bankers, waiters, real estate agents, writers, or chefs. He does not define us as wealthy or poor. Nor does He identify us as wives, husbands, parents, or grandparents. These things, noble as they may be, are simply *not* who we are.

Nor do the sufferings of this world define us. God does not call us diabetics, arthritics, cancer survivors, anorexics, widows, orphans, or victims of abuse or rape.

Nor do our failures define us.   God does not call us business failures, divorcees, college drop-outs, or parental failures.

And most wonderfully, God does not define us by our past *or current sins*.   Even if we are still in the throes of battling these strongholds, God does not identify us as liars, hypocrites, thieves, cheaters, alcoholics, plagiarists, adulterers, fornicators, murderers, sorcerers, idolaters, or drug dealers. He does not define us as gluttons or cutters or child abusers or those who attempted suicide. We will all be tempted in different ways, yet those particular *temptations*, or our *fall* into those temptations, do not define us. And, since **God shows no partiality and is no respecter of persons** (Acts 10:34 AMP) and He **has no favorites** (Eph 6:9 NLT), He doesn't even identify us as pastors or preachers or ministers or missionaries!

All these things, whether virtuous or unrighteous, may be *things that we do*, but they are not *who we are*. They simply do not define us. As my husband says, they are simply labels that have been slapped on us – by others, by ourselves, by the world, by Satan. God does not call us by these labels; He does not think of us in these terms; He does not see us with those eyes.

God *knows* everything about us, both good and bad, yet He *still* chooses to embrace us and give us an identity *far above all of that*. God tells us that even right now, even in mid-process, we are **a new creation** (2Cor 5:17). We are commanded to put off our old self and put on our new self every day, but if we forget or get confused or even outright disobey His commands, our identity remains as God says: people made in the image of God, redeemed by the blood of His Son and adopted as His children, loved, cherished, and accepted no matter what is done to us, no matter what we do or don't do, certain of a secure place in heaven with Jesus at the Father's right hand! That's all!

God always accepts us and approves of us. He doesn't

always accept or approve of some of our specific behaviors – but He always accepts and approves of *us*. He takes us just as we are. He embraces *the whole of us* and showers us with all of His love. No amount of doing or growing could ever win us any more of His love or acceptance, for He has given it to us in infinite measure already.

God does indeed define us. And then, He calls us to make Him Lord of every area of our life. To partner with Him to seek victory over sin. Yet, even in the midst of the battles, in defeat or in triumph, in obedience or disobedience, our *identity* remains unchanged. We are simply victorious, because we are one with the Victor.

Truth #2: The State of My Heart

We've talked a bit about my unforgiveness, and we are going to delve into our sanctification more deeply in subsequent chapters, but I'd like to touch on some areas of sin exposed in my heart of stone testimony.

As I began to trust God more, bit by bit, then, very gently, the Holy Spirit began to expose some dark areas of my heart. He showed me that when I am believing the "I'm not good enough" lies, I am actually in a place of *pride*. I know this seems impossible, because "I'm not good enough" sounds like humility. But if I believe that I am not good enough, I am believing that I actually *am able* to get to a place where I am "good enough." I am believing that somehow I can really win His forgiveness and attain enough holiness and become righteous enough to actually gain His attention. I am believing that I can earn enough worthiness and can accomplish impressive enough deeds to actually deserve His acceptance. And those thoughts reveal that I am operating in pride. "I'm not good enough" is *false* humility. False humility is pride, which fortified my hardness of heart.

The Holy Spirit also revealed to me that I had chosen hardness of heart by my *rebellion*. By refusing to believe the Truth of what God says about me in His Word, I was in rebellion. Listen to how Zechariah explains it:

But they refused to pay attention; stubbornly they turned their backs and stopped up their ears. They made their hearts as hard as flint and would not listen to the law or to the words that the LORD Almighty had sent by his Spirit through the earlier prophets. So the LORD Almighty was very angry.
Zechariah 7:11-12 NIV

I was calling God a liar. I had stubbornly stopped up my ears and made my heart like flint.

"Today, if you hear his voice, do not harden your hearts as you did in the rebellion."
Hebrews 3:15 NIV

In order to break through this hardness of heart, God required me to obediently and humbly accept His voice, His Word spoken in Scriptures. Anything less than this is rebellion.

Transparency Requires My Honesty About My Pain

Not only did God call me to honesty about my heart sins, but He also called me to honesty about my raging emotions, my broken heart, my pain, my sufferings, griefs, and dashed hopes. Who was I fooling? God already knew all this about me anyway! My denial of these realities was deception about my identity, and this denial blocked my intimacy with God.

Sometimes, what life has dealt us is so painful that we reach a place where we refuse to acknowledge it. This pain may be the result of our own sin or failure, it may be the pain that someone else has inflicted on us, it may be the trials of this fallen world, or it could be any combination. We may lock this pain up in a secret room in our heart, throwing away the key, never intending to visit that place of pain again. We may barricade it, work to suppress all memories of it, and effectively create a room of stone. The more rooms of stone, the more the flow of God's love and His Spirit through our heart is impeded. Our connection to God will be hindered, and intimacy with Him obstructed, until those secret rooms are opened to the Lord and we have invited Him in to heal us.

Is it scary, thinking of opening one of these rooms? Yes, for me too. Every time Jesus knocks at one of my hidden rooms, my emotions range anywhere from apprehensive to petrified. You too? Why do we have all this fear? I have listed a few possibilities:

- Perhaps we have figured out how to live with the locked room, and cannot imagine what life will be like with that room opened to Him.

- Perhaps we cannot trust Jesus' comfort to be greater than revisiting the pain.

- Perhaps we are unable to fully forgive the one who inflicted the pain.

- Perhaps we don't want to admit our sinful response to the pain. We don't want to admit that through our unforgiveness and bitterness, we have hurt others also.

- Or perhaps we can't imagine the healing that Jesus has planned for us when we open that door. We can't fathom the garment of praise to replace the spirit of despair that He offers us when we surrender. We can't see the light at the end of the tunnel, so we are afraid to even enter.

Truly, what an honor for Jesus to point to a room and say, "That one." He wants so much for us to trust that He will be greater than our pain. When He has knocked at a dark area of our past that He wants to enter and heal, He promises,

"I will go before you
And make the rough places smooth;
I will shatter the doors of bronze
And cut through their iron bars.
I will give you the treasures of darkness
And hidden wealth of secret places,
So that you may know that it is I,
The LORD, the God of Israel,
Who calls you by your name."

Isaiah 45:2-3

His intent is to guide us through a sweet painful walk and to give us the treasures of healing and a new level of closeness with Him — so that we indeed will know that *it was* He who called us by name onto that rich and painful journey.

Truth #3: Our Uniqueness

We are precious and honored in His sight, uniquely created for a purpose that no one else on earth can fulfill. Julie Woodley, trauma counselor and founder of *Restoring the Heart Ministries,* expresses it this way:

> My imposter self finds my identity in past achievements and the applause of others ... Has it ever occurred to you that to remain as your "poser self" you are bringing the world an imposter of who God created you to be? In all of this hiding something so very precious is lost — something the world so desperately

> needs – you, just you. Who God created you
> to be! ... God has given us all a unique calling
> and role that will reveal something about Him
> that no one else can reveal in the same unique
> way ...[6]

God desires to reveal Himself to the world – *through us.* He is infinite in His facets, and created each one of us to reflect a part of Him that *no one else can reflect!* Julie Woodley uses the word *unrepeatable.*[7] And we can only reflect that part of Him that He has assigned to us when we are honestly accepting of ourselves in all totality – faults and failures included – and allowing His glory to be revealed in the way that He has healed and restored us.

"Behold, I stand at the door and knock; if anyone hears My voice and opens the door, I will come in to him and will dine with him, and he with Me."
Revelation 3:20

He knocks, but we must open the door to our locked heart. Healing can begin when we invite Him in. And His healing means that He will break the hardness and make a way for us to receive His precious love. To dine with Him. What sweet abiding. The richest of communions. And in that sweet communion of dining with Jesus is when He begins to unveil our uniqueness and the specific gifting, calling, and purpose that He has for each of us.

As we acknowledge any hardness of heart and co-labor with Him to dismantle the barriers, will we then always be in a place to receive His love? No, we are imperfect humans. But as we grow up in this area of softening, we will receive more and barricade less. We will begin to be more sensitive to His Spirit and recognize when we have erected a new barricade – or when He is knocking at the door of an old one. We're going to continue to address the barricades throughout this book. We've already begun dismantling them by implementing the critical times of solitude and soaking. And right now, God is giving us an opportunity to wield our sledge hammer at the lies that contribute to the barricade — lies about who He is, and who He says we are.

God Is Giving Us a Choice

Right now, God is giving us a choice. Will we choose to cast down those lies and believe the truth of His Word?

We can continue to believe those lies and remain mired in a state of self-pity. We can persist in denying that we are striving to earn His love and acceptance, and thus remain trapped in false humility and pride. We can shrug and say that it's not such a big deal to think those "I'm unworthy" thoughts. We can continue to insist on our own way and persist in our rebellion. In short, we can continue to fight on the enemy's side.

Yes, that's what I'm saying. If we choose to persist in our beliefs that we are unworthy of His attention, that we are not good enough, righteous enough, or valuable enough, then we have successfully aligned ourselves with the enemy. We have just secured victory — *for the other side.* We are being used by Satan to **steal, kill, and destroy** — *our own selves.*

God is giving us a choice. Choose obedience, or remain in rebellion. Choose humility, or remain in pride. Believe truth, or believe lies. God is calling us to confront those lies, to acknowledge that we have believed those lies, to repent of believing them, to reject them, and to *choose* to believe the truth of His Word.

And we know that the Son of God has come, and has given us understanding so that we may know Him who is true ...

1 John 5:20

Jesus came to earth and suffered, died, and spent three days separated from the Father, bearing the punishment for our sin, **so that** God could establish a relationship with us. **So that** we may **know** Him, as He really is, truly and honestly. **So that** we could receive an **understanding** of His nature and ways. **So that** we can have deep intimacy with Him. **So that we may know Him who is true.**

Jesus didn't die for us to have life with God *only in eternity*; He died so that we could have intimate relationship with Him *right now* while we are still on earth. Deep is indeed calling to deep because He *yearns* to spend time with us.

"I don't want your sacrifices – I want your love; I don't want your offerings – I want you to know me."
Hosea 6:6 TLB

God does not want sacrifices, performances, great exploits, generous offerings, good deeds, or impressive accomplishments for the Kingdom. Listen to the cry of His heart. *"I want you to know Me."*

Questions Chapter 3: Toppling Barriers to Intimacy

Memory Verse:

What, then, shall we say in response to this? If God is for us, who can be against us? He who did not spare his own Son, but gave him up for us all--how will he not also, along with him, graciously give us all things?
Romans 8:31-32 NIV

1) Do you feel God is against you? Somehow, in some areas of your life, do you sense that He is not fighting *for* you? Don't try to deny these thoughts or pretty them up.

Allow the Holy Spirit to speak to your heart, remembering that there are no secrets in the secret place. Journal what the Holy Spirit shows you.

Read Romans 8:26-39, out loud and from the depth of your heart, boldly and confidently, in your secret place of His Presence. Do this every day until Jesus has transformed you and your heart believes it.

2) Re-read the section *Why Doesn't He Shield Us From All the Works of the Devil?* Use your own words to answer this question. Then read James 1:2-4. Journal what this passage teaches on the purpose of trials, and what response God expects of us.

If these questions and issues are not settled in your heart, it may help to read *Triumph Over Suffering,* which dives into Scriptures on suffering to help us understand adversity and to discover where God is in our pain.

3) Are you entertaining thoughts, attitudes, or deeply held beliefs that you are not deserving enough, worthy enough, valuable enough for His attention? Spend time alone with the Lord, asking the Holy Spirit to expose any thoughts like this in your heart.

Journal how humility is necessary to accept the two-fold truth:

- We could *never* be worthy enough, deserving enough, holy enough
- *And* He wants desperately to be with us anyway!

Re-read the bulleted items at the end of the section *Where Are You?* Implanting these truths deeply into your heart will be necessary to move into deeper intimacy and abiding. You may want to write them down on an index card and post them or carry them with you, reading them multiple times a day until your heart begins to receive these truths.

4)   What does it mean to you that being covered by the blood of Jesus means not *camouflaged*, but *embraced*?

5) Ask the Lord to reveal the state of your heart. Circle which one best describes the state of your heart, and journal why:

- Marble: cold and hard, requiring a chisel and hammer to carve.
- Flint: hard enough to be used in making weapons; prone to shatter when exposed to excessive heat.
- Shale: breaks apart in layers and sometimes crumbles.
- Chalk: porous, water (representing the Holy Spirit) can squeeze into some crevices.
- Limestone: soluble in water (Holy Spirit).
- Clay: soft putty in the Potter's hands.[8]

6)   Throughout the chapter, I mentioned some of my own sins that led to my hardness of heart, including pride, rebellion, unforgiveness, distrust, fear of rejection and fear of failure leading to striving and earning, and locking Jesus out of rooms of pain in my heart. Prayerfully consider each of these, and journal what the Lord shows you. Then take the time to thank Him for His revelation, repent of the state of your heart and the underlying sins. Realize that only He can change your heart, and ask Him to give you a new heart. End your time meditating on Ezekiel 36:26 in stillness before Him.

7) Who does God say He is? Who does He say you are? Search out Scriptures to answer these questions, and write them in your journal. Then, go to Appendix 1 and see if there are any additional Scriptures you would like to add. Write a summary of these truths, post it or carry it around with you and read it daily until your heart believes it!

Will you align your heart with Satan – or with God? When you commit to believe what God says in His Word, write out a covenant prayer to the Lord.

Part II

Intimacy
Through Surrender

John Li

John Li

Chapter 4
Surrendering
To His Sovereignty

As the deer pants for streams of water,
so my soul pants for you, O God.
My soul thirsts for God,
for the living God.
When can I go and meet with God?

Psalm 42:1-2 NIV

We may quote this verse often. But just how *desperately* do we want God?

As we read through this psalm, we see that the psalmist is describing a time when he is in a dark place, a place of enemy attack. His soul is downcast, disturbed ... I think that perhaps he is describing himself as a hunted deer, running for his life, gasping and panting, unable to continue without a drink from a stream of water.

How desperately do we want God? Is it merely a curiosity? Or are we as a hunted deer, panting for God?

Are our motives to glorify ourselves, to lift ourselves up as spiritual heroes who hear oh-so-well from God? Or do we truly have a fierce, yearning passion to simply *know* our Creator and Savior?

24Then Jesus said to His disciples, "If anyone wishes to come after Me, he must deny himself, and take up his cross and follow Me. 25For whoever wishes to save his life will lose it; but whoever loses his life for My sake will find it."

Matthew 16:24-25

Some think that taking up our cross means simply surviving the painful circumstances of our lives. But that's an attitude of self pity and the mentality of a victim. I think that Jesus' statement in verse 25 explains what taking up our cross *really* means: to lose ourselves inside of Jesus. When we deny ourselves, take up our cross, and follow Him, we die to ourselves. We become more intimate with Him. Our lives become more hidden with Christ in God; He, in turn, more totally consumes us. As we decrease, He increases. It seems to me that to reach each level of decrease will require a new level of surrender.

Will we go in search of this greater intimacy? How parched are we? Are we panting for water brooks? Delirious with thirst? Are we hopelessly empty without Him? Are we willing to go where He is calling us in response to the way He has loved us? **If anyone wishes to come after Me ...**

What holds us back? For me, I find that many times my struggle with surrender is rooted in rebellion against His sovereignty. I want my own way. I have devised a plan, and I think it's a good one. Things aren't working out the way I expected, and I intend to fix that. I may be unwilling to relinquish control to Him.

For the most part, I *think* that I am walking a life of full acceptance of His sovereignty. But when trials expose my heart, I may suddenly find myself wrestling through a surrender once again. When faced with another call to surrender, it seems that my choice here will tip the balance in my intimacy walk. Therefore I do not underestimate the importance of seeking Him deeply and persistently during those times until He has indeed transformed my heart. Every refusal to bow my heart to His sovereignty erects a barrier between us that He simply will not cross. And with every surrender to that sovereignty, He seems to throw open the floodgates of heaven to give me more of Himself.

The Holy Spirit may be tickling your conscience already. What part of your life are you reluctant to relinquish to His control? Yes, I suspect that it's the thing that first popped into your head. The thing that perhaps you quickly shut down in denial. "No, couldn't be that." "He wouldn't want that." "I already surrendered that long ago." Oh, yes, dearly beloved. I'm afraid that's the one. You may want to write it in the margin right now ...

It may be something huge. Or a seemingly more minor thing. But it's not minor to God. His name is Jealous ...

We may feel that we have surrendered this particular thing already – and we may well have. But there could be another part of it, another angle, or a deeper level, that God is calling us to right now. Whatever it is, it is hindering us from a deeper connection with God. And it will stand there, in the way, like a roadblock, until we remove it.

It could be a piece of a Scripture verse that we are choosing to ignore, that we think doesn't apply to us. (Hint: It probably does.) Or maybe this unsurrendered area is something that is causing an issue with our spouse that simply won't go away. Or it may be causing repeated strife with our children. It could be our battle to uphold our reputation – or our fear of losing it. Or maybe this unsurrendered area is a refusal to forgive and give grace.

What would our lives look like if we *really* surrendered

everything to the Lord? I mean not just our "heart" or our
"life," as we may glibly pray. But truly deeply *everything*.
Go ahead and circle what the Lord is highlighting for you
as you read through these bullets.

- Our job or our schooling. What would it mean
  to work with all our heart, as if God was our boss,
  not man (Col 3:23)?

- Our marriage. What would it mean to seek to meet
  our spouses' needs, and depend not on our spouse,
  but on God, to meet all of our needs (Phil 4:19)?

- Our kids. What would it mean to admit that we
  want them to look good to others so that we look like
  good parents? To place them in God's hands, to quit
  trying to shape them into little images of us, to
  relinquish that control (Ps 127:3, Phil 4:6-7)?

- Our friendships. How would it look if God picked
  our friends for us, and told us how much time to
  spend with them and what the time spent with them
  would entail? How would these relationships be
  different if we poured into our friends, instead of
  waiting for them to pour into us (Rom 12:10)?

- Our spouse. What would our life look like if we
  depended completely upon God to *select* our spouse
  for us (Pr 3:4-5)?

- Our money and possessions. What would our lives
  look like if we really lived like the earth was the
  Lord's, and everything in it (Ps 24:1)?

- Our priorities. Is giving glory to God really our
  number one pursuit (Rev 4:11, Eph 1:12, 1Pt 2:9)?

- Our health. What would happen if we made God
  our Chief Physician and put Him in charge of our
  doctors, medications, and medical plan (2Kg 5:1-14)?

What would happen if we put God in charge of our bodies? How would our eating and exercise change (1Tim 4:8)?

- Our family relationships. What would our families look like if we forgave those who have wronged us – deeply and truly from our hearts – and then asked God to love them *through* us (Mt 18:35)?

- Our reputation, position, status. How would we behave if we were trying to please God and not men (Gal 1:10)?

- Our plans and dreams and desires for our life. What would we do differently today if our only plans were what God has assigned us (Mt 7:21)?

- Our scars and wounds and pain. How much courage would it take to let Jesus into those areas of our hearts that we have walled off from Him? Will we open up those doors that we have bolted closed, and invite Him in to explore and touch and heal (Isa 61:1)?

Surrender requires a profound trust in God. Trusting that He will do a better job in the driver's seat than we are doing. Admitting that with us in the driver's seat, things aren't going quite so well. Recognizing that there are just too many things that we are powerless to control.

It will be difficult enough to surrender our *own* lives. But I think it may be even more challenging to trust Him with the lives of those we love. Does surrendering a loved one to God mean that we turn our backs and walk away? No, surrendering doesn't mean abandoning. It does not mean that we no longer care.

Surrender is motivated out of love – such deep love for the person that we are willing to get out of the way, and let God sit in the driver's seat. To trust that He has our loved ones' best interests at heart, that His heart is inclined towards them. To trust that He knows what He is doing, that He knows every moment of the future, and that He never stops working. To trust that even if it may *appear* that He has forgotten them, He has never taken His hand off them.

It may be easy to trust when we are not in trials, when there appears to be no danger, when life is smooth and peace prevails. But full surrender holds fast to trust in time of trial also. I am reminded of a tightrope walker ...

Charles Blondin crossed a tightrope over Niagara Falls several times: in a sack, on stilts, on a bicycle, even blindfolded. One time he crossed pushing a wheelbarrow full of potatoes. After that feat, he asked the audience if they believed he could carry a person across in the wheelbarrow. They enthusiastically believed. But his invitation to anyone to climb into the wheelbarrow was met with silence. None *really* trusted him to wheel them over the Falls.[1]

Go back to the previous page and prayerfully read through that list of bullets again. How deep is your trust of God? Will you trust Him to wheel you over Niagara Falls?

Let's pause and let the Holy Spirit search our hearts. Don't be afraid. Ask the Holy Spirit to show you right now what you have been holding back. Yes, I mean *right now*. Not when you're finished reading the chapter. Quit reading. Close the book and be still before Him. Join me again when you have heard from Him.

God is calling me to surrender:

_____

What is God calling you to surrender? Go ahead and write it in. I am praying that by the end of this chapter, you will be ready to surrender it.

I think that God is calling me to write "my time" on that line. I can sense the fear creeping over me as I hear Him calling me to surrender it. I can hear my usual arguments welling up inside me again. What if I obey what I *think* You are calling me to do, and then I am so overwhelmed that I don't have enough time alone with You? And then I become tense and stressed and functioning out of performance instead of in response to Your love? What if I don't maintain Your priorities, and I fail in my responsibilities as wife or mother? What if I've heard wrong, and You are not calling me where I think You are?

I feel a need to manage my life, to be sure everything gets done in its proper place and time. Do you hear the control in my voice? God hears it, too.

Wow, there is a huge undercurrent of fear of failure. What if I hear wrong? Is God ready to punish me for blowing it? Will He abandon me in the middle of a project that He did not assign me? And what will happen to my reputation when everyone finds out I heard wrong?

Additionally, this is a major issue of trust. Can I trust the Lord to correct me if I have heard wrong and I am embarking on something that He has not commanded? Can I trust Him to come *with me* down that mistaken path, gently guiding me back onto His plan? Can I trust Him to be greater than all my mistakes and failures, to be strong when I am weak, and to work all things for my good – and His glory? Can I trust that He knows what I need more than I do – and can I trust Him to orchestrate the events in my life and to ensure that all my needs are met?

I choose to embark on this journey of surrender. I'll write "my time" in that line. I will make a decision to *choose* to surrender my time, and ask the Lord to work this to completion in my heart.

> *Lord, I choose to surrender to You the control of my time. I give You my schedule book, my clock, my waking up and lying down, my going in and my coming out. I don't always hear You clearly. And even though my heart desires to always obey, I am sure there are times I "don't hear clearly" out of disobedience rather than out of muffled hearing. So I release control of my time to You. I trust You to remain with me in failure and to guide me back onto Your path if I have strayed. I trust that Your power will be made perfect in my weakness. And – this is the most difficult – I trust You to speak to me so clearly that I do not miss time alone with You, for You know better than I do how much I need that alone time to receive Your unconditional love, encouragement, strength, correction, and guidance. Amen.*

Okay, you all keep me accountable. And now it's your turn. Don't be afraid or embarrassed. God isn't surprised or disappointed, for He already knew it any way. It is only His kindness and grace that brings Him to reveal this to us. He will be ever so gentle with us as we wrestle through this with Him. I believe He is simply delighted that we are *willing* to wrestle with Him. His pulse is racing with expectation and excitement. His heart is so full of love for us that I think it may burst if He can't soon release it to us. It is our surrender that will open the floodgates to let His love in. Write your prayer of surrender in your journal.

Don't feel ashamed if you are struggling to surrender. I really mean that. Come with me to the Garden of Gethsemane to understand why I say that.

They came to a place named Gethsemane; and He said to His disciples, "Sit here until I have prayed." And He took with Him Peter and James and John, and began to be very distressed and troubled. And He said to them, "My soul is deeply grieved to the point of death; remain here and keep watch." And He went a little beyond them, and fell to the ground and began to pray that if it were possible, the hour might pass Him by. And He was saying, "Abba! Father! All things are possible for You; remove this cup from Me; yet not what I will, but what You will."

Mark 14:32-36

I'm not sure we can fully grasp the intensity of this prayer. The Amplified says **He began to show grief and distress of mind and was deeply depressed ... "I am almost dying of sorrow"** (Mt 26:37-38). Luke, the physician, tells us that the agony over His surrender was so great that He sweated blood (Lk 22:44). Hematohidrosis is a rare occurrence documented in the medical literature, "a condition in which capillary blood vessels that feed the sweat glands rupture, causing them to exude blood, occurring under conditions of extreme physical or emotional stress."[2]

If Jesus labored this fiercely in prayer in order to be certain of the Father's will and to surrender to that will, I think it must not be a sin to struggle here. It must not be a sin to ask God if there is any other way, to ask for confirmation that we have heard Him correctly, and to ask others to pray for us as we struggle. I think that perhaps we may sin if we refuse to *engage* in the struggle. We may sin when God reveals an unsurrendered area, and we deny it, or rebel, instead of engaging with Him and asking Him to work in our hearts. We sin when we do not reach God's intended culmination of the struggle, "Not my will, but Yours be done."

Walking Out Our Surrender

For me, sometimes choosing surrender is a great wrestling that may take some time, hours or even days. But choosing surrender is only the first step. After we *choose*, the real battle begins, as God calls us to walk it out. We know how Jesus had to walk out His surrender. For me, it seems that God begins to orchestrate events in my life to give me ample opportunity to walk that surrender out. Tests, you may say. If my antenna is up, if I am sensitive to His Holy Spirit, sometimes I see those tests coming with great clarity. Other times, it will only be in retrospect that I see that what I just endured was a testing of my surrender. We won't always pass all these tests. But it's not failure if we *learn* from it. John C. Maxwell, in *Failing Forward*, writes these words of encouragement:

> Failure ... is not someplace you arrive. Just as success is not an event, neither is failure. It's how you deal with life along the way. No one can conclude that he has failed until he breathes his last breath. Until then, he's still in process, and the jury is still out.[3]

God works out in the physical what we have committed in the spiritual. And each time we make a choice to walk out that new surrender, He strengthens Himself in us, He fortifies His stronghold, and He gives us the experience and courage to choose His path again the next time. Let's run in such a way as to win the prize (1Cor 9:24).

I think that rebellion against *His sovereignty* is a major stumbling block to surrender. Surrender and sovereignty. Hard to fathom both those words in the same sentence. Let's use the rest of this chapter to explore sovereignty in detail, so we can understand what surrendering to His sovereignty really means.

I think that accepting God's sovereignty is most difficult when we are in a trial. Because we may feel that God has rejected or abandoned us, or doesn't care enough about us to intervene, we may say that God "allowed" the suffering. But "allowed" is really not used in the Bible to explain how God works. The Bible uses words like **decree** and **ordain**, as we studied together in *Triumph Over Suffering*. "Allowed" seems to indicate that God conceded the battle to Satan. "Allowed" seems to indicate that God just gave up, that somehow we weren't worth fighting for. And that is simply *not* who God is. Let's look at God's sovereignty with a different perspective.

Adonai

Sovereignty. Unlimited power. Undisputed authority. Dominance, preeminence, rule, supremacy, control. These words cause me to stop and take a breath. Yet, as I mull over God's sovereignty as demonstrated in the Bible, these words still seem a bit hollow. They may suffice to describe the sovereignty of an earthly king, but when we take the whole counsel of the Bible, it seems to me that they fall short of explaining *God's* sovereignty.

I think that the true depth of the name *Adonai*, of "Sovereign" as that word applies *to God*, is vastly beyond what we can comprehend on a human level. I think that perhaps the name *Adonai* encompasses three seemingly divergent aspects:

- How God *rules*

- With *unfathomable love*

- While He simultaneously allows us our *free will*.

I know what you're thinking. Free will is the *opposite* of sovereignty. Well, in human terms, perhaps. But we're not talking about human sovereignty. We're talking about *God's* sovereignty. We're talking about *Adonai*.

It's hard to comprehend these three things going on simultaneously. And yet, because God is love, His sovereignty *includes* His perfect love for us. His love encases every attribute – including His sovereignty. So just what happens when we blend His rule with His perfect love and then incorporate into the mix our free will? Let's go to the Word to see.

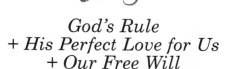

God's Rule
+ His Perfect Love for Us
+ Our Free Will
= ?

Who has measured the waters
in the hollow of His hand,
And marked off the heavens
by the span,
And calculated the dust of the earth
by the measure,
And weighed the mountains
in a balance
And the hills
in a pair of scales . . .

Isaiah 40:12

This God, who holds the oceans in the hollow of His hands, and measures the heavens by the span of His arms,

... emptied Himself, taking the form of a bond-servant, and being made in the likeness of men. Being found in appearance as a man, He humbled Himself by becoming obedient to the point of death, even death on a cross.

Philippians 2:7-8

This God, who lifts up the mountains and weighs them on His scales, who stretched out His arms obedient to the point of death, gave *us* a precious gift, the choice to obey Him, or not:

"From any tree of the garden you may eat freely; but from the tree of the knowledge of good and evil you shall not eat ..."

Genesis 2:16-17

He knew what we would choose — and He *still* gave us that gift!

O LORD, you have searched me
and you know me.
You know when I sit and when I rise;
you perceive my thoughts from afar.
You discern my going out and my lying down;
you are familiar with all my ways.
Before a word is on my tongue
you know it completely, O LORD.

Psalm 139:1-4 NIV

He knows every thought in our minds before we even think it. He knows every word before we even say it. He knows every piece of our hearts, the light and the dark, whether we are aware of those areas or not. He alone knows the past, present, and future. This God, who lifts up the islands like fine dust, who emptied Himself for us, who knew the rebellious choice we would make, gave us the will to make that choice. *This* is Biblical sovereignty. I say with Job,

Can you fathom the mysteries of God?
Can you probe the limits of the Almighty?
They are higher than the heavens –
     what can you do?
They are deeper than the depths of the grave –
     what can you know?
Their measure is longer than the earth
     and wider than the sea.

Job 11:7-9 NIV

Stop and catch your breath. Jot a few notes in the margin or in your journal, then we're going to explore some more.

The LORD foils the plans of the nations;
     he thwarts the purposes of the peoples.
But the plans of the LORD stand firm forever,
the purposes of his heart through all generations.

Psalm 33:10-11 NIV

His plans alone stand. But look at that verse again to see where those plans originate: in His heart. My friend Angelique puts it succinctly: *His heart* dictates His plans. And this God, *whose plans are the purposes of His heart,* chose *these* plans for Himself:

So the Roman cohort and the commander and the officers of the Jews, arrested Jesus and bound Him ... Then all the disciples deserted him and fled.

John 18:12 NASB, Matthew 26:56 NIV

This God, who ensures that His plans are fulfilled *according to the purposes of His heart,* who chose to be betrayed, arrested, bound, and deserted, then gives *us* a choice, to receive Him, or to reject Him:

But as many as received Him, to them He gave the right to become children of God, even to those who

believe in His name, who were born, not of blood nor of the will of the flesh nor of the will of man, but of God.   John 1:12-13

He is orchestrating the plans *of His heart.* He lays His heart bare, giving us the power to accept or reject Him – knowing ahead of time full well what we will choose. Every time in our lives that we are faced with a decision to surrender, He puts Himself in this place of vulnerability. Can you fathom this love? I surely cannot; I cannot understand Him. And no wonder,

> **"For My thoughts are not your thoughts,**
> **Nor are your ways My ways," declares the LORD.**
> **For as the heavens are higher than the earth,**
> **So are My ways higher than your ways**
> **And My thoughts than your thoughts."**
> Isaiah 55:8-9

This is Biblical sovereignty. This is what *Adonai* means. Take a few minutes to ponder these truths, and journal your thoughts. Then we'll continue.

[He] lives forever and ever, who created heaven and the things in it, and the earth and the things in it, and the sea and the things in it ... And He put all things in subjection under His feet ...
                    Revelation 10:6, Ephesians 1:22

This God, who created *all* things, who reigns over all rule and authority and power and dominion, created men such as these:

One of the officials nearby struck him in the face... Some began to spit at Him, and to blindfold Him, and to beat Him with their fists ...
                    John 18:22 NIV, Mark 14:65 NASB

This God, who created all things for Himself, created these men to strike His face, spit upon Him, and beat Him – in order to save the world He so loved. *And* this same God offers us this choice:

"If it is disagreeable in your sight to serve the LORD, choose for yourselves today whom you will serve: whether the gods which your fathers served which were beyond the River, or the gods of the Amorites in whose land you are living ..."

Joshua 24:15

If it is disagreeable to serve Him. This God, our Creator, who offered His face to be beaten and spit upon so that we could spend eternity with Him, tells us that if it is **disagreeable** to us to serve Him, then we can serve any god we choose!? This is God's sovereignty? This is Adonai? Pause and ponder this, and take some time to journal.

I can make no sense of this – and no wonder. Adonai is beyond my human comprehension. His ways are inscrutable. Unsearchable. Unfathomable. The thinking of my pea-brain mind is utterly futile. Let's go on.

Do you not know? Have you not heard?
Has it not been declared to you
**   from the beginning?**
Have you not understood
**   from the foundations of the earth?**
It is He who sits above the circle of the earth,
And its inhabitants are like grasshoppers,
Who stretches out the heavens like a curtain
And spreads them out like a tent to dwell in ...
He it is who reduces rulers to nothing,
Who makes the judges of the earth meaningless.

Isaiah 40:21-24

This God, who calls us **grasshoppers**, does not allow a sparrow to fall to the ground unnoticed. This God, who reduces judges to nothing, submitted Himself to their hideous human judgment:

After having Jesus scourged, he handed Him over to be crucified. Then the soldiers of the governor took Jesus into the Praetorium and gathered the whole Roman cohort around Him. They stripped Him and put a scarlet robe on Him. And after twisting together a crown of thorns, they put it on His head, and a reed in His right hand; and they knelt down before Him and mocked Him, saying, "Hail, King of the Jews!" They spat on Him, and took the reed and began to beat Him on the head.

Matthew 27:26-30

They beat Him on the head. This God, who sits above the circle of the earth, who was stripped naked and scourged for us grasshoppers, gives us the choice to obey or disobey, to accept or reject Him:

"I have set before you life and death, the blessing and the curse. So choose life in order that you may live, you and your descendants, by loving the LORD your God, by obeying His voice, and by holding fast to Him ..."

Deuteronomy 30:19-20

But each one is tempted when he is carried away and enticed by his own lust. Then when lust has conceived, it gives birth to sin; and when sin is accomplished, it brings forth death. Do not be deceived, my beloved brethren.

James 1:14-16

How could we disobey Him? Deny Him? Refuse Him? And yet we do. Every day. Why would He allow this? I have no explanation, **to Him belong counsel and understanding** (Job 12:13).

I am taking a big gulp right about now. To Daniel next.

> **His dominion is an eternal dominion;**
>> **his kingdom endures**
>> **from generation to generation.**
> **All the peoples of the earth**
>> **are regarded as nothing.**
> **He does as he pleases**
>> **with the powers of heaven**
>> **and the peoples of the earth.**
> **No one can hold back his hand**
>> **or say to him: "What have you done?"**
>>>> Daniel 4:34-35 NIV

What did He do with those hands that no one can hold back?

> **So he then handed Him over to them to be crucified. They took Jesus, therefore, and He went out, bearing His own cross, to the place called the Place of a Skull, which is called in Hebrew, Golgotha. There they crucified Him, and with Him two other men, one on either side, and Jesus in between.**
>>>> John 19:16-18

This God, who regards us as nothing and yet stretched out His hands and inscribed us on His palms, has bestowed upon us free will—and all the accompanying responsibilities:

> **So then, each of us will give an account of himself to God ... For we must all appear before the judgment seat of Christ, that each one may receive what is due him for the things done while in the body, whether good or bad.**
>>>> Romans 14:12, 2 Corinthians 5:10 NIV

This is Biblical sovereignty. This is Adonai. We try to comprehend His divine purposes coupled with His bottomless love and our free will, but as humans we cannot even begin to grasp this. Indeed there will someday be a time when our mouths are silenced, when we finally see that His righteousness and judgments are completely perfect, when **every mouth may be closed and all the world may become accountable to God ...** (Rom 3:19).

What I have learned from these verses?

God's Rule
+ His Perfect Love for Us
+ Our Free Will
= God's Sovereignty,
completely unfathomable to my human mind

- His power? Limitless.

- His love? Without bounds.

- Our free will? Clear and definite.

- Our comprehension of Adonai? Exceedingly limited.

Head to your secret place of His Presence and let the depth of these truths soak into your heart.

Defining God's Sovereignty

We can see from these passages that God's sovereignty is not the same as control in a human sense of the word. God's sovereignty is *beyond* control. Just like there is nothing in the human existence that can adequately explain or grasp the incarnation, I think that there is nothing in the human existence that can adequately explain *God's* sovereignty.

We can also see from these passages that God allows us to make our own choices. We are responsible for how we govern our lives. He allows us this precious dignifying gift while *simultaneously* fulfilling *His* purposes. Whether our choices will be righteous or sinful, His plan has already taken them into account.

God's sovereignty is the delicate interplay between His purposes and our free will, overlaid with His unconditional love. He does not violate our free will, yet He simultaneously ensures that we exercise our free will in a way that furthers His vast eternal plan – while pouring out His love for us at the same time. How can He possibly do that? That is precisely where our limited human understanding grinds to a halt. Because we, as humans, could never accomplish such a daunting task, we cannot possibly fathom how God could do it. But instead of writing this off as impossible because we cannot comprehend it, I am asking you *by faith* to accept that this God, the Mover of Mountains, the One who cups the oceans in the hollow of His hands and spreads out the heavens like a tent around us, for whom nothing is impossible, is able to do just that – and does it every day. Ponder this:

It seems to me that God chooses to limit Himself in many areas in His dealings with mankind. For example,

- Jesus came to earth and emptied Himself of His divine powers, choosing to do only what the Father commanded Him to do (Ph 2:7).

- God depends on *us* to be the body of Christ, His hands, His feet, His voice on this earth (1Cor 12:12-27).

- God calls us to co-labor with Him (1Cor 3:9; 2Cor6:1).

- God works through the prayers of His people (2Cor 1:10-11).

Does He *need* us? Not in an absolute sense of the word. He is infinite and of course He has no need for humans in order to accomplish anything. But He *chooses* to limit Himself, and in that respect, He *does* need us to bring His Kingdom to fruition.

God could indeed easily override our will. But He *chooses* not to. He allows us to make our own decisions, to rebel or to obey, to resist or to submit, to fight or to surrender. He has chosen to invite us to *work together* with Him, to *partner* with Him, to *co-labor* with Him (1Cor 3:9, 2Cor 6:1, 1Th 3:2). You may ask, But why? I think the answer to that lies in His impossible-to-comprehend unconditional love for us.

He does as He pleases with the powers of heaven and the peoples of the earth ... He humbled Himself by becoming obedient to the point of death, even death on a cross ... As many as received Him, to them He gave the right to become children of God.
Daniel 4:35 NIV, Philippians 2:8, John 1:12

He sovereignly does as He pleases, going to His death for us ... and then leaves it to us to choose whether we will receive His profound offer.

You see, *who God is* doesn't stop with His absolute sovereignty, and *who God is* isn't touched by our free will. Since **God is love**, His sovereignty *includes* His unconditional love for us. God takes His undisputed authority, intertwines it with our free will, and then overlays it with His perfect love. *God's*

sovereignty is an interplay between His purposes and our free will, an interplay that is infused with His irrevocable love. I think we'll need some quiet meditation time again.

Our Response to God's Sovereignty

So the question remains: How will we exercise our free will? God does not force Himself upon us as Lord of our hearts. He gives us the choice: to submit our will to His, to bow to Him as our Lord and Master, or to reject Him and rebel against Him.

Our salvation is the entryway into a journey of growth in Jesus. When we make our initial choice to repent of our sins, to trust Jesus as our Savior, and surrender our life to God, we then embark on a lifetime of deeper surrenders. This is our journey of sanctification, and with each step we are being conformed to the image of Christ. With each transformation we are brought into deeper intimacy with the Lord.

For this is the will of God, your sanctification ... God has chosen you from the beginning for salvation through sanctification by the Spirit and faith in the truth.
1 Thessalonians 4:3, 2 Thessalonians 2:13

The Amplified says that it is the will of God that you be **consecrated, separated and set apart for pure and holy living** (1Th 4:3). How does this sanctification happen? By the work of the Holy Spirit as we *believe in, adhere to, trust in, rely on* His Truth (2Th 2:13 AMP). What does this mean in our everyday lives?

- In Jesus we are already holy and blameless, yet we can choose to *grow* in holiness and blamelessness and *cooperate* with Him as He conforms us to His image (Ph 2:14-15).

- In Jesus we are set apart from the world, yet we can

choose to *separate* ourselves from the world and to *dedicate* ourselves to God.

- In Jesus we are pure, yet we can choose to *remove filth* from our lives and seek to *live chastely*.

- In Jesus we are the righteousness of God, yet we are not without sin. When we do sin, we can choose to *repent*, seek His *forgiveness*, and seek *right relationship* with God.

Jesus gives us His righteousness, making us holy and blameless; our part is to daily surrender to the sanctification. Surrendering to the sanctification is making Jesus our *Adonai*, the Lord of our heart, the Master of every aspect of our life. Surrender is to give Jesus rule over us, over our desires, our hearts, our minds, our lives, our purpose and plans. During our time on this earth, as His sanctification process continues in us, we grow closer to Him; He carries our sanctification on to completion until the day of Christ Jesus (Phil 1:6).

Stuck in the Agony

If you're like me, there are times when I want to surrender, but I don't know exactly how to get there. I spend some time in the agony part, but I can't figure out how to get to the "Your will be done" part. I think we've figured out that surrender can't be forced, manufactured, coerced, or faked. God knows the deepest most concealed thoughts of our hearts. **He knows what lies in darkness** (Dan 2:22 NIV).

I do not want to rest in a place of unsurrender. I know that my rebellion must tear at His heart. I know that withholding my surrender is a roadblock keeping me from drawing closer to the Lord. It obstructs our relationship.

It interferes with my ability to hear more clearly from Him – and can even block my hearing completely. I know that it thwarts me from receiving His love and joy and peace. What can I do to move from a place of unsurrender to a place of surrender?

If the Holy Spirit has given me revelation that I am not aligned with His will, or that I am holding something back, and I can't seem to come to that full surrender, I must first repent of my refusal to surrender. I may ask others to pray with me. I keep seeking Him; I pound on His chest and pester Him, crying out to Him to change me. I do not want to stop until He has worked surrender in my heart. With my own feeble human efforts, I try as best I can to align my actions, words, and thoughts with His. And then, sometimes totally exhausted, I simply pray, "Lord, I am willing to be made willing. Do whatever it takes." And then I wait for Him to move.

Only Grace Extricates Us From the Miry Clay

I waited patiently for the LORD;
And He inclined to me and heard my cry.
He brought me up out of the pit of destruction,
Out of the miry clay,
And He set my feet upon a rock
Making my footsteps firm.

Psalm 40:1-2

Yes, He **fashions the hearts**, and it is **God's will that we should be sanctified**, but in the end, it is only the **kindness of God** that leads us to repentance (Ps 33:15, 1Th 4:3, Rom 2:4, 2 Tim 2:25). He *grants* us repentance. He is the one who fashions our hearts. He is the One who molds us, shapes us, sanctifies us. It is only the power of His Holy Spirit at work within our hearts that graciously brings us to repentance and surrender. When we have bowed our hearts to His sovereign will, He begins, by His grace, to transform us and to bring us to surrender. As we trust Him to work, as we do our part to obediently choose His path again and again as best we can, as we have faith to believe that it is *His will* that we be sanctified and as we pray according to that will, the Lord will indeed honor our prayer. He will do whatever it takes to bring us to surrender.

A word of caution: I have found that if I am unable to come to surrender, and I truly and deeply pray to be made willing, God will indeed do whatever it takes to bring me to surrender. And my journey may then become very rocky. I would choose no other way, though, because I know that He will walk me through it, and the greater level of intimacy with Him at the end of that walk will be extraordinary.

Surrender Requires Humility

Not long ago, I was struggling with a surrender of forgiveness – forgiveness of myself. My friend said to me, "Celeste, it's really a matter of humility. You are not accepting that Jesus did *everything* on the cross." Indeed, she was right. I was stuck in a place of pride, thinking that there was something I could – or should – do to earn my own forgiveness. Her words of Truth removed the veil from my heart and enabled me to embrace the humility of accepting that there was nothing, *nothing*, I could do to make up for my sin.

Surrender Requires Trust

Sometimes, our own intelligence, knowledge, experience, and wisdom can block us from coming to surrender. It is no wonder that Jesus tells us to humble ourselves and become like little children (Mt 18:3-4). I have invited my friend Jade, an astute woman with a dual doctorate in metaphysics and religion, to describe how she needed to trust as a little child. This precious woman knows over twenty languages (yes, you read that number correctly) and has written and been published in three of those languages. Before she came to Christ, she had already read the Bible many times, as well as the Torah, the Qur'an, the Taoist scrolls, and other ancient sacred writings. In her search for God, she had reached a point where her intelligence could carry her no farther. She realized that coming to Christ would be by grace through faith, or not at all. She penned these words the day after her salvation.

Amazing Grace has always brought me to tears. The song was a beautifully piercing reminder that I would not be found and that I was beyond saving. Above all, it was auditory proof ensuring my life stayed behind an invisible wall separating me from "normal" worthy people.

Because of the invisible wall, I stopped short of and hesitated giving my life to Him. I was also waiting in hope that someday I might feel genuinely "touched" by His Spirit. I mistakenly erected another barrier between myself and Him, thinking I had to experience that "genuine feeling" to tell me that I was worthy of being saved.

1 June 2013 is the date of my rebirth into my new life with Christ. That afternoon, before I turned my life over to Him, I walked with a Christian girlfriend. As we shared our histories, thoughts and concerns, it became increasingly clear to me — an epiphany — what Grace through Faith means.

My "ah ha" moment crystallized as I heard a voice within tell me to go ahead, take the leap, trust in blind faith, and rest assured there would be ground below to catch me. He held my heart as I took the leap. Instead of falling, He made me fly! He actually exalted me by making me fly. I'm supposed to exalt Him, but He exalted me with Eternal Life in Him!

In my heart, I understand how my journey was His

plan all along, made all the more perfect exactly as it was orchestrated, by Him. I am excited that I have been found. I embrace with open arms and an open heart the layers and qualities of joy He is giving me. I know I will fall, that I am unworthy, and because of that, He holds me up to be righteous. He has also given me a ravenous hunger to ingest His Words and I have not stopped reading and re-reading the Books of the Old and the New Testaments. Understanding leaps off the pages as never before, and His Words are an inexplicable treasure of joy, comfort, and enlightenment, affecting my entire worldview.

Grace through Faith ... it is a tremendously extraordinary miracle in its profound simplicity, keeping me humble and grateful to my Savior, Jesus Christ. He is attuning my ears with a boldness I have never experienced before. I no longer need to hesitate. I am His Child. I am His Warrior. I embrace my new life in Him!

Jade Yu, PhD
Royal Palm Beach, Florida

Yes, Jade, indeed, the Lord raises up those who are humble. He **lifts up those who are bowed down** (Ps 146:8). And He exalts those who are repentant:

> **"This is the one I esteem:**
> **he who is humble**
> **and contrite in spirit,**
> **and trembles at my word."**

Isaiah 66:2 NIV

He has His eye upon those who are repentant, who are humble and contrite. He will honor them, free them, deliver them, draw them to Himself. On the day of her salvation, this transformed woman stayed up all night reading the Word, devouring Deuteronomy, Esther, Proverbs, Ezekiel, Hosea, Joel, Habakkuk, Malachi, the Gospel of John – and Job twice! As she continues to read, the Spirit is uprooting Satan's lies and teaching her God's truths, radically changing her *entire worldview.*

What a profound first time surrender! You can so clearly see His hand of grace. But realize also the depth of grace necessary for all our *subsequent* surrenders:

... as you have received Christ Jesus the Lord, so walk in Him.

Colossians 2:6

How did you receive Jesus? *By grace through faith.* And the only way to walk in Him, the only way to come to a new level of surrender, is *by His grace through faith.* Unable to visualize the full outcome, yet trusting, as Jade did, that His capable hands will be there to catch us, is a walk of faith trusting His grace. It will be a working of the Holy Spirit in our heart, which begins when we invite Him in. We make the *choice* to surrender, and the Holy Spirit works in our heart to bring that surrender to completion.

The Trap of Token Surrender

I have seen this too many times, both in myself and in others, to gloss over it here. This token surrender can happen when God is calling us to surrender, and we surrender only a piece of what He is calling us to, instead of the whole thing. Francis Frangipane in *The Three Battlegrounds* expresses it this way,

> There will be pressure from your flesh, as well as from the demonic world itself, to minimize or ignore what God is requiring of you. You may be tempted to surrender just a token sin or some minor fault, while allowing your main problems to remain entrenched and well-hidden.[4]

If we give a token surrender, we may *think* that we have surrendered all He is calling us to, and then become entrapped in this web of deception. We may fool ourselves that our surrender is complete. It may be a long time before we see our own deception.

Come with me to hear my friend Chuck's testimony illustrating this idea of token surrenders. Chuck is one of my Triumph Servant Leaders and is serving the Lord in many areas, but it has been a difficult journey from when he first accepted Jesus as his Savior at age eleven. His childhood was scarred with the pains of a father who nightly drank and then left him alone in a car in the dark while he cheated on his wife. Drafted into the military at 19, Chuck experienced all the horrors of serving in the Vietnam War. His best friend died in his arms. The Vietnamese child that he adopted died in a bombing before he could bring her to the States. I'll let Chuck pick up the story here.

I began to drink heavily when I came home from Vietnam. Re-enlisting in the Air Force, I received award after award, decoration upon decoration, the youngest and fastest promoted member – but I still stayed in touch with the booze. I was asked to join the "elite and outstanding" Air Force Recruiting Service, rubbing elbows with generals and colonels and sharing the radio waves with Wolfman Jack in NYC – but I was still devoid of real happiness.

I worked as a Junior VP at a bank, and was promoted to work for the Under Secretary of the US Treasury. Wow, did I have it all – until my life came to a crashing end in the stock market crash of 1979. With a new home, two cars, a wife and two children, but without any income, I deceived myself that I was "humbling myself" by taking a teaching position. But it was only a token surrender, and I continued my relationship with Jack Daniels and Jim Bean.

Teaching wasn't for me, and I further deceived myself that I was "humbling myself" again as I became a contractor. Yet once again it proved to be only a token surrender. A successful career, another new home, great cars and wonderful income didn't satisfy; my family was crashing because of my drinking. My wife gave me an ultimatum:

quit, or she, the kids, and the business would disappear. I did, and I remain sober today, over 30 years later. Yet I still did not return to Christ.

I survived heart surgery in 1993, but that didn't bring me to surrender. Next, stomach ulcers caused such great internal bleeding that I was pronounced "dead" for nearly twenty minutes, received a glimpse of heaven and was told, "You're not done yet." In a nod of token surrender, I acknowledged that "something special" had happened here, but deep in my heart I continued to deny Christ.

In 2001, I had surgery for a huge Abdominal Aortic Aneurysm. The surgeon told me later that he prayed during the entire surgery because he didn't expect me to survive. This was a wake up call for me, and my wife and I enrolled in a Bible study, The Alpha Series. As the lead pastor shared his Vietnam experience and we made eye contact, I knew that it was time to stop running. The Holy Spirit opened my heart; I began to weep uncontrollably, and this time it was no token surrender. Not long after, my church showed a video of the Washington DC Vietnam Memorial at their Fourth of July service. The camera scanned the memorial, then focused on a name: Michael J. Price, my best friend who had died in my arms. Sobbing, God spoke to me – thirty-three years later.

Since my true surrender to the Lord, I have hosted Bible studies in my home, taught The Alpha Series and Crown Financial, authored several books, become an ordained minister, and worked in a drug and alcohol rehab center. I recognize how God has prepared me to serve Him and to assist others by using the skills and talents He gave me.

I now understand the meaning of "obedience" from personal experience. In 2007 I stepped out in faith, leaving a wonderful employment and income. Within 48 hours God birthed Today's Promise in my heart, a national ministry designed to mentor and coach couples as they build healthy, strong, and lasting marriages.

Chuck Dettman
Executive Director and Founder
of Today's Promise

You can see how God orchestrated many trials to repeatedly reveal the state of Chuck's heart and to expose his little surrenders for what they really were: tokens. This long journey of token surrenders did culminate in his final deep surrender to Jesus, and the fruit of Chuck's true surrender is the enormity of his Kingdom work.

Deeper and Deeper Surrenders

You may be surmising by now that surrender is not a one-time event. We make our very first choice to surrender, and then enter into a lifetime of surrendering. I'd like to introduce you to my friend John C., and let him describe his journey through deeper and deeper surrenders. John's childhood was marked by abandonment after abandonment; his adulthood by three marriages. When he married Phyllis ten years ago, they both agreed to place God in the center of their marriage. But although this was a critical decision, it wasn't the complete answer.

Yesterday my wife and I had another terrible argument. I felt I could give no more; I had done my best. As I continued in Bible study, and read about surrendering to God, a light went on – a very bright light. "Surrender your marriage to God; surrender Phyllis to God; surrender your problem to God and take care of yourself," the Lord said to me.

I felt I had direction. So every time the problem came up, I surrendered it to God. But after a short time, I found that my surrendering was not the same; it had lost something. I started to doubt. Did I really surrender? Have I been using God to get what I want? Am I losing my faith in God? Confusion and frustration came strongly. I did not know where to turn.

I took a ride to the beach, talking out loud to God. On the way my mind was filled with hate and resentment. But when I arrived, my mind went back to surrender. I thought

I had surrendered. I thought I had given everything. What was wrong? I began to pray for God to help me, to guide me. What came next had to be God.

God took me back to the beginning of my life. Now I have thought about my past often, but this time the journey back into my childhood was different. When God walked me through it this time, I was flooded with emotions. I relived my entire life right there on the beach – this time with God walking with me, and this time experiencing all the emotions from which I had tried to escape.

God was faithful not only to stay with me through this journey, but also to reveal to me what He wanted me to surrender. I am not to simply surrender Phyllis or my problems; what I must surrender to God is ME. The part of me that is filled with all the emotions from the very beginning of my life. It was not easy, but as God led me through that surrender, I felt a peace come over me.

I am 84 years old, and I had been suffering from things that happened to me when I was 3,5,9,15. What purpose could God have had? I began to smile, knowing that I had just had an intimate encounter with Him as never before. And, as I left the beach, I sensed that He was up to something.

Last Tuesday my wife and I invited two people who are battling cancer into our home. One of them looked so worn; when she spoke, I could feel her pain. The other needed help to walk and spoke so softly we almost couldn't hear him. I wanted to help them; I was sharing their pain. We sat at the table and talked for a while, watched part of The Truth Project, and talked some more. Soon both of our guests were laughing and telling stories; their voices had gained strength. Yes, God does have a purpose, and I saw His purpose at the table. God did not create me to solve marriage problems or to solve Phyllis' problems. He created me to do just what I was doing right now. He put me at peace, and showed me where He wanted me to serve.

My daily prayer now is to keep surrendering my past to Him, and to tell Him how grateful I am.

John C.
Jupiter, Florida

I think John C. would agree with me that the depth of the encounter he had with the Lord on the beach that day would never have happened without the pain of his childhood. As he opened his heart to God, He came to know the Lord as never before, meeting Him as Healer and Faithful One. And it seems that it was through the pain of his past and the healing of his present that God gave him a piece of His heart. God enabled John to experience God's own heartache for the pain of His people. And as if this wasn't enough, God also gave him Kingdom work, using him to reach these people and touch their place of pain.

Surrendering to His Plan

As God pours His love into our hearts, He will begin to teach us that in His sovereignty, He ordains our trials, He hand-picks them, perfectly tailored for each one of us *individually*, in order to give us more of Him. And as His loves flows through us, we will treasure the truth that He has ordained, pre-determined, chosen — and protected — every moment of our lives.

Sovereignty is as if God is saying, *"I am responsible. If you are angry about anything in your life, you take it up with Me. Don't blame other people, don't blame the world, don't blame Satan. Pain and suffering are not My cherished plans. Yet, I am in control, and My plan in My timing will come to pass. I am the Supreme Ruler of the Universe. You take it up with Me."*

And when we do that, when we come to God in our pain, He will speak to us. He may or may not give us understanding. He may or may not open our eyes. But there is one thing He will always do. And that is to pour His love into us, and to give us Himself.

But why, you ask, does He then not simply protect us from all the workings of Satan? Yes, I have asked that question many times myself also. I think that the answer lies in His infinite love. He wants fellowship with us so so desperately that He doesn't want to wait until we reach heaven. He doesn't want to wait until the end of the world. He wants to give us a foretaste of it right now. And in order to receive more of Him, we find that the only safe place is abiding in Him.

Additionally, the purpose of all that He created is to glorify Himself. As we yield ourselves to His hands, He will bring forth His glory in us and through us, and we will then share in His glory.

Now if we are children, then we are heirs – heirs of God and co-heirs with Christ, if indeed we share in his sufferings in order that we may also share in his glory.

Romans 8:17 NIV

Jade, whom you met a few pages back, summarizes Job in these words: "No matter how much Satan works to trip us up, no matter how violently he attacks, no matter how hard he tries to confound us and drive us away from God, in the end, he will only further God's plan. He is God's servant – a created and fallen being, yet still completely God's servant." Indeed. Colossians agrees:

For by Him all things were created, both in the heavens and on earth, visible and invisible, whether thrones or dominions or rulers or authorities—all things have been created through Him *and for Him*.

Colossians 1:16, emphasis added

All things have been created *for Him*. Psalm 119 expounds, **All are Your servants, all things serve You, everything serves Your plans** (Ps 119:91 NKJV, NIV, NLT). Satan and his forces of darkness will always be His servants, unwittingly furthering His purposes and plans.

How Will You Respond to Adonai?

"Thou art worthy, O Lord, to receive glory and honour and power; for thou hast created all things, and for thy pleasure they are and were created."
Revelation 4:11 KJV

He created everything, including you and me, *for His pleasure.* He then rescued us from Satan and brought us to Himself *so that* we would declare His praises:

But you are a chosen people, a royal priesthood, a holy nation, a people belonging to God, that you may declare the praises of him who called you out of darkness into his wonderful light.
1 Peter 2:9 NIV

Created to give Him pleasure. *Redeemed* to declare His praises.

... He said, "It is finished!" And He bowed His head and gave up His spirit ... And behold, the veil of the temple was torn in two from top to bottom; and the earth shook and the rocks were split.
John 19:30, Matthew 27:51

He tore the veil in two to invite us to enter into intimacy with Him. His work on the cross is finished. Yet He commands us to **work out your salvation with fear and trembling** (Ph 2:12). He commands us to *cooperate* with Him in our sanctification. To do the hard work of surrender. To bow our hearts to *Adonai*, who stands at the door and knocks. He has only one question for you now: Will you open the door for Me?

Will you open your heart in deeper surrender to the

Knocking One? Will you invite Him into that place of deep intimacy with you, will you invite Him to dine with you? Will you choose that place of deep abiding?

"I'll Go First."

In His sovereignty, God accomplishes His plan *without* violating our free will – because of the depth of His love for us. Yet, because of that same incomprehensible love, He invites us to surrender to His sovereign plan, because He knows that His plan is the most blessed plan *for us*. Go back to what you have written in that surrender line at the beginning of the chapter. Are you ready to surrender it?

God's cherished desire for us is a depth of relationship with Him that is a never-ending circle. He pours His love into us, which enables us to surrender more, which opens the door for us to receive more of His love and intimacy and revelation of who He is, which leads to deeper surrenders as we are able to trust Him more, which leads to more openness to His love, which results in Him overflowing us with His love once again, which leads to greater intimacy...

Beautiful in its simplicity, breathtaking in its intensity, a self-perpetuating cycle that brings us closer and closer to Him and fills us more and more with His Spirit . . . How will that cycle start? There must be an initial beginning, right? How do we step into this place of endless giving and receiving with our Creator and Savior?

This is how that cycle starts. God says, *"I'll go first."*

"I'll go first." God entered the cycle by dying so that we may live. By His death we may enter into relationship with Him. By His death we can plunge deeper into Him.

God *already* went first. He has set the cycle into motion. The next step is yours.

Will you pray with me?

Lord, I choose to surrender

to You. I lay it at Your feet, trusting it to You. I release it to Your control. I trust that Your plans are perfect, for me and for those I love, and I embrace those plans. I trust myself to Your sovereign loving hands, to mold me and shape me into the image of Your Son, whatever it takes. Amen.

Questions Chapter 4:
Surrendering to His Sovereignty

Memory Verse:

"For My thoughts are not your thoughts,
Nor are your ways My ways," declares the LORD.
For as the heavens are higher than the earth,
So are My ways higher than your ways
And My thoughts than your thoughts."
Isaiah 55:8-9

1) Explain in your own words Biblical sovereignty, God as *Adonai.*

Re-read the section *Surrendering To His Plan.* What does it mean that Satan and his forces of darkness will always be God's servants, unwittingly furthering His purposes? Apply this concept to a current trial in your life.

2) Read Genesis Chapter 32, and Matthew 26:36-46. Think about your own journey of surrender as you worked through this chapter. How did submitting to His sovereignty factor into your surrender ?

3) Surrender requires humility. Describe a time that demanded a walk of humility to reach full surrender.

Surrender requires trust. Describe a time when God called upon you to utterly trust Him in order to surrender.

If you are struggling with your surrender now, does pride or distrust feed into your inability to surrender?

4) Re-read the section *The Trap of Token Surrender.* Ask the Lord to reveal to you if any of your surrenders – recent or in the past – have been tokens. Realize, though, that although these tokens may have been small, they may also have been important preparation for a much greater surrender.

God may speak to you as you are quiet and listening. He may allow you insight by the words that slip out of your mouth, for **out of the overflow of the heart the mouth speaks** (Mt 12:34 NIV).

Or, as He did with Chuck, He may orchestrate events in your life to repeatedly bring up the same area of surrender. If God has revealed that your surrender is a token, or incomplete, or that you have simply taken it back after relinquishing it to Him, ask Him to reveal any deep heart sins holding you back from full surrender.

5) Re-read the section *"I'll Go First."* God has indeed gone first. Describe this cycle as it is at work in your life. Have you entered into the cycle with Him?

For me, grappling with surrender and sovereignty has not been easy. If you are still wrestling here, it may help to read over those chapters in *Triumph Over Suffering.*

John Li

Chapter 5
Demolishing the Idols
That Thwart Our Fellowship

What do righteousness and wickedness have in common? Or what fellowship can light have with darkness? What harmony is there between Christ and Belial? ... What agreement is there between the temple of God and idols? For we are the temple of the living God. As God has said: "I will live with them and walk among them, and I will be their God, and they will be my people."

2 Corinthians 6:14-16 NIV

He is a jealous God, and He will expose idols that we've set up in His temple. He will not allow idols to thwart our intimacy with Him.

We may think of idols as carved images – these *are* idols – but idols are even much more ubiquitous and insidious than that. Idols can be anyone or anything that we put our trust in, that are more important to us than God, that we rely on for security, that drive us to lie to protect or to control ... or that we cannot release to God's control. To better understand idolatry, come with me to Peru ...

A number of years ago, I went with my family on a mission trip to Peru. On our final day, I was laid low with a stomach virus, so I was forced to remain back at the hostel while my husband and teenage kids traveled with the team into town.

Now before this day, if you had asked me if I trusted God with my family, I would have said absolutely. I had surrendered them to Him – many times, actually. Deeper and deeper each time. I would have said that God is trustworthy and that I completely trusted Him to take care of my family. Even if something happened that the world would not call "good," I believed that I was able to trust that He was indeed always working for my good and for my family's good, and that He would certainly bring good out of the worst of situations. But my level of trust was about to be tested.

Our lead pastor had told me that the team would be back to the orphanage by three o'clock. But they did not show up at three. Four o'clock arrived. Then five and six. I was in a strange land and could not speak the language. There were no phones. There was no way to check up on them. No messenger to send out. By the time darkness fell at seven o'clock, my utter lack of trust in God was completely exposed. I was a wretched mess.

My heart was laid bare before Him. The Holy Spirit revealed that my trust in God was only a head belief. The Holy Spirit exposed the lie that had lain hidden in my heart: God could not be trusted with my family.

Celeste Li
Jupiter, Florida

In all honesty, I would have never recognized the fear and distrust entrenched in my heart without the fire of the

trial. God knew what was there. Satan did, too. Only I
was oblivious. God wanted to expose it.

That night in the hostel in Peru, I fell on my face and
repented. It was a serious wrestling in my heart, as I cried
and I praised and I cried and I read Scripture and I cried
and I worshipped, vacillating for hours back and forth
between trust and fear.

I wish I could say that He had the victory. But although
there were glimpses of His Light working to penetrate the
darkness in my heart, He never fully broke through. In
retrospect, I see that I was never able to thank Him for the
situation, whatever the outcome would be. Yes, worship and
praise are critical in a trial, and if our hearts can do that,
God is certainly at work within us. And thanking Him in
the trial is another level – thanking Him for His salvation
and mercy and grace and forgiveness and eternal life. But
thanking Him *for the trial?* Thanking Him because I *trust*
His plan to be perfect for His Kingdom, and good for me
and mine? Rejoicing in *His painful plan?* That's a whole
different level entirely.

**Consider it pure joy, my brothers, whenever you
face trials of many kinds ...**
James 1:2 NIV

Yep, that's the heart that He desires, all right. And my
heart didn't pass the test.

I know what you must be thinking, "But you wrote a
book on that!" Indeed I did. And at this moment of testing,
I lost a major battle here. Nevertheless, God wouldn't call
this "failure." It would have been failure had I not *learned*
from this.

As I look back over the five years since that night in
Peru, I see that my journey of trust has been peppered with
both victories and losses. Sometimes, Jesus is triumphant
in my heart. Other times, even as recently as a few weeks

ago, I do not reach a place of deeper trust in Him before He ends the test. Discouraged, I need to remind myself of the teachings of Pastor Todd Mullins from Christ Fellowship Church:

> See yourself as God sees you: you are more than a conqueror ... You are a contender, one who has the potential to become a champion ... Failure is not final ... What you do after you get knocked down is critical. Being challenged is inevitable. But being defeated is optional.[1]

Oh, you want to know the rest of the Peru story? I didn't mean to keep you in suspense. At 9PM the bus arrived. The team was exhausted and famished, but unharmed. Just a bit late, that's all. Six hours late.

The team may not know why they were six hours late, but I sure do know at least one of the reasons. God gave me six hours in order to expose my heart, to bring me to repentance, and to give me an opportunity to trust Him – *before* I learned that they were safe. Six hours to surrender them to Him – not to *abandon* them, but to *release* them to His care. He graciously gave me those six hours. It wasn't nearly enough time.

God has a word for something or someone we are unable to surrender to Him. He calls it an *idol*. He calls it *rebellion*.

His Name Is Jealous

You shall not worship any other god, for the LORD, whose name is Jealous, is a jealous God.

Exodus 34:14

What a remarkable Name of God: Jealous. The Hebrew is *Qanna*. *Qanna* does not mean that God is suspicious, distrustful, or envious. My *Hebrew Word Study* says that

Qanna means that He "will not tolerate the worship of other gods. This word is always used to describe God's attitude toward the worship of false gods, which arouses His jealousy and anger in judgment against the idol worshippers."[2] I have asked my friend Rosa to share with us how she encountered the Lord as *Qanna.*

My husband had an affair with my best friend. This double betrayal destroyed me emotionally and mentally. I didn't know what to do; I felt lost and completely alone. I searched the Bible for answers, asking, "Why, Lord, why? I gave to the poor as You said to do, I opened my doors for years to teach the unsaved, I preached to my family, I attended church, I read the Word daily – why?"

He answered Me, "I AM FIRST!!"

*It was then that I realized that I had placed my spouse first, my family second, and then my God last! I had it all backwards for years. Everyone and everything else came before Him. He is **a jealous God** (Deut 4:24).*

I repented, asked His forgiveness, and laid everything at His feet. Now that He is first in my life, I have grown so much closer to Him. I seek Him more now than I ever did. I hear Him more clearly, I feel His Presence more powerfully, I read the Word for hours at a time. I am able to give Him all the glory and honor through my trials, and I thank Him for my trials. I have learned that no matter what I go through, He is always with me. When I recently broke my wrist, I cried out to my God, and He was there. I saw His silhouette image kneel before me and touch my face. As He said, "I am here, My child," I experienced a flood of His peace. I know it is because He is now first in my life that my encounters with Him are so much richer and deeper.

Rosa Ortiz
Triumph Prayer Team
West Palm Beach, Florida

I have known this sweet woman for a number of years. When the double betrayal struck, Rosa had been no stranger to hardships, for she was a stage five cancer survivor. Yet the trial of the cancer did not bring her to recognize her idolatry of her spouse and family; the brokenness from the betrayals did. As I watch this dear woman's walk with Christ, and see her spiritual growth and the deepening of her relationship with Him, there is no question that her surrender is what opened her to receive His love and His Presence so much more sweetly. As Rosa endured heart-wrenching betrayal, and allowed her heart to be supernaturally healed by Jesus, she fellowshipped in the sufferings of Christ. This enabled her as nothing else could to receive a piece of God's heart. Rosa can now relate to God's deep heart pain as the prophet Hosea did; those who have never been betrayed cannot.

We belong to the Lord. We are rightfully His. We have given our hearts to Him. But when we give our hearts to an idol, He passionately desires to win our hearts back, for idolatry is not His plan for His precious children. He created us, and in His all-loving omniscience, He knows what is best for us: our complete devotion to Him. This exclusive adoration opens the floodgates for us to *receive* the unending love and protection that He has already given us. His name is Jealous – for our good, as well as for His.

Identifying Mammon

With Jesus, it's all or nothing:

"No one can serve two masters; for either he will hate the one and love the other, or else he will be loyal to the one and despise the other. You cannot serve God and mammon."

Matthew 6:24 NKJV

I selected the New King James translation because it uses the word **mammon**. Other versions translate it "wealth" or "money." The Amplified says **deceitful riches, money, possessions, or whatever is trusted in.**

Whatever is trusted in. Whatever we *rely* on for our security, peace, happiness, or protection. This is deeply convicting and extremely critical. We cannot serve both God and the world. Incomplete surrender means that we are not surrendering at all, for we cannot be partway there. By Jesus' definition, if we have one foot in the world, we are of the world. We cannot serve the world and serve God. We cannot put things of the world first, and also put God first. We cannot depend on the things of the world for our peace and contentment, and also depend on God for our peace and contentment. We cannot trust *ourselves* for security and protection, and also trust *God* to protect us and keep us secure. We cannot rely on ourselves to sustain us, and also rely on God to sustain us. We cannot live for what the world has to offer us, worldly accolades and excitement and purposes, and also live for God's purposes. It's one or the other. We choose.

Idolatry is whatever we cannot surrender, whatever we cannot *trust* God with. Whatever causes us to lose sleep at night. Whatever we cannot trust Him *to take care of.* Recall my testimony in Peru. *Whatever we fear losing.*

Let's take a look at that word mammon. It is a Babylonian word, *mammonas*, and it is actually the Babylonian god of materialism. Mammon is "the personification of riches."[3] The root word of *mammonas* is "confidence."[4] Mammon is more than just possessions; mammon is anything that we *put our confidence in*, anything that we *trust.* If we have one foot in the world, if we are choosing to serve the world, if we are trusting the things of the world to provide us with security, peace, or purpose – God calls this *idolatry.* If we are relying upon our own abilities to build up our reputation or our status or our business or our relationships, if we are dependent upon what others think of us for acceptance and approval, if we are seeking the approval of men – God calls this *idolatry of self.*

Refusal to surrender is idolatry. It means that something or someone in our lives – maybe even we ourselves – are more important to us than God is. It means that God is not first in our lives. It means that we are bowing down to the god of mammon. The Apostle John elaborates:

Do not love the world or anything in the world. If anyone loves the world, the love of the Father is not in him. For everything in the world – the cravings of sinful man, the lust of his eyes and the boasting of what he has and does – comes not from the Father but from the world. The world and its desires pass away, but the man who does the will of God lives forever.

1 John 2:15-17 NIV

James puts it this way:

You adulteresses, do you not know that friendship with the world is hostility toward God? Therefore whoever wishes to be a friend of the world makes himself an enemy of God.

James 4:4

We can love the world, or we can love God. We can be friends with the world, or friends with God. Scripture tells us we can't love both.

Let's Pray

Any number of people or things can be idols. Let's pause and ask the Holy Spirit to search our hearts.

> *Lord, only You can expose idols that we have erected in our hearts. Only You can give us hearts that delight in You. Please open our hearts to hear from You. Give us the strength and desire to demolish these idols, and please deposit in our hearts a joyful delight in You.*
> *Amen.*

Search me, O God, and know my heart;
Try me and know my anxious thoughts;
And see if there be any hurtful way in me,
And lead me in the everlasting way.
Psalm 139:23-24

The word **hurtful** can also be translated as **offensive**, **wicked**, and **grievous** (NIV, NKJV, ESV). My *Hebrew Word Study* says "a painful way, meaning a harmful habit like idolatry."[5] When we harbor idols, we hurt others, we cause pain to ourselves, and we grieve God's heart. *Please lead us, Lord, in the way everlasting.*

Before we go on, pause and make those prayers your own.

Idols Exposed

We're going to spend the next part of this chapter inviting the Holy Spirit to speak to our hearts and to expose any idols we may be harboring. As you read through this list, ask yourself some questions. Is there anything I am obsessed with? Anything that seems a little too important to me? Anything that I am spending too much time with –

perhaps to the exclusion of God-ordained assignments and responsibilities?

Don't rush through this list. Go slowly and prayerfully, giving the Holy Spirit a chance to speak. Circle anything that the Holy Spirit is nudging you about. And go ahead and write in the margin any additional idols the Lord brings to mind.

- Spouse, boyfriend/girlfriend
- Children, parents, grandchildren, relatives
- Friends
- Social life, relationships, approval of others
- Work, career, school, grades, education, awards, degrees
- Talents and gifts
- Ministry work, church service, volunteer work, Kingdom work
- The status of having a spouse, boyfriend, girlfriend
- Money, finances, wealth, savings, riches, possessions, home, vacations
- Position, status, reputation, accomplishments
- Our children's accomplishments
- How others view us, their opinion of us
- Sports stars, music stars, actors
- Activities, hobbies, watching or playing sports, socializing, shopping
- Phone, computer, movies, TV shows, books, video games, social media
- Body, appearance, exercise, physical health
- Alcohol, drugs, pornography, sex, food
- Our agendas, our plans for our lives, our plans for our kids' lives, our plans for our spouse or our concern over what our spouse is doing
- Ourselves

Many things on this list are not inherently bad or wrong. Indeed some of these are God-given responsibilities. But if we cannot step away from them, if they take priority over our relationship with God, we may be dealing with an idol.

Let's test ourselves with a series of questions, and see what the Holy Spirit may reveal. Go ahead and mark anything He is revealing.

Where Is Our Trust?

An idol can be something or someone that we depend upon for security. That we rely upon to meet our needs. The place we go for answers and solutions. Who we depend upon to rescue us from our trials, problems, or messes. Instead of seeking God, we may go to an idol for comfort, encouragement, or affirmation. Yes, God may place people in our lives to assist us or to comfort and encourage us in time of need, but we must ask ourselves, do I go to God *first?*

At times, our *motives* may be wrong in our relationships, and that may be a tip-off to idolatry. Are we seeking a particular relationship *so that* we can bolster our self-esteem and look good in the world's eyes? Or perhaps to receive understanding, encouragement, and compassion?

Those we rely on to fulfill our needs will always come up short, because they are only human, and cannot possibly satisfy our needs. We don't realize how desperately needy we truly are. We don't understand that satisfying our needs is like trying to turn a desert into a spring with merely a cup of water. Only God can transform our deserts into springs. *Only God* can truly satisfy.

"The poor and needy search for water,
but there is none;
their tongues are parched with thirst.
But I the LORD will answer them;
I, the God of Israel, will not forsake them.
I will make rivers flow on barren heights,
and springs within the valleys.

**I will turn the desert into pools of water,
and the parched ground into springs."**

Isaiah 41:17-18 NIV

When we look to God to meet our needs, He meets them with *Himself*. Because He is infinite, what He is giving (Himself) is infinite. And when God is our sole Provider of love, joy, and companionship, when He is our Source of contentment, satisfaction, and peace, when we look to Him for approval, acceptance, and encouragement – then, when others in our life bless us by adding their little cup of water to His almighty flood, it will be icing on the cake. We will be able to appreciate those sweet cups of water, because we have already been infinitely satisfied. We will recognize that He has provided those people, and we can receive the flow of His Spirit through them. And then, instead of sucking dry those relationships, we may discover that those relationships will soon begin to blossom.

What Do We Fear?

"You shall fear *only* the LORD your God."

Deuteronomy 6:13, emphasis added

What we fear may be an idol. If we fear our parents, they may be an idol. If we fear the opinions of others, people may be an idol.

What we fear *losing* may also indicate idolatry. If we fear losing our children or our jobs, they may be idols. If we fear getting bad grades, then awards may be an idol. If we fear poverty, then money may be an idol. If we fear failure, then success may be an idol. If we fear rejection, then people's approval and acceptance may be idols.

**For am I now seeking the favor of men, or of God?
Or am I striving to please men? If I were still trying**

to please men, I would not be a bond-servant of Christ.

Galatians 1:10

Identifying our fears, casting down those idols, and seeking the fear of the Lord is paramount to intimacy. Listen to how Isaiah explains it:

It is the LORD of hosts
Whom you should regard as holy.
And He shall be your fear,
And He shall be your dread.
***Then* He shall become a sanctuary ...**

Isaiah 8:13-14, emphasis added

When we walk in fear of the Lord, *then* He will become our sanctuary.

What's Constantly On Our Minds?

What do our thoughts revolve around? What are we addicted to? What are we unable to let go of? Something or someone that we crave, or go crazy for if we don't have, can be an idol. If we are working our schedule into ridiculous contortions in order to spend time somewhere, we could be dealing with an idol. Have we gotten off-balance? What would those closest to us say that we were obsessed with?

Worry and anxiety can point to idolatry. What do we worry about? What do we fall asleep thinking about? Whatever prevents us from falling asleep – or wakes us up from sleep – could be an idol.

I have noticed that there are times when I awaken with a barrage of thoughts that I cannot quiet. I may wake up obsessively worrying about my kids or my job or the book I am writing. Or I may be unable to quit rehearsing in my mind my packed schedule of everything

that needs to get done
that day. No matter
how hard I try, I am
unable to shut these
thoughts down and turn
my focus to God. For
me, this is an indication
that I may have fallen
into idolatry. But, if I
am able to easily place
all that in His hands, if I
wake up eager to spend
time alone with Him, I
sense that my focus is
right where God wants
it to be.

Of course, obsessive thoughts don't need to be only waking-up thoughts to throw up a red flag for me. Any time that I cannot quiet worrying thoughts and place my trust in God, I know I must ask Him to search my heart for idols.

Can We Give It a Rest?

Can we take a break from it? Can we give it a rest? Anything that we cannot step away from could be an idol. What are you unable to surrender to Him?

If missing someone or something causes frustration, anger, or irritability, we could be dealing with an idol. Can you be away from your boyfriend for a summer? Can you leave your kids with a sitter and go out to dinner with your husband? Can you skip your fishing trip this weekend? Whatever it is – can you put it aside for a while? What would you be like without it? If you can't give it up – or can't get your hands off it – you may be dealing with an idol.

One More Litmus Test

I've got one more litmus test to see if we can give it a rest: Can we make a decision to leave it alone *for one day out of the week?* I mean to *really* not work, to lay it all down, to take a Sabbath rest – whether it's resting from a job, from day to day responsibilities, from extracurricular activities, or even from ministry work.

Ministry work? How can work that God has clearly assigned to us be an idol? Well, it may have become an idol when *accomplishing* that work has become more important than *spending time with Him.* When God assigned us one particular job, but we added on ten other assignments. When the doing *for God* is more important than the relationship *with God.* Do not equate ministry work with relationship. It is a subtle but critical distinction.

Can we take a rest? God commands,

"Remember the sabbath day, to keep it holy. Six days you shall labor and do all your work, but the seventh day is a sabbath of the LORD your God; in it you shall not do any work, you or your son or your daughter, your male or your female servant or your cattle or your sojourner who stays with you. For in six days the LORD made the heavens and the earth, the sea and all that is in them, and rested on the seventh day; therefore the LORD blessed the sabbath day and made it holy."

Exodus 20:8-11

God created the entire universe in six days and had a Sabbath on the seventh. Why, then, am I unable to trust that He will indeed provide for me if I am working only six days and resting on the seventh? Why do I think that He's not going to be able to accomplish all that He desires

to do *through* me in just six days out of the week? Why do
I think that I need to work all seven? I am beginning to
realize that, for me, even Kingdom work can become an
idol. Perhaps God commanded the Sabbath rest as a way to
alert us to when we may be falling into the trap of idolatry.

I don't mean that we are to observe the Sabbath in a
legalistic sort of way. When we make Jesus the Lord of our
Sabbath, He will reveal to us individually how He wants us
to keep it holy. Pastor Tom Mullins of Christ Fellowship
describes it simply as "a rhythm of Sabbath rests." And I
love the rewards of walking in this rhythm with Him:

> **You shall surely observe My sabbaths; for this
> is a sign between Me and you throughout your
> generations, that you may know that I am the LORD
> who sanctifies you.**
>
> Exodus 31:13

We will study in upcoming chapters how our
sanctification leads to greater intimacy. God so desires us
to be sanctified, and to know Him as the One who sanctifies
us; it seems that He gives us the blessing of the Sabbath
rest to do just that. Listen to how Isaiah describes how the
rhythm of the Sabbath leads to deep intimacy with Him:

> **"If because of the sabbath, you turn your foot
> From doing your own pleasure on My holy day,
> And call the sabbath a delight,
> The holy day of the LORD honorable,
> And honor it, desisting from your own ways,
> From seeking your own pleasure
> And speaking your own word,
> *Then* you will take delight in the LORD,
> And I will make you ride
>   on the heights of the earth;
> And I will feed you
>   with the heritage of Jacob your father,
> For the mouth of the LORD has spoken."**
>
> Isaiah 58:13-14, emphasis added

Are you seeking intimacy and delight in the Lord? Do you desire to ride with Him on the heights of the earth? Isaiah writes that Sabbath rest is key.

Go back and look over the items that you have marked in this series of questions. Journal what the Holy Spirit is revealing.

Confusion Can Indicate Idolatry

If we are unable to clearly hear His guidance in a particular area, we may be battling an idol. Hear what God thunders to Ezekiel:

"Son of man, these leaders have set up idols in their hearts. They have embraced things that lead them into sin. *Why should I let them ask me anything?"*
Ezekiel 14:3 NLT, emphasis added

If our lives are in confusion, if we don't know what God wants us to do or don't know His will for our lives, we may have an idol. If we can't hear from God, we may have an idol. If one moment we think God wants us to do one thing and the next moment we think God wants us to be doing something totally opposite, an idol may be distorting His voice. If we have no purpose and don't know what God is calling us to, it may be because God is not on the throne in our heart. *We* may be on the throne of our heart – along with whatever else is more important to us than God. Idols may occupy *portions* of our heart. This means that part of our heart does not bow down to Jesus, but bows down to the idol. Our heart is divided.

What does this mean practically? If we are seeking God's guidance in an area that the idol has influence, we won't see with God's eyes – we will see with eyes of idolatry. We won't hear with God's ears – we will hear with ears of idolatry. As we seek God's answer, it may come back to us *distorted* by the idol.

You've met my friend Cathy in Chapter 2. To help us get a better understanding of how idols can block His voice, I have asked Cathy back to explain how an idol in her life had distorted God's answer to prayer.

Ever since I was a child, my family had moved about every five years. We would build a new house from the ground up. It was some kind of pattern that was as regular as clockwork.

When my husband Craig and I had been in our new home for five years, he was offered a job that would necessitate our move to another part of the state. Seeking God's will for this decision, we fasted and prayed together. Craig heard, "No." I heard "Yes." One of us was not hearing clearly. I felt certain it wasn't me, and prepared to talk Craig into moving. The new job would be paying all the costs of packing and moving – how could we turn that down?

We sought Godly counsel. Our Pastor's wife sensed that I was the one not hearing clearly from God, and that I was trying to control the situation. She spoke to me. "You can talk Craig into it, and you can get your way, but if you do, it will be harder to hear from God the next time." That scared me. I didn't want to lose hearing God's voice. It was too precious to me. Even though I did not hear the "No" that Craig was hearing, I let him make the decision. He did not take the new job.

One year later, the company that had offered Craig the job encountered financial difficulties and laid off many workers. Craig, as a new employee, would almost certainly have been laid off.

In retrospect, I see that the comfort of a repetitive pattern of constant moving had become my idol. I liked the idea of a fresh start, a new home every five years, and the opportunity to leave behind old problems. All these things had become more important to me than doing things God's way. These idols had obscured God's voice and barred me from hearing from Him. The shock of recognizing God's omniscience and the amazement of experiencing His protection so personally have taught me a lesson on idolatry that I did not soon forget.

Cathy Moesel
Inner Healing and Deliverance Ministry
Covenant Centre International
Palm Beach Gardens, Florida

Cathy's story illustrates with great clarity how an idol of our own agenda can truly block His voice.

Idolatry of Self

I think that the biggest idol we have may be ourselves. Idolatry of our self plays into many of the other idolatries we have been discussing. If our idol is success, work, status, or other's opinions of us, for example, that may be idolatry of reputation. Idolatry of self. Pride.

... but when they measure themselves by themselves and compare themselves with themselves, they are without understanding ... But HE WHO BOASTS IS TO BOAST IN THE LORD. For it is not he who commends himself that is approved, but he whom the Lord commends.

2 Corinthians 10:12,18 NIV

Satan tries to trap us into measuring ourselves instead of seeking the Lord's commendation. Comparing ourselves to others is one of his insidious traps. If we fear someone will get ahead of us in work, relationships, or wealth, if we fear someone's reputation may exceed ours, if we fear someone may be smarter than us, advance faster than us, or become more spiritually mature than us, then we may have fallen into the trap of idolatry of self.

If we are relying on our own abilities and personalities to foster relationships and to hold them intact, we may be idolizing ourselves.   If we are looking to ourselves to supply our own needs or to provide for our own joy or peace, we may be trusting in the idol of self.   And that idol will some day be toppled:

They will be turned back
And be utterly put to shame,
Who trust in idols,
Who say to molten images,
"You are our gods."

Isaiah 42:17

God calls us to deep deep dependence upon Him.   To acknowledge in our hearts that He has been the Provider of our job, abilities, talents, degrees, personality, and health – and to remain in a place of intense gratitude and untold awe.   To recognize that He and He alone has given us our spouse, children, parents, friends.   To accept that **in Him all things hold together** (Col 1:17); only *He* holds our relationships together.   God calls us to destroy the idol of self, to trust not in ourselves but only in Him.   To turn from self-reliance and independence, to choose utter dependence upon our Sovereign Almighty Lord.   That is intimacy.

And those who know Your name
**   will put their trust in You,**
For You, O LORD, have not forsaken
**   those who seek You.**

Psalm 9:10

Before we proceed, flip back to the bulleted list of possible idols in the *Idols Exposed* section. With these tests and questions fresh in your mind, prayerfully go through that list once again.   Circle anything the Lord is nudging you to mark.

Idolatry Can Be a Very Insidious Sin

Idolatry can be very sneaky. Many times we don't notice it and are unaware that we have been ensnared by it. We can be doing all kinds of "spiritual" disciplines – reading our Bibles, serving in church, doing ministry work – and *still* have one or more idols. Idols can stealthily worm their way into our hearts. It can begin innocently; an idol can be something that seems harmless at first – a sport, a hobby. Or it can even start as a God-ordained responsibility, such as taking care of our kids, working to support our family, or serving in church. But somehow, something happens in our hearts, and that good thing leaps up onto the throne in our hearts. Right next to our own selves on that throne.

Paul warns about idolatry and other sins in First Corinthians 10. He recounts God's anger against the Israelites for worshipping the molten calf, committing sexual impurity, grumbling, and testing the Lord, and then he cautions the Corinthians,

So, if you think you are standing firm, be careful that you don't fall!

1 Corinthians 10:12 NIV

I have heard it said that as humans, we are idol-makers by nature. If we think we've got this one licked, be careful that we don't fall.

Temptation of Idolatry After Victory

Recall when the Israelites were slaves in Egypt, they witnessed miracle upon miracle that culminated in their freedom. Plague after hideous plague and a dividing of waters whose renown resonates even today. Now what happened a very short time later? While the Presence of God was still mightily in their midst covering Mt. Sinai?

They left God. Completely abandoned Him. Bowed their hearts to an idol, their bodies to a golden calf. Great victory, followed by a plummet into idolatry.

Forty years later, after the Israelites had been humbled, purified, and equipped, and were about to enter the Promised Land, God warned them,

"Then it shall come about when the LORD your God brings you into the land which He swore to your fathers, Abraham, Isaac and Jacob,
> **to give you great and splendid cities**
>> **which you did not build,**
> **and houses full of all good things**
>> **which you did not fill,**
> **and hewn cisterns which you did not dig,**
> **vineyards and olive trees which you did not plant,**
> **and you eat and are satisfied,**

> ***then watch yourself,***
> **that you do not forget the LORD**
>> **who brought you from the land of Egypt,**
>> **out of the house of slavery.**

You shall fear only the LORD your God;
and you shall worship Him
> **and swear by His name.**
You shall not follow other gods,
any of the gods of the peoples who surround you,
for the LORD your God in the midst of you
> **is a jealous God;**
otherwise the anger of the LORD your God
will be kindled against you,
and He will wipe you off the face of the earth."
Deuteronomy 6:10-15, emphasis added

This is a sobering passage. How does it relate to us today? When God has delivered us from a stronghold, when He has given us release and freedom and has blessed us abundantly with His goodness and peace, ***then*** *watch yourself.* Stern warnings that when we are on the mountaintops, danger lurks. Right on the heels of victory comes a great risk of falling into idolatry.

Watch yourself, that you do not forget the Lord who redeemed you. Fear Him only. For His Name is *Qanna*, Jealous, and He demands our undivided devotion – for *our* good, not for His.

We so desire victory. The miracle answer. The healing that baffles the doctors. The check that arrives in the mail that saves us from financial crisis. The traveling preacher whose words pierce a loved one's heart. Why not? I admit that I pray this way too.

Do we think we are better than the Israelites? If God granted us the miracle we are begging Him for, the miracle that removes our hardships and suffering, that dries our tears, that lifts us from the valley to the mountaintop ... would we still seek Him with that desperate passion? If we weren't in such a place of need, what would we be worshipping? If we were no longer wandering in the desert, just how much would we be clinging to Him?

God Hates Idolatry

God commanded Ezekiel to prophesy to Israel,

"So as I live," declares the Lord GOD, "surely, because you have defiled My sanctuary with all your detestable idols and with all your abominations, therefore I will also withdraw, and My eye will have no pity and I will not spare. One third of you will die by plague or be consumed by famine among you, one third will fall by the sword around you, and one third I will scatter to every wind, and I will unsheathe a sword behind them. Thus My anger will

be spent and I will satisfy My wrath on them, and I will be appeased … Then you will know that I am the LORD, when their slain are among their idols around their altars …"

Ezekiel 5:11-13, 6:13

Israel was steeped in generations of idolatry. Idolatry in our own hearts can also be a very deep root, a massive stronghold. God sent the Israelites into captivity because of their idolatry. Likewise, when we are trapped in idolatry, we are already in captivity. We do not own the thing we idolize – it owns us.

God hates idolatry, for it defiles His sanctuary: us. Because of His infinite love for us, He will not tolerate idolatry in us. As He did with the Israelites, He will do whatever it takes to bring us back to Him – for *our* good. And even more striking to me is how idolatry grieves God's heart:

"I was crushed by their adulterous heart which has departed from Me, and by their eyes which play the harlot after their idols."
Ezekiel 6:9 NJKV

This word **crushed** in the Hebrew means "to break, to burst, to break in pieces, to break down, to break up, to smash, to shatter."[6] I am cut to the quick as I take this all in.

God's heart is shattered because of our idolatry. Broken in pieces. Can you see His tears? I think that our idolatry breaks His heart not only because our rejection wounds Him, but because *it also destroys us.*

Relying on God Instead of on Idols

God wants us to depend solely upon Him for everything
– for both ourselves and for those we love. He wants us
to rely on Him for sustenance, needs, food, relationships,
spouse, health, housing, job, money, protection. He desires
us to trust Him and His perfect plan for our life, whether
our lives look like we expected them to look or not. He calls
us to seek Him for answers, solutions, and the way out of a
mess. He demands that we look *only* to Him for approval,
acceptance, and love.

Not there yet? Me neither. But as I grow in Him, as He
continues His sanctifying work in me, the idols are coming
down, and He is teaching me what it means to love and
worship Him with all my heart, soul, mind, and strength.
Psalm 121 has helped me to demolish idols in my life, and
I'd like to share it with you.

> I lift up my eyes to the hills--
>   where does my help come from?
> My help comes from the LORD,
>   the Maker of heaven and earth.
> He will not let your foot slip--
>   he who watches over you will not slumber;
> indeed, he who watches over Israel
>   will neither slumber nor sleep.
> The LORD watches over you--
>   the LORD is your shade at your right hand;
> the sun will not harm you by day,
>   nor the moon by night.
> The LORD will keep you from all harm--
>   he will watch over your life;
> the LORD will watch over your coming and going
>   both now and forevermore.
>
> Psalm 121:1-8 NIV

We may think that our kids or our spouse or our friends are going to fill us with all the love we need. We may believe that if only we can earn our parents' approval, we will be accepted. We may be relying on our own hard work to provide for ourselves and our families. We may be trusting our own wisdom and abilities to rescue us from our troubles. We may even be looking to our jobs or our ministry work for fulfillment. But open your eyes! God calls this idolatry.

We may think that our help, our approval, or our fulfillment is coming from our idols. But we are deceived. Jeremiah calls idolatry a **discipline of delusion** (Jer 10:8). Isaiah declares that we are praying to **a god who cannot save!** (Isa 45:20).

Our help is from the Lord, the Maker of heaven and earth. Our fulfillment comes only from *relationship* with Him. And look what kind of help the Lord gives us! He will not let our foot slip, for He holds our hand. He watches over us constantly – He doesn't let down His guard by going to sleep for the night or even taking a little nap. He protects us from threats by day and attacks by night. He shelters us from all harm – yes, indeed, that word is *all*. For in His hands, He is working everything for good, and He has the final say in everything. Satan may mean it for evil, but He intends it for good. He watches over our entire lives, every going and coming, every end of a season and every start of a new one – both now and forevermore.

How does your idol stack up to that?

The Challenge of Destroying Idols

I find tearing down idols to be very challenging. Demolition of idols involves repenting of sin, humbling ourselves, surrendering. It entails abandoning our wishes and plans for our lives, and choosing God's plan. Living to glorify Him instead of living to glorify ourselves. Choosing dependency upon Him instead of insisting on accomplishing everything on our own abilities. As we demolish our idols, I find there is often agony involved, for I certainly find these deep heart transformations to be at times extremely difficult and excruciatingly painful. Paul speaks of putting to death the deeds of the body.

... for if you are living according to the flesh, you must die; but if by the Spirit you are putting to death the deeds of the body, you will live ... Now the deeds of the flesh are evident, which are: immorality, impurity, sensuality, idolatry, sorcery, enmities, strife, jealousy, outbursts of anger, disputes, dissensions, factions, envying, drunkenness, carousing, and things like these ...
Romans 8:13, Galatians 5:19-21

So why do *we* have to do it? Doesn't *He* do it all? Apparently not.

Notice who has to do the work of putting the deeds of the body to death: **you.** Notice how the work is done: **by the Spirit.** Only by His grace. It's a partnership, Him and us. He gives us the will and the strength, the guidance and courage and direction, but we have to be the ones to walk it out in the physical.

The Holy Spirit gives the *revelation* that we have deeds of the flesh that need to die. But somehow, we have to be the ones to surrender the idol. We have to walk away from the addiction. We have to turn from disobedience and choose to live by His commands. We have to humble ourselves and ask forgiveness for our anger. We have to choose to set our minds on things of the Spirit instead of things of the flesh. We have to release the unrepentant offender from our bitterness. We must relinquish our children to His control. We must submit our plans to His will. The Spirit does all the deep heart work, but we must cooperate

with Him. We can't do it without Him, and He won't do it
without us. It seems that when we take the painful steps
of putting to death the deeds of the flesh, we invite Him in
to transform us.

I think that putting to death these deeds *ourselves* is
even more difficult, and may be even more painful, than
if God would do it for us. For when we do it *ourselves*, we
have the choice to stop if smashing the idol becomes too
painful, if it is too humbling, if our egos are suffering too
greatly. We can quit, quench the Holy Spirit's conviction,
and return to our own selfish idolatrous path. This is
the same choice that Jesus faced in Gethsemane and at
Golgotha. He could have refused the cross. He could have
called down twelve legions of angels (Mt 26:53). Yet, for
our sakes, He did not. He laid His life down by His own
initiative (Jn 10:18). He *chose* crucifixion. And it seems to
me that when we *choose* obedience, when we *choose* to put
to death the deeds of the body, when we *choose* to destroy
an idol, we choose to share in His sufferings.

Are we willing? Are we willing to surrender not only
what is obviously sinful, what is clearly bad for us, but also
our desires for *good things* if they are not His will for us?
Will we choose *His* plan, even if it doesn't mean financial
security? Will we desire *His* plan, even if it doesn't mean
an easy life for our kids? Will we treasure *His* plan, even
if it doesn't mean healing right here and now? Are we
willing to allow His Light to expose our sin, are we willing
to repent, confess, and ask for forgiveness? Are we willing
to surrender our idol, our agenda, our plan, our life the
way *we* wanted it or expected it to be? And – are we willing
to do all this with great joy? **Consider it pure joy ... in
everything give thanks ...** (Jam 1:2, 1Th 5:18, emphasis
added). We trade a life of thrills and excitement and worldly
pleasures for eternal purpose and everlasting peace. **Do
not love the world or the things in the world ...**

The Flesh Is Weak

"Keep watching and praying that you may not enter into temptation; the spirit is willing, but the flesh is weak."

Matthew 26:41

For I know that nothing good dwells in me, that is, in my flesh; for the willing is present in me, but the doing of the good is not. For the good that I want, I do not do, but I practice the very evil that I do not want. But if I am doing the very thing I do not want, I am no longer the one doing it, but sin which dwells in me.

Romans 7:18-20

Let's pause a moment and clarify. This word **flesh** as used in the Bible can have more than one connotation, and we will need to understand the context of the passage to recognize the meaning.

In some passages, flesh is used to mean our physical body. Our physical body is *not* our enemy; we are not to attack it or battle against it, but we are to nourish and cherish it:

... for no one ever hated his own flesh, but nourishes and cherishes it, just as Christ also does the church, because we are members of His body.

Ephesians 5:29-30

But in many other passages, **flesh** means our inherently sinful nature, as in Romans 7 and Matthew 26:41 above. Let's go back to Romans 8 and read a bit further:

So then, brethren, we are under obligation, not to the flesh, to live according to the flesh— for if you are living according to the flesh, you must die; but if by the Spirit you are putting to death the deeds of the body, you will live. For all who are being led by the Spirit of God, these are sons of God.

Romans 8:12-14

Putting to death the *deeds* of the body does not mean putting *ourselves* to death. It means putting our *idols* to death. Remember the word *mammonas* that we studied at the beginning of the chapter. The god of materialism. The god of whatever we put our trust in. We are battling the spiritual forces of evil in the heavenly realms. Know who the enemy is.

Putting to death the deeds of the body does not mean that we pretend we have no sin. It does not mean that we deny the existence of our passions and desires, whether they are sinful desires or Godly ones. It does not mean stuffing down anything that we think – or know – is not pleasing to God. That is deception, and God seems to refuse to work in deception.

God wants us to come to Him in all truth, trusting Him to fully accept us and fully love us *just as we are*, weak flesh and all. He desires us to be transparent before Him, trusting that He already knows it all, and has not – and will never – reject us. He yearns for us to trust ourselves to His hands, to trust Him to mature us in Him and enable us to walk by the Spirit as He works through His all-accepting non-judgmental love.

But I say, walk by the Spirit, and you will not carry out the desire of the flesh.

Galatians 5:16

As we grow in intimacy, He enables us to walk by the Spirit with greater fluidity. One of the prices of intimacy with Jesus is the surrender of our idols. Those who know Jesus the deepest seem to have shattered the most idols. They have exchanged the earthly happiness that idols provided for God's supernatural joy. In their brokenness they learned intimate abiding.

But whatever things were gain to me, those things I have counted as loss for the sake of Christ. More than that, I count all things to be loss in view of the

surpassing value of knowing Christ Jesus my Lord, for whom I have suffered the loss of all things, and count them but rubbish so that I may gain Christ and be found in Him … that I may know Him and the power of His resurrection and the fellowship of His sufferings, being conformed to His death; in order that I may attain to the resurrection from the dead.

Philippians 3:7-11

How much brokenness will it take before we consider it all rubbish? Before we recognize that our idols will never truly satisfy? Before we value *knowing* Christ above all else? Before we truly desire to share in His sufferings and be conformed to His death in order to gain sanctification and intimacy with Him? For me, I think a lifetime.

Koinonia

The word **fellowship** in the Philippians passage above is *koinonia*. Also translated sharing or partaking, *koinonia* means "participation, communion, fellowship."[7] It is a fellowship that develops because people have *together* partaken of something too deep for words. *Koinonia* bonds people together on an intimate level. *Koinonia* is intimacy.

Koinonia is also what bonds us to Christ.

How can we puny humans bond to an infinite God? How could we *possibly* share anything in common? Man: finite, fading, momentary, passing … God: boundless, immeasurable, infinite, eternal.   How could we have anything in common? Yet God created us for *koinonia*, for deep fellowship with the Father (1Jn 1:3), with Jesus (1Cor 1:9), and with the Holy Spirit (2Cor 13:14).   His desire for *koinonia* with us is so acute that He said, seemingly recklessly, *"I'll go first."*

Since the children have flesh and blood, he too shared in their humanity so that by his death he might destroy him who holds the power of death -- that is, the devil -- and free those who all their lives were held in slavery by their fear of death.
                                                    Hebrews 2:14-15 NIV

Shared is *koinonia*. Since we have flesh and blood, Jesus shared in our humanity, initiating a deep penetrating fellowship with us. He desires *koinonia* with us so fiercely that He died for us to free us from Satan, to give us eternal life – and to enable us to enter into *koinonia* with Him. An unfathomable communion with the Father, the Son, and the Holy Spirit. God knows us fully – and *still* accepts us completely. He has *chosen* to fellowship with us.

Nothing in all creation is hidden from God's sight. Everything is uncovered and laid bare before the eyes of him to whom we must give account.
                                                    Hebrews 4:13 NIV

This God, from whom nothing is hidden, chose fellowship with us – right where we are. He doesn't require us to be pure or holy or sinless. He entered into fellowship with us when we were **dead in our trespasses and sins** (Eph 2:1).

Yes, God has said, *"I'll go first."* He initiated fellowship with us. Then, after sealing this fellowship, God said, *"You go next."* He invites us into deeper and more profound fellowship, so that we **may be filled up with all the fullness of God** (Eph 3:19). How do we enter into this deeper fellowship?   Let's hear how Peter explains it:

... He has granted to us His precious and magnificent promises, so that by them you may become partakers of the divine nature, having escaped the corruption that is in the world by lust.

2 Peter 1:4

Partakers is that same word again, *koinonia*. We are invited to fellowship in His divine nature, to share in deep penetrating intimacy with our holy and pure God.

Invited. *So that we may.* God's part is sure: His precious and magnificent promises that make this *koinonia* possible. But whether we develop deeply the *koinonia* that He offers us is in question. The choice is up to us.

Listen to how the Amplified translates this verse:

... He has bestowed on us His precious and exceedingly great promises, so that through them you may escape [by flight] from the moral decay (rottenness and corruption) that is in the world because of covetousness (lust and greed), and become sharers (partakers) of the divine nature.

2 Peter 1:4 AMP

We may become partakers – *if* we choose to flee from the corruption of the world. *If* we choose to flee from lust and greed. *If* we choose to flee from such rottenness as idolatry and evil desires. *If* we choose to flee from covetousness. Covetousness is ingratitude. Covetousness is envy and discontentment. When we are ungrateful and discontent, we fall into the snares of the world's corruption. When, by His promises, we escape this corruption, we become partakers of His divine nature. We grow in sanctification, abiding, intimacy. We receive more of His Spirit, more of Him.

Peter goes on to explain just how we escape this corruption:

... they have escaped the defilements of the world
by the knowledge of the Lord and Savior Jesus
Christ ...

2 Peter 2:20, emphasis added

The *knowledge* of Jesus enables us to escape the
defilements of the world. Growing in the true knowledge
of Jesus results in greater sanctification, deeper partaking
in His divine nature. Peter describes the qualities that
develop as we continue in this sanctification, and then he
declares,

For if these qualities are yours and are increasing,
they render you neither useless nor unfruitful in the
true knowledge of our Lord Jesus Christ.

2 Peter 1:8

As our Godliness is **increasing**, we will not be **useless
or unfruitful.** We will not be **ineffective, unproductive,
barren,** or **idle** (2Pt 1:8 NASB, NIV, NKJV, AMP). We
will be His earthen vessels, sanctified and filled with the
treasure of His Holy Spirit, used by Him for His Kingdom
and His glory.

Hardening Our Hearts

Now what may happen if God is calling us to demolish
an idol, to put to death the deeds of our flesh, and we decline
the invitation? God so desires us to put to death the deeds
of our body; He wants to fill us with His Spirit, so by His
kindness He brings us to repentance (Rom 2:4). He knows
what will be best for us, and in His great love and mercy,
He has predestined us to be conformed to the image of His
Son (Rom 8:29). He loves us so so much; He works very
gently. And if we don't fight Him, putting those deeds to
death will be easier. But when we hold on to our idols,
our plans and our ways, our fleshy passions and desires
that are not of Him – then He may need to pry our hands

off them. Sometimes, the prying off may be painful. As we fight Him, it may become even more painful. Because of the great love with which He loves us, He may ordain suffering to facilitate the prying off.

In Psalm 39, David writes about the transience of man and how God disciplines him:

With reproofs You chasten a man for iniquity,
You consume as a moth what is precious to him.
Psalm 39:11

I, too, have found this to be God's plan for me when He has exposed an idol and given me a chance to repent, and I have refused to surrender it to Him. His Name is Jealous, and because the idol was more precious to me than He was, in His fire He consumed that idol. He removed it from my life. The Message says it this way: **To purge us from our sin, our dearest idols go up in smoke.** This may sound awful – but recognize His heart! He is always working for our good; He knows it may be painful for a season, but the inflowing of His Spirit will be so healing and tender and magnificent beyond what we could possibly imagine. And He wants that for us. He knows that He is our one and only true treasure, and He wants to bless us with Himself!

"He must increase, but I must decrease."
John 3:30

Less of us; more of Him. He is the Everlasting Life. *Koinonia* is a melding, a merging of our lives into His.[8] And as we let Him take over our lives, we will come to a place where we won't know where ours ends and His begins. For we have died, and our lives are hidden with Christ in God. Apart from Him we can do nothing (Col 3:3, Jn 15:5).

Questions Chapter 5:
Demolishing the Idols
That Thwart Our Fellowship

Memory Verse:

Do not love the world or anything in the world. If anyone loves the world, the love of the Father is not in him.

1 John 2:15 NIV

1) Go back through the chapter and review the idols you have marked. Did you recognize the idol because you trusted in it? Or perhaps because you couldn't put it down? Explain how the Holy Spirit revealed an idol to you, and your work in demolishing it.

2) Read 1 John 2:15-17 in your Bible or in the section, *Identifying Mammon.* What does God say about living with "one foot in the world"?

3) Is there an area in your life where you are having trouble hearing from God? It could be idolatry hindering you. Ask the Holy Spirit to give you revelation here.

4) Jeremiah calls idolatry a **discipline of delusion** (Jer 10:8). Explain how idolatry is a delusion.

5) Is God calling you right now to put to death any deeds of the flesh?

6) Read Psalm 135:15-18. Referring to idols, the psalmist writes, **"Those who make them will be like them."** What does that mean to you?

7) Journal how demolishing an idol has opened you to deeper koinonia with Jesus.

John Li

Chapter 6
To Forgive as Jesus Forgives

*C*oming to forgiveness may be one of the most challenging of surrenders. Yet reaching the surrender of forgiveness is paramount in order to abide, because unforgiveness indeed blocks our intimacy with God. **If you do not forgive men their sins, your Father will not forgive your sins** (Mt 6:15 NIV). That verse is black and white. If we don't forgive, He won't forgive us. We will then stand unreconciled to God until we choose forgiveness. Brace yourself. This is going to be a heavy – and critical – chapter.

Do I need to forgive someone who never apologizes? How about someone who keeps hurting me again and again – in the exact same way? What about someone from my long ago past – can't I just keep that area quiet and buried? And who cares if I forgive myself?

As I struggled to make sense of God's command to forgive, those questions burned inside of me, demanding answers. As I wrestled with God and resisted coming to forgiveness, I learned firsthand that when I did not forgive, I could not be healed; I could not be set free and made whole. Unforgiveness held me in the deepest darkest pits of bitterness and despair. Unforgiveness ate away at my heart and soul, and even my physical body. Unforgiveness was the chain that bound me to anger, hatred, revenge, and hardness of heart. And what was most horrifying to me, unforgiveness was a barrier that blocked my intimacy with Jesus.

I have also learned that for very deep wounds, forgiveness comes in layers, and it may take a lifetime of forgiving to process through those layers. The first time we choose forgiveness, we forgive as best as we understand. Yet we are able to forgive only as deeply as our spiritual maturity allows us. Then, as we grow in Christ, He will call us back to forgive on deeper and deeper levels. Don't be discouraged! It doesn't mean that we didn't forgive fully the first time, but that we have grown up in the Lord, and are now able to forgive in deeper measure. And each time we choose another layer of forgiveness, it seems we are inviting Jesus to enter our lives as never before. He responds to our invitations by flooding us with new and surprising levels of intimacy with Him.

Signs of an Unforgiving Heart

Before we are tempted to slip into denial about unforgiveness, let's look at some clues that may indicate that our forgiveness process is still incomplete. Ask the Lord to reveal, and go ahead and circle anything that pertains to you.

- Feelings of resentment, retaliation, or revenge
- Bitterness or hatred
- Avoidance of a particular person
- Anger at that person
- Criticizing or gossiping about that person

- Secretly rejoicing in our hearts that something bad has happened to that person

None of that resonates? Let's look at some more subtle signs that there may yet be an undercurrent of unforgiveness in our hearts:

- Passive aggressiveness with a particular person
- Replaying the offense in our minds
- Being defined by the offense
- In our conversations with others, frequently referring back to the offense and how we have already forgiven – or avoiding talking about the person altogether

Are you still with me? Hold on tight while we take a look at some more vague symptoms that can be even harder to pinpoint as a root of unforgiveness. I call them "vague" because sinful roots other than unforgiveness can lead to these symptoms as well. I also call them "vague" because they may not necessarily be directed at the person we have not forgiven, so it may be harder to recognize that unforgiveness may be the cause. Realize that unforgiveness can damage our relationships – and not just the relationship with the unforgiven one. In a way we can hardly understand, unforgiveness can also taint our other relationships (Heb 12:15), and unforgiveness profoundly hinders our relationship with God (Mt 6:14-15). Let's take a look at these vague symptoms:

- Anger in many unrelated circumstances or with unrelated people
- Overreacting, especially to seemingly insignificant things
- Depression
- Blaming
- A critical spirit
- Lack of joy
- A cold heart
- An inability to receive or express love

Feeling a bit of conviction? Yes, me too. Fasten your seatbelts. We're going to crank it up a notch.

The Black Heart of Revenge

If you're like me, you may be willing to admit unforgiveness, but really reluctant to admit revenge. That word is just dripping with black darkness, and I really do not want to admit any part of it. But where unforgiveness lives, revenge can also lurk, hiding from our consciousness. We may think we have forgiven – and indeed we may have made much progress here. We may have forgiven as completely as we could at the time – but there may yet be deeper layers. Grab your pen, and let's take a spiritual check-up together:

- How do we talk about that certain person when they are not present? Do we speak with love and respect, or with criticism?

- Do we find an excuse to gossip about that person? Do we cloak gossip in a disguise of "teaching" or as a "prayer request"?

- Do we brag about the good that we have done in arenas where they have hurt us, holding up their failures in unspoken contrast to our good?

- Does something inside of us do a little dance of revengeful excitement when something bad happens to that person?

- Let's listen to our words when that person is present. Are our words edifying, or do we speak with well-camouflaged put-downs? Is our speech peppered with little digs, or sarcasm masquerading as wit?

- Are our subtle attacks against them to protect

ourselves from being hurt by them again? Do we act like the best defense is a good offense?

- Are we sarcastic? Jackie Kendall, author and speaker on the topic of forgiveness, declares, "Sarcasm is a reflection of an angry and offended heart."[1]

Revenge is a means of control. We may not even be aware of it, yet we may be working to exert our power over someone by holding the offense over them. We may not want to let them off the hook. We can do this overtly, by refusing to accept their apologies and gestures of repentance, or by declining to accept the ways they try to make up for it. Or we can be very clandestine about it – overtly accepting their apologies, but still holding it over them deep in a secret area of our hearts. An area we deny even exists. An area that God alone sees.

Do I have your attention now? Remember the very first person who popped into your mind when you read the title of this chapter? You know, the face you pushed aside, as you reasoned that God was not talking to you about *that* person. The one you think you have *already* forgiven – or maybe the one who hurt you so much that the world would never *expect* you to forgive. Yes, that one. Is God knocking at your heart? In a step of faith, write what the Holy Spirit is speaking to you right now:

What Exactly Is Forgiveness?

My *Greek Word Study* gives some interesting definitions for the word translated as forgiveness:

> To send forth or away ... to let go from one's
> power, possession, to let go free, to let escape,
> to let go from obligation ... to remit a debt ...
> To forgive sins is not to disregard them or do
> nothing about them, but to liberate a person
> from their guilt and their power.[2]

Clearly, forgiveness is holding the wrongdoer completely responsible – but *releasing* them so that they are no longer responsible to *us*, but are responsible to *God*.

Forgiveness is a deep spiritual process involving our recognition of our unforgiveness, our willingness to forgive, and God's heart work. We cannot *make* ourselves forgive. We cannot manufacture forgiveness. All we can do is *choose* forgiveness and ask the Holy Spirit to bring forgiveness to completion. We must be *willing* to receive His transforming power in our hearts. We make that initial decision to forgive, and then step into a lifetime of forgiving. We co-labor with God in an on-going lifelong process.

Ken Sande, founder of *Peacemaker Ministries*, explains it this way.

> Forgiveness isn't forgetting. Forgetting
> is a passive process, letting a matter fade
> from memory merely with the passing of
> time. Forgiving is an active process involving
> a conscious choice and a deliberate course of
> action ... When God says that he "remembers
> your sins no more" (Isaiah 43:25), he doesn't
> mean he *can't* remember our sins. Rather,
> he is promising he *won't* remember them ...
> he chooses not to mention, recount, or think
> about our sins ever again. Similarly, when
> we forgive, we must choose to draw on God's
> grace and consciously decide not to ... dwell
> on this incident ... bring up this incident and
> use it against you ... talk to others about
> this incident ... [or] allow this incident to

stand between us or hinder our personal relationship.[3]

A few words of clarification here. Please don't think that when we "choose not to dwell" on the offense it means that we simply stuff it. God calls us to *process* the heart wounds and reach a place of forgiveness in order to release and choose not to dwell. Additionally, choosing not to dwell does not mean that we will never speak of the offense, for the Holy Spirit may at times lead us to speak out our testimony, perhaps when we have reached some depth of forgiveness and have received Jesus' healing touch. As we travel through this chapter and the next, the Holy Spirit will give clarity to this journey.

The Process of Forgiveness

Here's how the forgiveness process may look:

- *Step 1:* Honesty. Accept the truth that we were hurt, that we were wronged, and admit to God the depth of our pain. Confess to God our inability – or outrignt refusal – to forgive.

- *Step 2:* Repent of holding on to unforgiveness, and ask God to forgive us for our unforgiveness.

- *Step 3:* Release. Choose forgiveness. Make a decision to release the wrongdoer from our bitterness and vengeance.

- *Step 4:* Transformation. Ask the Holy Spirit to transform us, to bring our heart to forgive, to free us from unforgiveness, to deliver us from the stronghold of unforgiveness.

- *Step 5:* Healing. Jesus' touch heals the wounds in our hearts.

If you're like me, you'd like to just skip to Step 5 and have the healing right away. Yep. Tried it. Didn't work. I also tried skipping Step 1, the honest assessment, by minimizing, excusing, and denying. But that didn't work either. We're going to look at these steps in more detail later in the chapter.

This Sounds Hard – Do We _Really_ Need To Forgive?

Can't we sort of push it under the carpet and "act like good Christians" and pretend it all didn't happen? We can. But that's not forgiveness. Nor is it God's plan, since that is a walk of denial, which is deception.

I think I can understand your pain, and how hard it is to choose the path of forgiveness. But please understand that it was never God's cherished plan for you to be wronged, betrayed, injured, attacked. God's cherished plan is the Garden of Eden before the fall: perfect sinless bliss, no crying or pain, simply peace and joy as we walk with Him in the cool of the day.

Humankind has rejected the life God originally designed for us. We live in a fallen world, where we hurting people proceed to hurt each other. Yet, as God looks down at the mess we created, the fact that it is all our fault doesn't make His heart grow cold toward us. He loves us passionately, desperately; His heart is deeply grieved when any of His precious people are in pain. And out of His love and pain, He set about restoring our relationship with Him, putting into action the plan He ordained before the foundation of the world.

It's not human nature to forgive someone who has harmed us, crushed us, scarred us. And yet, for reasons that we may not yet fully understand, God does indeed *command* us to forgive. Let's study a few Scriptures and ask the Holy Spirit to implant this in our hearts.

Therefore, as God's chosen people, holy and dearly loved, clothe yourselves with compassion, kindness, humility, gentleness and patience. Bear with each other and forgive whatever grievances you may have against one another. Forgive as the Lord forgave you.

Colossians 3:12-13 NIV

God commands us to forgive, and explains what occurs in the spiritual realm when we do not forgive: God will not forgive us. Jesus explains this plainly,

"For if you forgive men when they sin against you, your heavenly Father will also forgive you. But if you do not forgive men their sins, your Father will not forgive your sins."

Matthew 6:14-15 NIV

This verse is not speaking about losing salvation, but about not receiving God's forgiveness. If we forgive others, God forgives us. If we won't forgive others, God won't forgive us.

Additionally, if we don't forgive, we will live in torment. Jesus explains this in the parable of the unmerciful servant, who was forgiven an unsurmountable debt, and then refused to forgive his fellow servant a miniscule debt (Mt 18:21-35). Jesus ends the parable with this ominous statement:

"And his lord, moved with anger, handed him over to the torturers until he should repay all that was owed him. My heavenly Father will also do the same to you, if each of you does not forgive his brother from your heart."

Matthew 18:34-35

The King James says **delivered him to the *tormentors.*** I've heard it said that when we don't forgive, it's like drinking poison and hoping *the other person* will die. Whether we realize it or not, we will be tormented until we choose to forgive *from our heart.*

We can see from these verses that the reason God commands us to forgive is *for our own good:* so that our heavenly Father will forgive us, and so that we do not live in torment.

Chester and Betsy Kylstra, founders of *Restoring the Foundations*, take it deeper. "God asks us not only to forgive, but to be willing to take the initiative for reconciliation when needed. Scripture offers no loopholes. God covers forgiveness from both directions."[4] Forgiveness is so important to God that He commands us to forgive if someone has wronged us — and to *seek* forgiveness if we have wronged someone:

"Therefore, if you are offering your gift at the altar and there remember that your brother has something against you, leave your gift there in front of the altar. First go and be reconciled to your brother; then come and offer your gift."
Matthew 5:23-24 NIV

Now that we've laid some foundations, we're going to look at the steps of forgiveness in more detail.

Step 1: Honesty

As difficult as it may be, we've got to start at Step 1, admit our unforgiveness and assess with complete honesty.

Cynthia Kubetin, a survivor of childhood sexual abuse, details the reason honesty is so critical to forgiveness: "You can only forgive as deeply as you acknowledge the offense."[5] It's that simple. We've got to accept all the hideousness of the offense and the enormity of our pain, for we can only forgive to the depth that we *understand* what we are forgiving. I'm going to go medical here to draw a parallel.

If we are cut with a knife, and the wound is simply stitched up on the *outside*, without the proper examination, cleansing, and stitching of the *inside*, a pocket will be left underneath the external stitches. This pocket can fill up with infection. Similarly, we can be in denial about the depth of our pain and our wounded hearts. If we avoid taking the time to admit our pain and to cry out to God in our anguish, if we just cover it up and pretend it isn't so bad, we can develop an emotional abscess. This emotional abscess can ooze out bitterness, revenge, and displaced anger. It can explode with emotional outbursts and inappropriate levels of anger to even minor offenses.

Medically, in order to treat the abscess, those superficial external stitches must be removed, the depth of it must be examined and the infection cleaned out, and the stitches placed again – this time from the inside out. Emotional healing will look much the same.

Clearly it would have been wiser to have taken care of the wound correctly the first time around – but truly, when it comes to emotional, mental, or spiritual wounds, we humans rarely seek the best healing the first time around. Later, when "infection" has set in and is oozing out, it can demand much courage to revisit these places of pain. Yet I know of no other way.

Sometimes we may not be ready to go the full depth at this time – and that is okay. We will allow Jesus to gently lead us as far as we are ready to go during this season. Trust Him. He will not take us anywhere He has not prepared and equipped us to go, and He will walk with us every step of the way.

Step 2: Repentance

Repent? If I am the one hurt, why would I need to repent? Doesn't the other person need to repent? Stick with me here.

There are three areas here I want to address. The first is repenting for our persistent unforgiveness. I realize that some of you may have been injured in heinous ways, some of you may have been wounded as children, and some of you may have been tormented with repeated long-term injuries. Please realize that God is gracious, and He knows that forgiveness may take time. Yet, there seems to come a time when God *does* call us to repent from holding on to our unforgiveness. If God is knocking at the door of your heart right now, this may be the season that He is offering to walk you through this process of forgiveness.

The second area I want to address is repenting for any ungodly thoughts, words, or actions *in response* to the injury. If someone has hurt us, and our response is uncontrolled anger, retaliation, revenge, or hardening of our heart, God calls us to repent of our ungodly response. This may be a difficult step for those who have been wounded deeply or at a very young age. Please don't think that I am saying that the person who wounded you has no need to repent! But recognize that their repentance is between them and God. God will still hold them completely responsible. *Our* walk through this process of forgiveness has nothing to do with *the other person's* repentance; it has nothing to do with their accountability. They remain accountable to God.

The third area of repentance is pretty tricky. This third area is to repent of any of our ungodly actions, no matter how small, related to the offense. It is a call to repent of any part we may have played in the incident, even if that part is a very small fraction of the entire situation. Some of you may have *nothing* to repent of in this area, particularly if you were a young child when you were hurt. If you were abused – either as a child or as an adult – you bear no guilt for the abuse. It is not your fault *in any way*. If the one who hurt you, or someone who knows about the injury, has told you that it is your fault, *that is Satan's lie.* Whether you were a child or an adult when you were abused, the abuse is not your fault. Nothing you did, and nothing you didn't do, ever gives anyone the right to abuse you – physically, mentally, emotionally, or sexually. You bear no guilt for someone abusing you; do not repent for someone abusing you. Repent for holding onto unforgiveness: yes. Repent for someone abusing you: no.

Whatever situation of unforgiveness we are working through, we will need to rely on the Holy Spirit to guide us. We will seek the Holy Spirit's revelation to learn how to take responsibility for only our part, and to leave the wrongdoer's part between them and God.

Step 3: Release

"I'll forgive if he apologizes ... if he never does it again ... if he promises to ..." *Conditional forgiveness* is not really forgiveness at all. True forgiveness is *choosing* to pardon, *releasing* the wrongdoer from our bitterness and vengeance. *Sending away* all hurt, revenge, hatred, anger, and resentment. We may need to make this choice hundreds and hundreds of times. Every time our anger surfaces, it is simply another call from the Holy Spirit to release again. Don't give up! As we persist, God will work forgiveness deeper and deeper into our heart and soul.

I have heard that if we are unable to release the wrongdoers from our unforgiveness, we may be interfering with their relationship with God by demanding that they answer to us. When we forgive and release, they now no longer answer to us; they must answer only to God. We no longer require them to stand before *us* for an accounting. They will stand before *God* for an accounting. When we put the one who has hurt us in God's hands, it frees us to keep our eyes focused on Jesus and our own relationship with Him.

Does this mean that we *trust* them again? No. Forgiveness does not equal trust. Forgiveness is a *choice to release*. Trust must be *earned*.

Does forgiveness mean that we develop a friendship again? That we enter back into deep relationship? Not necessarily. Full restoration of relationship will require *the other person's* repentance and transformation.

If the other person has not sought God in repentance, we will need to ask the Holy Spirit to direct us into the level of relationship that He wants for us at this time. Without their repentance and heart transformation, our relationship will most likely remain void of deep connection – but that does not always mean that the Holy Spirit will completely shut down this relationship. He may direct us to maintain the tenuous connection because He is at work in this relationship in ways that we cannot see at this time.

If the person is not safe, the Holy Spirit certainly may direct us into no contact at all. However, forgiveness means that we do stand ready to restore relationship when the person has come to repentance. Restoration of relationship may be gradual, and of course be led by the Holy Spirit.

A Debt That Can Never Be Repaid

Our choice to release entails acknowledging that
the wrongdoers can never make up for the offense. It is
recognizing that they owe us a debt that they can never
repay – and then choosing to release them from that debt.
Cynthia Kubetin expresses it this way:

> Forgiving is a decision regarding a debt.
> When I forgive, I decide that I am not going
> to attempt to collect a debt that you owe me.
> I am not going to punish you in an attempt to
> feel better.[6]

And Ken Sande expounds on this idea of debt release
this way:

> Forgiveness can be costly. When someone
> sins, they create a debt someone has to pay.
> Most of this debt is owed to God. In his great
> mercy, he sent his Son to pay that debt on the
> cross for all who would trust in him. But if
> someone sins against you, part of their debt
> is owed to you. This leaves you with a choice.
> You can either take payments on the debt or
> you can make payments.
>
> You take payments on a debt from others'
> sin in many ways. You might withhold
> forgiveness, dwell on a wrong, be cold and
> aloof, give up on the relationship, inflict
> emotional pain or gossip, lash back, or plot
> revenge ...
>
> Your other choice is to make payments on
> the other person's debt, releasing others from
> penalties they deserve to pay. Sometimes
> God empowers you to do this in one easy

payment. You decide to forgive, and by God's grace the debt is swiftly and fully canceled in our heart and mind. But when you have been deeply wronged, the debt it creates can be too large to pay at once. You may need to bear the impact for the other person's sin over a long period of time. This might mean fighting against painful memories, speaking gracious words when you wish to say something hurtful, working to tear down walls and be vulnerable when you still feel little trust, or even enduring the consequences of an injury the other person is unable or unwilling to repair.[7]

I must admit that I have spent a long time struggling with forgiveness. For me, the catalyst I needed to begin the forgiveness process was realizing that God has forgiven *me* a debt that I can never repay. Yes, there are people who owe me a debt that they can never repay – but compared to the debt that I have been forgiven by God, *their debt is nothing.*

Step 4: Transformation

I often hear people declare that they have forgiven, but as they share their forgiveness process, it seems they are merely stuffing the offense, pretending that it didn't happen. I believe that true deep forgiveness is impossible without God, for forgiveness is from the heart, and only He fashions our hearts (Mt 18:35, Ps 33:15). It seems that we cannot *manufacture* forgiveness. Our part is to *choose* to forgive, to walk out that choice daily, to acknowledge that we cannot forgive without Jesus' work in our heart. Our job is to ask Him to transform us – and then to wait. We wait on the Holy Spirit to deliver us from unforgiveness and to give us forgiveness in its place.

Step 5: Healing

Healing comes from an encounter with Jesus – and often multiple encounters over weeks, months, even years as He touches our hearts and heals our places of deep pain. This healing process generally takes longer if ...

- The pain inflicted was over a protracted period,
- The injury is ongoing now,
- The pain occurred at a young age, or
- Someone very close to us wounded us.

Sometimes, healing is indeed the fifth step in the process. Other times, Jesus begins His healing process before we even begin honesty, repentance, and release. Perhaps He graciously intervenes when the offense is particularly heinous, or if we were a young child when we were hurt, or maybe when we are as yet unsaved and do not have the Holy Spirit in us to enable us to choose forgiveness.

Sometimes, Jesus' healing touch comes unexpectedly, without any apparent effort on our part. Other times, God may call us to work through the pain perhaps by means of a specific Bible study or with a Christian counselor.

Sometimes, only one encounter with Christ brings us to full healing. Other times, that touch is just the first of many encounters with Jesus that will be necessary to reach completion of healing.

I have found it helpful to *ask* Jesus for healing. Asking helps me to remain in a place of expectant humility. Asking prepares my heart to hear how He may be calling me to partner with Him in the healing process. And asking opens my heart to receive His healing as it flows forth. Let's take a quiet moment alone with Him and ask Him to heal our wounds and broken hearts.

I'd like to introduce you to my friend Arica, an amazing young woman of faith and perseverance. As we follow her story, let's see if we can pick out the various steps of forgiveness here.

The welcome home of our new baby was nothing short of a nightmare. My husband had completely hidden his drinking from me for about two years. But that night, he couldn't hide it anymore. He had overdone it, and because he had been caught, he acted out. He had been out of line in arguments before, and quick to defend himself or to argue, but there had never been such threats or violence before. I want to make it clear that nobody was left with bruises by blunt hits, but there was enough fear and physical force put into it all for consequences to be put into effect. Suffice it to say that the night ended with him being arrested and court ordered away from his family for two and a half months. There was no contact allowed, by voice or by sight, with any of our children – age 5 years, 2 years, and 5 days old. I was allowed to speak on the phone with him, and then in the last few weeks to meet in person to work things out.

The things exposed were hard to swallow. My husband of seven years, a Godly man, the man I loved, was a closet alcoholic and had lied straight to my face for two years! My husband just pushed me around a mere five days after giving birth! The father of my children got rough with our boys and now he couldn't have contact with them – or with his newborn baby girl – for two and a half months!

I certainly had had plenty of suspicions that he had been sneaking, hiding something, but I could never prove anything. I could never catch him, and could not even find anyone else to back up my reasonings either. I had been praying for a long time, "Lord, You know what the truth is, You know what is going on. If he is hiding something, please, Lord, reveal it in a way that You know will make things better. All I ask, Lord, is that you please protect my children and myself through it, and give me the strength I will need through every step. Help me to make the right choices so things can be better, and so our marriage can be used by You. In Jesus' Name, Amen."

So this nightmare was an answer to my prayers. God was working. Yes, He answered. He did His part, and He answered my prayers the whole way through. Now, it was my turn to do what He was calling me to do.

The choice was mine: to forgive, or to hold on to hurt and resentment in my heart. It was a choice that put the future of my marriage on a teeter totter and our children's lives in the balance. It was a defining moment . . . for me, for my husband, for our three children. Hurt was what I felt. Resentment was what I thought was RIGHT!! I had a reason to hold onto hurt and resentment! I didn't need to forgive . . . or did I? God was calling to my heart. I knew what I had to do. I knew what was really right . . . but it was still my choice. God was not going to force me.

It wasn't an easy choice to forgive. It didn't just roll off my heart without pain. There were many hours of hurt and tears and questions. Tons of prayers and a constant conversation with God. Wonderful advice sought and given from Christian women in my life. The things I had to forgive felt like I was climbing over mountains. Each time the thoughts would come, I would choose to forgive again, each time a new mountain. But I was choosing to climb, and God, my gracious God, kept His part and helped me. He still helps me climb those mountains. Choosing to forgive was the choice I knew I needed to make. I needed to trust my Lord to get me through it. To do what He called me to do. If I am to be used by Him, I must listen to His word and His way, not my word and my way. And He will bless that . . . and I am pleased to say that He has and He is.

It has been almost nine months since that explosion when my family was turned upside down. But things are better than they were before this whole thing started. My husband attends recovery and I attend Al-Anon, which helps me to *focus on me and my issues. My children are so happy, and our marriage is stronger than before. I am not saying that all this has come to us easy, but we both have our eyes and hearts in the right direction. We are both trying the best we can to do our part, and God is blessing.*

Arica
Jupiter, Florida

Did you catch Arica's honesty? How about her repentance for her own sins? Release of her husband? And God's transformation and healing? The wounds are deep. The process of forgiving and healing, already quite lengthy, has only just begun for this couple.

As Arica processed forgiveness, she encountered remembrances of the same offense repeatedly, day after day, week after week, until forgiveness flowed easily through her heart. Jackie Kendall calls this "The 490 Principle."

Then Peter came and said to Him, "Lord, how often shall my brother sin against me and I forgive him? Up to seven times?" Jesus said to him, "I do not say to you, up to seven times, but up to seventy times seven."

Matthew 18:21-22

Jackie Kendall interprets Jesus' words to mean that we must forgive 490 times – *for the same offense!!* That is a lot of forgiving to do – and yet, for us humans, that is often what it takes, especially for wounds that are excruciatingly painful. Choosing to release again and again and again – 490 times. Jackie Kendall believes that is why the painful memories, flashbacks, and dreams keep recurring – to lead us to the 490th time of forgiveness.[8]

Positioning Ourselves To Receive the Spirit's Work

Can we speed up the forgiveness and healing process? Well, we do know it is the sovereign unpredictable uncontrollable work of the Holy Spirit, yet we can *position* ourselves to receive His deliverance and healing:

- Get ready to hear: Keep immersing in Bible study, prayer, solitude, soaking, praise and worship, accountability, serving, and connecting with our church family. This will put us in a position to hear.

- Face the truth: Sometimes, healing is delayed because we are not yet ready to face the raw truth in all its pain. We may resist revisiting deep injuries that we have walled off in our hearts. We may be fearful; we may not be able to trust that God will be able to comfort us in the pain. When Jesus was teaching His disciples to forgive seventy times seven times, they recognized their need for greater trust in Him in order to be able to forgive in this way. Their prayer was, **"Increase our faith!"** (Lk 17:5). If we keep growing in Christ, He will fully prepare us and equip us to follow Him down the path of acknowledging the truth.

- Repent of holding on to unforgiveness.

- Repent of your part, even if your part is only a small part. For example, your spouse may have left the marriage – and God does hold your spouse fully accountable for that – but God still calls you to repent of your own sins in the issue, perhaps disrespecting your spouse, or putting your kids first, or letting your anger rage unchecked, or not spending enough time nurturing your marriage.

- Forgive even if the world and the people of the world say that the offense is unforgivable. Even when we are inflicted with the most heinous of wounds, God *still* calls us to forgive. "Realize, however, that God is gracious; He knows some injuries are so heinous that we will need time and space to come to forgiveness."[9] Yet His requirement that we forgive still stands. As we develop our relationship with Christ, we will become strong enough to choose to forgive.

- Acknowledge with all humility that *we* cannot produce a forgiving heart; only Jesus can grant our hearts the ability to forgive.

- Pray blessings over the wrongdoer. Blessings? Certainly. Jesus commands us, **"Bless those who curse you, pray for those who mistreat you"** (Lk 6:28). As we pray, ask the Holy Spirit to reveal how to bless that person – *specific blessings unique for that person.* He will show us just how to pray. Why does this help speed up the forgiveness process? I don't exactly know – but somehow I think it is not possible for the heart to hold both bitterness and blessings at the same time.

What Can Hinder the Forgiveness Process?

Sometimes, we can have a desire to complete the forgiveness process, but somehow are blocked. Let's discuss a few possible barriers to forgiveness.

Confusing Forgiveness With Trust
Can Block the Forgiveness Process

Forgiveness does not equal trust. We *choose* forgiveness, but trust must be *earned.* Releasing someone from our unforgiveness, from our bitterness, from our revenge, does not mean that we trust them. It does not mean that we put ourselves in a place to be hurt again. It does not necessarily mean that we become friends again or choose to spend time with that person or even ever see them again. Forgiveness can be completely one-sided as we walk through the forgiveness process with God alone.

Forgiveness does not depend upon the repentance of the other person. Trust is different. Trust must be earned, and trust is part of a restored relationship.

Confusing Forgiveness With Reconciliation Can Block the Forgiveness Process

Reconciliation is indeed God's goal, but forgiveness does not equal reconciliation. Reconciliation is healing and restoring the relationship.

A restored relationship requires repentance on *the other person's part also.* I don't believe it is possible to have much depth of relationship with one who has wounded us and is still denying the offense or refusing to repent. God commands us to maintain a forgiving, unconditionally loving, nonjudgmental relationship with them, but it will probably be void of deep connectedness. The Lord will lead us in the details of that relationship as He heals us.

When we forgive, we release the other person from the debt they owe us and ask the Holy Spirit to bring forgiveness into our hearts. Then we wait, standing firm in our shoes of peace, ready to begin reconciliation when the other person repents and asks for forgiveness.

Confusing Forgiveness With Accountability Can Block the Forgiveness Process

Chester and Betsy Kylstra explain that forgiveness does not mean that we release them from accountability. When we forgive, we still hold them accountable for their actions; we do not erase the consequences. We release them from bitterness and revenge, but not from their accountability or consequences. "Forgiveness is not saying the offense is 'okay' ... [It] does not negate holding the offender responsible for his actions."[10] For example, if a friend had an accident in my car, I am to forgive and release him from my anger and bitterness, but still hold him accountable to make restitution for the damages. And God's wisdom may lead me to refuse to lend him the car again.

Condemning Judgment
Can Block the Forgiveness Process

Sometimes we may have chosen to forgive, but we are holding on to judgment. We may be judging the person for hurting us, and may pridefully believe that *we* would never hurt someone that way. We may feel disdainfully superior, thinking of ourselves more highly than we ought (Rom 12:3). We may be so puffed up with our own self-righteousness that we can't even see that we have hurt others also.

Shame
Can Block the Forgiveness Process

Shame may cause us to hide our secrets, fearing rejection. Secrecy may prevent us from even completing Step 1 of the forgiveness process. It can hinder us from admitting and acknowledging the truth of the injury.

Anger With God
Can Block the Forgiveness Process

Sometimes we may have forgiven the person, but we may still be disappointed with life or even angry with *God.* Stay with me here – as good Christians, we really don't want to admit that we are angry with God. But let's pause a moment and allow the Holy Spirit to examine our hearts. Are we disappointed that life is not happening as we imagined it would? Are we frustrated at things that are beyond our control? Are we angry that life is not going according to our plan? Are we angry at God for not protecting us, for not intervening when we know He certainly could have? Are we rejecting His sovereign plan? Are we bitter because the world is unfair? Of course life is unfair! God never said this fallen planet would be fair – He said *He is just.* Submitting to God's sovereign plan – whether it makes sense to us or not at this time – and releasing God from our anger, bitterness, expectations, and demands – can clear the path to receive His transformation and healing work of forgiveness.

Unrepentant Wrongdoers
Can Block the Forgiveness Process

Sometimes those who wound us do not apologize, they don't ask for forgiveness, and they even continue an on-going offense. This can certainly be a stumbling block for *our* forgiveness. Yet Jesus forgave *on the cross,*

"Father, forgive them; for they do not know what they are doing."

Luke 23:34

And we are commanded to *forgive as Jesus forgives.* Yes, forgiving someone who is unrepentant or who continues in the same sin will be a monumental undertaking. Yet forgiveness cannot depend upon the other person's repentance.

If it is possible, as far as it depends on you, live at peace with everyone.

Romans 12:18 NIV

As far as it depends on you. We forgive simply because God commands it.

Let's pause a moment and ask the Holy Spirit to reveal if any of these are blocking your forgiveness. Make some notes in your journal or in the margin as He reveals.

What If We Cannot Even <u>Choose</u> To Forgive?

Throughout this chapter I have talked about the impossibility of "manufacturing" forgiveness.[11] It seems to me that we cannot *force* ourselves to forgive, especially if the pain is very deep, or if one very close to us has inflicted the pain. We can't talk ourselves into forgiving or persuade our hearts to pardon. Is there anything we *can* do if we are stuck right here, unable to *choose* to forgive?

When I recognize that I am stuck in unforgiveness, when I am struggling with that choice to let go, I spend more time repenting. I invite the Holy Spirit to search my heart, and I come out of denial. I get really honest with God, and I don't gloss over my unforgiveness, bitterness, resentment, hardness of heart, or revenge. I read through the Gospel accounts of Jesus' death, focusing on His blood that purchased my forgiveness. Then, I entreat God to make me *willing* to forgive. My prayer sounds much like my prayer when I am struggling to surrender: "Lord, I am *willing* to be *made willing* to forgive. Please give me the ability to forgive." Then I open my heart for the Holy Spirit to do His work, and I watch and wait.

I'd like to share with you how my journey of forgiveness first started.

I knew the Scriptures on forgiveness. I knew God commanded me to forgive. I had spent many many agonizing years trying to forgive, but was simply unable. Finally, at a time of desperation, my heart cried out in grief and pain, admitting with all humility my inability to forgive, and begging God to make me able to forgive. I will never forget that moment. He gave me His healing <u>first</u>, forgiving all of my sins and failings. One heartbeat later, but seemingly simultaneously, He enabled me to forgive. At that sacred moment, He healed the gaping wound in my heart. He forgave me my sins, and I forgave. Also, at that *very moment, the Holy Spirit came into my heart for the first time, as I received Jesus as my Lord and Savior.*

Celeste Li
Jupiter, Florida

A word of caution: If we are in unforgiveness, and we earnestly pray for God to make us willing to forgive, we may be in for a rough journey. He may open our eyes to ways that we have hurt people in order to bring us to a place of humility and readiness to forgive. Or He may allow Satan to sift us like wheat in order to expose deep heart sins such as pride, distrust, or control that could be blocking forgiveness.

Layers and Layers of Forgiveness

Let's say that we have indeed processed through all of the forgiveness steps, confronting the truth, repenting, choosing forgiveness, and receiving the Holy Spirit's transformation and the Lord's healing touch. We may have had a deep spiritual sensation of release or a lifting of a weight as Jesus freed us from the bonds of unforgiveness. We may even know with certainty that we have encountered Jesus' precious healing touch in those raw areas of our hearts. Is the journey complete? Have we finished with forgiveness? Maybe. Maybe not.

One day we may encounter the one who hurt us, or recall a memory of the offense, or endure a dream or a flashback, and the pain may well up inside us all over again. Perhaps even feelings of bitterness, revenge, and hatred return and we may feel unable to release them. What happened? We may ask ourselves, Did I not forgive "properly"? Did I not repent enough? Did that encounter with the Lord really happen? If I have forgiven, why am I experiencing all this pain?

We may well have completed the portion of the forgiveness journey that God had ordained for us at that time. But it may be time to tackle the next leg of the journey. The Holy Spirit may be showing us that although much transformation and healing has taken place, Jesus has not finished His work in us yet. The pain may simply be God's way of acknowledging that we have grown in Him and are ready for the next level. Let's pick up the story of my forgiveness journey, which really illustrates this concept of layers of forgiveness. I think of it as traveling down a spiral staircase, deeper and deeper into the heart of God.

I started years ago at the moment of my salvation with the first step of forgiveness: releasing the people to God. For me, that was huge, and it took many years for me to take that very first step. When I did, I encountered the Lord as never before, and I thought that my forgiveness was complete.

But much later, the Holy Spirit brought me to new revelations that there were areas of unforgiveness that I was still holding on to. I had forgiven in general, but not specific memories, instances, moments. He walked me through it, and this time, it did not take me so many years.

But months later, the Holy Spirit showed me that I still harbored resentment. Why? I asked. Didn't I cover everything? The Holy Spirit revealed that I had forgiven the actions, but not the <u>people</u>. Wow. That was really deep. It took a bit for me to reach forgiveness there.

Was I finished yet? Nope. The Holy Spirit soon began to reveal to me the judgments I held against them. I was prideful that I had not sinned in this same way, so I held condemning judgment. I considered myself better than them, thinking, somehow, that my sins were less sinful. Oh, there was much to process with the Lord that time.

Another time He revealed my secret desire for revenge. I wanted to hold something over their heads. Somehow, I believed the lie that by not quite releasing them, I maintained some type of power over them. Admitting my revenge to the Lord was very challenging. Of course, He already knew it, but somehow I thought I could hide that part of my heart from Him.

Yet another time He revealed my deep fear. I feared that if I forgave, I would open myself up to further pain. While that may or may not have been true, what was important here was that I did not trust God to be greater than my pain. I could not put myself in that vulnerable place of trusting that if I was hurt again, He would protect and comfort. I felt I needed to keep control over the situation, over the people, because I could not trust God to protect my fragile heart. Not trusting God is a very deep root indeed.

He later revealed my stubborn refusal to reconcile, because that would require me to humble myself and ask forgiveness for my sin of holding onto unforgiveness. To ask forgiveness for my sinful response of walling myself off. He showed me the idol of myself and my reputation, and I have to admit that I did not want to expose my sins to those who had wronged me. I wanted to remain this holy and upright person that I pretended to be.

He also reminded me that people are not the enemy. Satan is the enemy. I had fallen into Satan's trap of battling the wrong enemy. Our battle is not against flesh and blood...

Each time the Holy Spirit revealed, and I repented, He drew me ever so much closer into His heart. Each time, I was sure that I had covered it all. Each time, I received His heart transformations and healing encounters, and

each time, I thought that forgiveness was complete. What else could there possibly be? But again and again we revisited the same issue. Traveling down that spiral staircase, reaching a landing of rest, but then called down to another level again, deeper and deeper into the Lord's heart.

So here I stand, many years deep into the process. And this week, the Holy Spirit said, "It's not finished yet." Ugh! Still not finished? I could not imagine what else could possibly be blocking me from completion of forgiveness. Once again, I had absolutely no idea. Once again, I went to prayer and fasting to hear His voice, seeking Him to reveal what only He knew.

He said, "You're angry with Me." I argued with Him a bit. Futile, of course; He's always right. He reminded me that He took full responsibility for everything on this earth. He went on to say, "You have been hurt, and your sinful response to your pain has left your life in a big mess. And although you accept My sovereignty, you don't like what I have chosen for your life. I call that rebellion."

As I was on my face repenting, God explained, ever so gently, that those who had hurt me were His servants.

How are they Your servants? I was desperate to know. The Lord explained that only He knew my heart, and that He was using them to expose the deepest darkest depths of my heart. Satan meant it for evil, but God meant it for good. God desired to expose the core of my heart that had remained hidden from me, the darkest sins of pride, control, and fear, the horrid sins of not trusting Him, of idolatry, of rebellion. God, not violating their free will or mine, yet ultimately sovereign and abounding in love for me, desired to expose the dark areas of my heart, to bring me to repentance, to cleanse me and deliver me and heal me, to drive out darkness and fill me with His Spirit. He wants deep relationship with me that fiercely. He wants to infuse me with His Spirit in greater and greater measure, so He will do whatever it takes to expose my heart. He chose to use the evil of this world as His servants. Only He knows what will be required for my heart to be laid bare. And He will ordain not one tear more.

I desire to accept His perfect plan for my life. Every moment, past, present, and future. Now that I can see these situations with His eyes, He has given me a deep gratitude for these people. For I know, I am certain, that without their influence upon my life, my sins would remain hidden, blocking me from receiving Him in deeper and deeper measure. I trust that only He knows what it will take.

Celeste Li
Jupiter, Florida

Jackie Kendall explains, "You can forgive as effectively as your faith is strong."[12] When we first forgive, we are only able to forgive what we understand at that moment. As we become more spiritually mature, as our trust in the Lord grows, the Holy Spirit will lead us through deeper and deeper layers of forgiveness. It's not that we have failed the process the first time; on the contrary, we have passed with flying colors and are ready for the next level.

I have heard it said that people harbor unforgiveness when their pain exceeds their faith.[13] The deeper the wound, the deeper the relationship with Jesus that will be necessary to heal it.

How Will We Know That We Are Progressing On the Forgiveness Journey?

Look for fruit such as this:

- The relationship no longer elicits pain.

- We are praying for God to have mercy upon them.

- We are able to pray deep and specific blessings for them.

- We *want* restored relationship. We are praying for them to come to repentance so that our relationship can be reconciled.

There are two other litmus tests, but they are not for those who have just embarked on the forgiveness and healing process. These tests are reserved for those hearts where Jesus has been working for a long time, for people who have received intense healing from the Lord:

- Has the Holy Spirit brought us to a place of understanding and compassion? Has He given us insight into the depth of the pain *the one who hurt us* has experienced that has driven them to inflict such pain on us? This is not a place of excusing – those who wound remain responsible and held accountable for their actions. This is not a place of blind trust or release from consequences. This is simply a place of broken-heartedness for the wrongdoer, understanding the pain that drove them to make those sinful choices. As author and radio host Glenda Watson puts it: we recognize, without judging, that, "Hurting people hurt people. Wounded people wound people. Broken people break people."[14]

- How do we react when the one who has hurt us enters the room? I don't mean simply that we have moved from rage to indifference – although that is a huge accomplishment. What I mean is, did we avoid them? Did we pretend they didn't exist? Or are our hearts breaking for them? Are we wearing our shoes of peace and standing ready to begin the process of reconciliation when they repent and ask for forgiveness? Are we actually excited to see them, hoping that this is the moment and that they are ready for restoration to begin?

Understand that completed forgiveness is not dependent merely on us doing our part of *honesty, repentance, and release* in the forgiveness process – it is also dependent upon God doing His part of *transformation and healing of our hearts* in that forgiveness process. For reasons we may not fully understand, Jesus' healing may take a long time. Wait on the Lord; trust in His perfect timing.

Recognize also that completed forgiveness does not mean a fully restored relationship. **As far as it depends on you ...** (Rom 12:18). A *restored relationship* requires repentance and true change *on the other person's part* also.

But don't wait for their repentance and change – forgive as Jesus forgives, and recognize the powerful spiritual bonds. As the Holy Spirit completes forgiveness in our hearts, those who have hurt us will be released to perhaps seek repentance and forgiveness themselves. And in addition, we will be set free ourselves, for bonds of unforgiveness held *us* captive as well.

There is one more area of forgiveness we will address before we leave this chapter: forgiving ourselves.

Forgiveness of Self

I had repented. And repented and repented and repented. Seventy times seven. For the same sin. My husband called it the "Lady Macbeth Syndrome." The need to wash my hands over and over and over again to get rid of the stain of sin. Why did I struggle with this persistent guilt?

I found myself talking to my friend Stephanie Cassatly. Her book, *Notice of Release,* chronicles her journey of forgiveness of the man who murdered her mother. Stephanie is connected with *The Forgiveness Project,* and since God has deeply anointed her in this ministry, it's hard to hide unforgiveness from her. "Celeste, your persistent guilt is because you are not able to forgive yourself." Forgive *myself*?

I pondered this a bit. I realized that I had gotten a bit mixed up. I was tangled up *repenting* seventy times seven – but the "seventy times seven" is how many times we have to *forgive* someone, not how many times we have to *repent*. How many times do we need to repent for a particular sin? *Only once.* I think God makes this very clear,

If we confess our sins, He is faithful and righteous to forgive us our sins and to cleanse us from all unrighteousness.

1 John 1:9

That verse is very straightforward. We confess, He forgives and cleanses.

So why was it so hard for me to forgive myself? Why couldn't I let myself off the hook? Why did I need to keep washing and washing my sullied hands?

I think maybe it had to do with my desire to *make up for* my sins. That doesn't sound so wrong. Sounds like restitution, which is a good thing, right?

I think it had to do with wanting somehow for the punishment to match the crime. Well, that may be a little bit off, hmm?

I think maybe it had to do with wanting to *earn* my forgiveness. Oh. Something *is* wrong here.

Stephanie went on to say, "And the only way to forgive yourself is through a walk of humility."

Oh, yes, she indeed is right. It was *pride* that was preventing me from receiving His grace. His forgiveness comes by grace, received through my utter humility, or not at all.

As far as this sin was concerned, I had to admit that it was over. Finished. I blew it. I couldn't undo it, make up for it, fix it. There was *nothing* I could do. Only Jesus can bring beauty out of the ashes. I can't. All I could contribute was the ashes.

I repented of pride and chose to receive the free gift that He was offering me. I received His forgiveness and forgave myself all at the same moment. Pride had been blocking me from receiving the gift of His grace. Trauma counselor Julie Woodley says it this way: "To forgive yourself takes a lot of courage. Who are you, after all, to let yourself off the hook ... Only the love of God makes it possible."[15]

I realized that I have no right to forgive myself for my sins. I am only able to forgive myself because God has forgiven me and He commands me to forgive myself. I am not worthy of forgiveness – God's or my own – it is a free gift of His grace. He gives me grace, and I, in obedience, give myself grace.

"Jesus Plus"

When we do not forgive ourselves, we are saying that Jesus' death is not sufficient to cover all our sins. We are declaring that our sins are so great that we need Jesus *plus* something else to be forgiven. I have heard this sin called "Jesus Plus."

If we are looking at ourselves with condemning judgment, we are holding ourselves to a higher standard than God does! If we are burdened with guilt, self-hatred, or worthlessness, then unforgiveness of self may be the root. God indeed commands forgiveness – and I believe that includes forgiving ourselves. Chester and Betsy Kylstra write, while "there is no Bible verse that directly instructs us to forgive ourselves . . . certain principles expressed in the Bible strongly encourage self-forgiveness."[16]

So we've made some mistakes. Maybe we think we've failed as a spouse or a parent. Perhaps we've even committed some pretty huge sins. So, what, you think that God isn't big enough, powerful enough, and loving enough to redeem that?

When we have fallen into the "Jesus Plus" trap, we are trampling on the precious blood of Christ, which has been shed for *all* of our sins. When we repent, God releases us. And if God releases us, who are we to hold ourselves in bondage?

Does forgiving ourselves mean that we have no responsibility for our sin? Oh, no. Remember what we discussed earlier in the chapter. When we forgive someone, we still hold them responsible. "This is not a place of excusing – the wrongdoer remains responsible and held accountable for their actions." What does it mean that we are still responsible and accountable?

There are times when God may call us to confess to an accountability partner. There are times when God may call us to make restitution, perhaps to pay for damages if we have broken something. There are times when God may call us to apologize to someone we have hurt and to ask forgiveness. There are times when God may call us to confess to those in authority and receive the consequences of our sin. Forgiving ourselves does not absolve us from whatever steps God may be commanding us to take.

There are also times when there is nothing to do but accept God's forgiveness and to forgive ourselves. For me, these times are the hardest. When God has assigned me nothing, absolutely nothing, to do. At these times, there is nothing that can be done, but to give Him the ashes and receive His grace in facedown humility.

My daughter Jenna, now a sophomore in college, has had a front row seat to my own struggles to forgive myself. One evening, reading some non-Christian poetry, this astute woman discovered a hint of some deep truths of God. She extrapolated a bit, and adapted it for me: "Feeling overly burdened by shame, sin, and guilt is to doubt God's capacity to forgive, and the generosity of His love."[17]   Her words have pierced my heart.

Persistent Guilt

If the Holy Spirit is calling us to repentance, we will sense *conviction*, not oppressing guilt or shame. Satan will attempt to use persistent guilt and unforgiveness of self to overpower us and destroy our calling. And if we refuse to forgive ourselves, we have just won a victory – *for the other team*.

I have a few questions that I ask myself to help me determine if I have indeed accepted God's forgiveness and forgiven myself:

- Do I look back at that sin, mistake, or failure with deep peace?

- Do I look back at it with *gratitude* that it happened?

- Do I *like* myself?

- Do I like myself as that woman who blew it? Do I

love her? Can I see her with eyes of compassion? Can I take her into my arms easily, or would I rather forget her?

If we have begun to let the sin define us, that could be a hint that we may have fallen into unforgiveness of our self. Remember what we studied in Chapter 3, *Toppling Barriers to Intimacy*. Our identity is who God says we are in Jesus: a child of God, redeemed and made whole, chosen and adopted and infused with the Holy Spirit. His treasured child whom He is passionate about and wants to spend time with. If we are obsessed with a sin, if we define ourselves by this sin, if we have a need to hide in shame – or a need to tell everyone about it – then we may have fallen into persistent guilt.

Stephanie explained to me that one of the reasons that it may be hard to forgive ourselves is because at some point, we have become both the perpetrator and the victim. We may have hurt others by our sin, and dealt with that as the Holy Spirit led. But we have also hurt *ourselves* by our sin. We may have to forgive our self for hurting our self. I think, maybe, this is where the "seventy times seven" comes into play again. We may need to forgive and release *ourselves* "seventy times seven" *for the same sin* before forgiveness of ourselves is completed in our hearts. Layers and layers of forgiveness, traveling down that spiral stairway into His heart. As we grow in Him, He calls us to deeper levels of forgiveness, and when we journey there with Him, we enter a deeper level of intimacy with Him.

Understand that persistent guilt is false guilt; it is an attack by the forces of darkness in an attempt to steal our peace, to kill our relationship with God, and to destroy the Lord's calling and the Kingdom work that He has assigned to us. Expect Satan to keep pestering you about that sin – he is an expert in attacking through shame and false guilt. Even seasoned Christians can succumb to this attack, and begin to believe Satan's lies that God has no use for them, that their ministry is now ineffective, that they can no longer touch people for God. But that is not God's plan! God always has a plan and purpose for us, a destiny that takes into account all of our wounds, sins, shortcomings, and failures.

But he said to me, "My grace is sufficient for you, for my power is made perfect in weakness." Therefore I will boast all the more gladly about my weaknesses, so that Christ's power may rest on me. That is why, for Christ's sake, I delight in weaknesses, in insults, in hardships, in persecutions, in difficulties. For when I am weak, then I am strong.

2 Corinthians 12:9-10 NIV

The key weapons we have against this persistent guilt are humble acceptance of His forgiveness, forgiveness of ourselves, and walking with Jesus into our destiny.

Go into your secret place of His Presence and ask Him to reveal to you if you have been unable to forgive yourself. Sit still before Him, letting Him wash you with His bottomless capacity to forgive, and His infinite generosity to love.

Entering the Battlefield Again and Again

Yes, in this world we will have trouble (Jn 16:33). Pain is inevitable. There will be many offenses that require forgiveness, large and small, and God calls us to live a life of constant forgiveness.

The first time the Holy Spirit walks us through deep forgiveness is, in some ways, the hardest, because we cannot possibly imagine the blessing of release from captivity that is waiting for us on the other side. Afterwards, subsequent calls to forgiveness may be easier, because we know the deliverance and divine healing that we will receive as we work through the process again – and that gives us great hope and drive.

But in other ways, forgiveness may become harder each time, because God will be calling us to a deeper level, a more challenging battle, a more painful memory. However, as we work together with Jesus and He wins these battles in our hearts, we grow in forgiveness; we uproot unforgiveness at a deeper and deeper level.

As we work through the forgiveness process, we may be surprised to discover that it is not simply one person or one event that we are working on to forgive. We may find that the roots of unforgiveness have permeated many aspects of our life. We may find that we are harboring unforgiveness of a whole host of events with a particular person, or even with a whole additional string of people and events.

As we grow in Christlikeness, as we grasp deeper truths, the Holy Spirit will enable us to forgive in greater measure:

- When we see ourselves with God's eyes and realize how many people *we* have hurt

- When we really and truly realize that our forgiveness is total and complete for *all* of our sins

- When we recognize that our forgiveness is not because we deserved it, and not because of anything we have done

- When we see that God's forgiveness is solely because of His love and mercy and grace ...

... then our forgiveness towards others will begin to flow out of God's forgiveness to us. I have heard it said that we are most like Jesus when we forgive.

Equipped to Be a Forgiver

There are so many people with a distorted view of God, a caricature that has been crafted by Satan's lies and their own painful experiences. Those lies may be blocking them from coming to the Lord. They desperately need to know the truth, that their heavenly Father is a God of love and grace and forgiveness. It is inevitable that offenses will come (Mt18:7). When we choose to forgive, when the healing power of His forgiveness flows freely through our heart to theirs, they may experience the mercy and grace and love of God. It may even be the first time they have ever experienced this. And His grace touching their hearts – through His forgiveness flowing through ours – just may be the instrument that He uses to draw them to Himself.

Questions Chapter 6: To Forgive As Jesus Forgives

Memory Verse:

Be kind and compassionate to one another, forgiving each other, just as in Christ God forgave you.

Ephesians 4:32 NIV

1) Define forgiveness in your own words. Be sure to also include what forgiveness is not. Where are you on the spiral staircase of your forgiveness journey?

2) Re-read the section *The Process of Forgiveness*. Which step is most challenging for you?

3) Read Matthew 18:21-35. Why do you think unforgiveness is torment?

Ponder how our own unforgiveness is bondage *for us*. Explain how when we forgive, we set the other person – and ourselves – free.

4) Re-read the section *What Can Hinder the Forgiveness Process?* Are any of these hindering you from forgiving right now?

5) Ask the Holy Spirit to reveal if you are struggling with unforgiveness of self. Explain how pride can thwart our ability to forgive ourselves.

6) Go back to page 201, to the name you wrote on that blank line. Spend some time with the Lord to fully forgive and release this person into His hands. Do the same for any others God has brought to mind through this chapter. Write your commitment to forgiveness in your journal as a reminder, in case the enemy tries to accuse you later of holding onto to unforgiveness.

Part III

Intimacy
Through Sanctification

Chapter 7
The Life of the Heart

We've used this word "heart" loosely throughout the book to represent such diverse things as our emotions, our will, and our desires. Let's take some time to explore what Scripture teaches us about the heart, for we will need a deep understanding of the heart to tackle Part III, *Intimacy Through Sanctification.*

What Exactly is "The Heart"?

Clearly, the heart is most critical, for Proverbs tells us,

Above all else, guard your heart, for it is the wellspring of life.

Proverbs 4:23 NIV

Our hearts are our wellsprings of our lives. The King James says **out of it are the issues of life.** The NLT says it plainly, **it affects everything you do.** As I read through the Word, I see quite a diversity of activities and assignments of the heart. As you ponder these points, circle anything that strikes you:

- Understanding, wisdom, and discernment are found in the heart – but foolishness, stubbornness, and abominations are also found there (Pr 14:33, 22:15, Dt 29:19, Pr 26:25).

- We hide God's Law in our hearts, we set our hearts to learn His Law, and in our hearts we meditate (Ps 119:11, Ezra 7:10, Ps 4:4).

- Our innermost thoughts, desires, and passions are in our heart, as well as our impulses and imaginations (Ps 37:4, Eccl 11:9, Ps 73:7).

- Our heart is the place of sorrows, bitterness, anger, and vengeance – and also the place of gratitude, tranquility, compassion, and forgiveness (Ps 13:2, Eccl 7:9, Col 3:12, Pr 14:30, Mt 18:35).

- Our heart is the seat of pride, rebellion, and wickedness – and also the seat of humility, trust, and integrity (2Chr 32:26, Jer 5:23, 1Sam 17:28, Col 3:12, Pr 3:5, Gen 20:5).

- Courage and fear lodge there, as well as love and hate, purity and deceit (Ps 27:14, 27:3, Deut 6:5, Lev 19:17, Mt 5:8, Pr 12:20).

- Our plans, purposes, and intentions reside in our hearts (Ps 33:11, Jer 23:20, 1Chr 29:18).

- When we are deceived, a veil is over our hearts; when the Holy Spirit convicts us, we are pierced to the heart. It is the Lord who opens our hearts to respond to Him (2Cor 3:15, Acts 2:37, 16:14).

- When our hearts turn from God, we harden them (Ex 8:32).

- The heart that God desires is clean, broken, contrite, fully devoted, and inclined toward Him (Ps 51:10, 51:17, Ps 119:112).

- God tests our hearts, humbles them, and circumcises them (Pr 17:3, Ps 107:12, Deut 30:6).

- We speak to God in our hearts, search for Him with all our hearts, and believe with our hearts (1Sam 1:13, Jer 29:13, Rom 10:9-10).

- When we are obedient, we do the will of God from our hearts (Eph 6:6).

- Realize also that Satan was the one who put betrayal into Judas' heart and deceit into Ananias' heart (Jn 13:2, Acts 5:3).

When we accept Jesus as our Lord and Savior, He dwells **in our hearts through faith** (Eph 3:17). Our hearts are also the home of His Spirit:

Because you are sons, God has sent forth the Spirit of His Son into our hearts, crying, "Abba! Father!"
Galatians 4:6

As we can see, the heart encompasses many aspects; in this chapter we are going to focus on two areas. First, we will spend some time focusing on the part of our heart that encompasses our emotions, for I think we will find quite a connection between our emotions and our ability to grow in intimacy with Jesus. Then, toward the end of the chapter, we will hone in on the submission and sanctification of our hearts.

Emotions Can Reveal the State of Our Heart

We've touched on the importance of being honest with God about the pain in our hearts. Sometimes, however, we can be unaware of our heart pain. But even if we are unaware, it seems that the heart cannot be silenced. Whether we are alert to the condition of our heart or not, our heart pain affects our actions and thoughts, it influences and harms our relationships, and it interferes with our relationship with God. How can we become aware of the deep pain in our heart? We can observe three areas:

- The speech that unexpectedly tumbles out of our mouths – the words, as well as the tone – can expose our hearts. **"For out of the abundance of the heart the mouth speaks"** (Mt 12:34 NKJV).

- Our actions, deeds, choices, and how we *react* instead of *respond* to a situation, can give a glimpse into the condition of our hearts. **"For out of the heart come evil thoughts, murders, adulteries, fornications, thefts, false witness, slanders"** (Mt 15:19).

- Our emotions can reveal deep heart pain, or even entrenched heart sins. **How long must I struggle with anguish in my soul, with sorrow in my heart every day?** (Ps 13:2 NLT). If we allow Him, God can utilize our emotions to reveal the state of our heart.

I think we can fairly easily see the connection between our words and our heart, and between our actions and our heart. Emotions can be trickier, though. Come with me as we explore this connection between emotions, the state of our heart, and our intimacy with God.

I must admit that I ran from my emotions for many years. They were painful, uncontrollable, and often frightening. It didn't seem "right" for a Christian to have these kinds of emotions. I didn't know what to do with them, so I stuffed them inside and pretended they didn't exist. But one day the Holy Spirit really grabbed my attention. He told me that denying my emotions was not walking in truth. When I pretended that I didn't have any negative feelings, I was simply lying to myself – and to God. God called it deception. He called it sin.

Additionally, I discovered that stifling unpleasant emotions led to hardness of heart. When I ignored, denied, or stuffed my emotions, instead of taking them to God for Him to give me understanding and healing, I walled off my heart to God and others. I was hardening my tender heart into a stony one. A heart of flesh or a heart of stone. It was my choice.

But does this really matter? Can't my heart just remain ... private? I may want it to, but I'm afraid it cannot. I've invited my friend Richard to explain how the state of our heart simply won't remain private. As Triumph Servant Leader, co-founder of our church's Cancer Support Groups, and primary leader of our community's Big Heart Brigade, Richard is indeed in the public eye. He knows what it's like for eyes to see into his heart.

I have heard intimacy defined in this way: in-to-me-see. I ask myself, what do people see when they look at me? Do they see Jesus? We may think that our facades can fool people – and at times perhaps they do. But people are often able to see past our masks and into our hearts. And when they look into our hearts, if they see Jesus, that's a good indication of profound intimacy with Him.

Richard Ekey
Founder of Men's Branch of Triumph
Palm Beach Gardens, Florida

Let's look at how we can utilize the honest expression of our emotions to encounter God, to expose deeper sins, and to develop our deep connected relationship with Him.

Encountering God Through Emotions

In First Kings, Elijah has just killed all the prophets of Baal, and Queen Jezebel vowed to take his life. Elijah ran for forty days and forty nights to Mount Sinai, the mountain of God. In this desperate time of panic, I wonder if maybe Elijah ran to what might have been his own secret place of God's Presence.

Then he came there to a cave and lodged there; and behold, the word of the LORD came to him, and He said to him: "What are you doing here, Elijah?"

He said, "I have been very zealous for the LORD, the God of hosts; for the sons of Israel have forsaken Your covenant, torn down Your altars and killed Your prophets with the sword. And I alone am left; and they seek my life, to take it away."

1 Kings 19:9-10

Notice the depth of Elijah's honesty. Depression, self-pity, anger, fear. It's all there. That honesty led to an astounding encounter with God.

So He said, "Go forth and stand on the mountain before the LORD." And behold, the LORD was passing by! And a great and strong wind was rending the mountains and breaking in pieces the rocks before the LORD; but the LORD was not in the wind. And after the wind an earthquake, but the LORD was not in the earthquake. After the earthquake a fire, but the LORD was not in the fire; and after the fire a sound of a gentle blowing. When Elijah heard it, he wrapped his face in his mantle and went out and stood in the

entrance of the cave. And behold, a voice came to him and said, "What are you doing here, Elijah?"

1 Kings 19:11-13

God's Presence was preceded by a mountain-shattering wind, an earthquake, and a fire, and *then* God spoke to Elijah in a gentle whisper. How deep must Elijah's relationship with the Lord have been, that he would hear and recognize that the voice of the Lord was the *gentle blowing* that came on the heels of the great wind, the earthquake, and the fire!

Now watch the tenderness of the Lord. The Lord must have known his heart was still full of pain, and that he needed to release all that pain before he was ready to receive God's comfort. God invited him to again share what was in his heart, and Elijah answered with total honesty.

Then he said, "I have been very zealous for the LORD, the God of hosts; for the sons of Israel have forsaken Your covenant, torn down Your altars and killed Your prophets with the sword. And I alone am left; and they seek my life, to take it away."

1 Kings 19:14

Interesting. Elijah said nothing new. I love how God wants to hear everything from our perspective. Of course He is omniscient and knows it all, but He desires to personally hear our pain with His own ears. **He heard my voice out of His temple, and my cry for help before Him came into His ears** (Ps 18:6). He wants to hear every little detail, as many times as is necessary for the release to be complete.

And God's gentle answer? He reassured Elijah that there were still 7000 in Israel who had remained faithful to God. He gave Elijah further assignment to confront kings in their sinfulness. And He provided for him a protégé to train who would assist him to the end of his life (1Kings 19:15-18).

I wonder what a **gentle blowing** is. Surely it must be difficult to put into words what it sounds like when God speaks to us. These words in the Hebrew are translated many different ways in the various Bible translations: **a gentle whisper, a still small voice, a low whisper, a sound of gentle stillness** (NIV, NKJV, ESV, AMP).

A sound of gentle stillness is my favorite. I would venture to say that Elijah was probably no stranger to pouring out his emotions to God. He seems to have so developed his sensitivity to the Lord that he was able to discern God's voice despite the strong wind, the earthquake, and the fire.

Emotional Turmoil Can Expose Our Heart

I think a real life example can explain this best.

Christmas was approaching, and my church was asking for volunteers to serve. We had a houseful of out-of-state relatives coming in for Christmas. The thought of the work involved with the visitors coupled with time at church serving gave me a pit in the bottom of my stomach.

Frustration, fear, anger, and confusion boiled in me. Anxious thoughts paraded through my mind unchecked. I tried to be a "good Christian" and pretend all those feelings didn't exist. I even asked God for supernatural strength to accomplish all this. Nothing happened.

I have to admit that I didn't know exactly what the emotions were at the time, but I knew they were negative. I probably just called it "feeling overwhelmed." At first I didn't know to use them as a means to encounter God. But eventually, after I had poured out my frustrations to Him (feeling very un-Christian the whole time), God quieted my spirit and revealed to me my anger and fear. Anger because I felt I had no control. Fear because I was afraid I would "look bad" in church if I wasn't volunteering for Christmas, and would "look bad" to my relatives if I wasn't prepared for them and wasn't constantly at home with them. The Holy Spirit then led me to realize that I was more concerned with what others thought of me than what God thought. That my reputation – before my church and before my family – had become my idol.

Convicted, I spent some time in prayer and repentance. I studied passages in my Bible to remind myself how much God hates idolatry. I surrendered my reputation and my agenda to Him. I asked Him to teach me to depend on Him and to remember to seek Him for all decisions, big and small. I thought, "Now certainly the supernatural strength or some miraculous answer will come." It didn't.

However, His answer to my unasked question did come a few days later. The pastor I was serving under asked me about volunteering for Christmas services. To my surprise, I didn't become upset or defensive, and my response helped me to realize that God had indeed done a work in my heart. I simply told the pastor that I didn't know; I was still praying about it. Then he said, "Don't you have a pile of relatives coming in for Christmas?" I admitted I did. "That's your Christmas ministry this year. You belong at home with them. Knowing you and your family, I am sure there will be a lot of talk about Jesus over Christmas!" And as God's peace washed through me, I knew that this was His answer, spoken through the words of that pastor.

Over the next few weeks, I was asked quite a few more times when I would be serving for Christmas. It was easy to answer with great peace, for I had heard from God. Even when the question came as an accusation or even an attack, I had no need to defend myself. Trusting God to be my Defense and my Shield, I was not flustered. I knew that for me, being at home serving my relatives for Christmas was the center of His will for me.

Celeste Li
Jupiter, Florida

It was clear that I needed to go to God with my turmoil, and that I needed the Holy Spirit to help me to identify exactly what the emotions were. He gave name to them, and that gave me clarity. He then traced them back to the root of idolatry of my reputation, and after I had repented, He so sweetly answered my unasked question of where *He* wanted me for Christmas.

Now don't miss the testing that followed: the number of times I was asked about serving for Christmas. Satan intended these times to be a trap, to bring me back to idolatry, fear, and confusion. But God intended the tests to strengthen my trust in and reliance upon Him. The tests were not to show *God* the state of my heart, but to show *me*. The peace that remained showed me that He had indeed uprooted a bad root and transformed a piece of my heart.

Does that mean that I'm finished with the sin of idolatry of myself and my reputation? I wish it were that simple. No, over the years, still more and deeper roots have been exposed and uprooted ... I suspect with yet more to come.

God Meets Us Where We Are Emotionally

I find the Psalms to be beautiful examples of using anger, fear, depression, pain, frustration, disappointment, grief, or other difficult emotions to encounter God. Let's listen in to David in Psalm 13.

> ¹ **How long, O Lord? Will you forget me forever?**
>   **How long will you hide your face from me?**
> ² **How long must I wrestle with my thoughts**
>   **and every day have sorrow in my heart?**
>   **How long will my enemy triumph over me?**
> ³ **Look on me and answer, O Lord my God.**
>   **Give light to my eyes, or I will sleep in death;**

⁴ **my enemy will say, "I have overcome him,"**
   and my foes will rejoice when I fall.
⁵ **But I trust in your unfailing love;**
   my heart rejoices in your salvation.
⁶ **I will sing to the LORD,**
   for he has been good to me.

                                   Psalm 13:1-6 NIV

Well, that's pretty impressive. From anger and fear to
hope and trust in six short verses. I am wondering, How
did David do it?

I speculate that this psalm was probably not penned
when David was young in the Lord. As we trace David's
life, we realize that this man after God's own heart spent
much time in the Lord's Presence. He utilized music and
worship to develop intimacy with God. He knew personally
the Lord's salvation from the jaws of death again and again.
Others have speculated that as a young shepherd, perhaps
during long night watches, he learned the treasures of
stillness in God's Presence. This psalm seems to reveal
what he had learned over many years; it seems to be a
reflection of a deep, trusting relationship with his Lord.

Let's follow his lead, for it is indeed a good template for
us to emulate. Through verses one to four, David's anger
cascaded. He was completely honest before God. He held
nothing back. This is where we must start. Right where we
are, in truth, naked before Him who knows it all anyway.
Sometimes, when I bring my painful emotions to God, my
tirade goes on for much longer than four verses. David's
too, as we will see as we study his psalms.

But somehow, between verse 4 and verse 5, the psalm
changes its tone. What happened in that space between
verse 4 and verse 5? Exactly what happened during that
pause? Perhaps David chose worship even in the midst
of his pain and trial. Or perhaps honestly spilling out his
heart to God birthed a dynamic encounter with the Lord.
Perhaps David made a conscious choice to trust God, even

when God seemed absent, silent, or sleeping. Perhaps David repented of doubt and disbelief. Perhaps the Holy Spirit simply reached down and touched David's heart with His enormous love. Whatever happened, it appears that David came away from this prayer time comforted, strengthened, reassured of God's love and protection – and even singing.

Difficult Emotions Can Drive Us Away From God – Or to Him

Come with me to Galilee ...

... the boat was already a long distance from the land, battered by the waves; for the wind was contrary. And in the fourth watch of the night He came to them, walking on the sea. When the disciples saw Him walking on the sea, they were terrified, and said, "It is a ghost!" And they cried out in fear. But immediately Jesus spoke to them, saying, "Take courage, it is I; do not be afraid."

Peter said to Him, "Lord, if it is You, command me to come to You on the water." And He said, "Come!" And Peter got out of the boat, and walked on the water and came toward Jesus. But seeing the wind, he became frightened, and beginning to sink, he cried out, "Lord, save me!" Immediately Jesus stretched out His hand and took hold of him, and said to him, "You of little faith, why did you doubt?" When they got into the boat, the wind stopped. And those who were in the boat worshiped Him, saying, "You are certainly God's Son!"

Matthew 14:24-33

When did Peter become frightened? **Seeing the wind.** When he took His eyes off Jesus and put his focus on the turbulence. The result of his fear? He began to sink. Peter had already witnessed Jesus calm the storm (Mt 8:23-27). He had just now been given a command to **take courage**, and an assignment from God (**"Come!"**) – yet he was suddenly unable to complete that assignment because he had taken his eyes off the One Whom Even The Winds And Sea Obey. With his eyes no longer on Jesus, the problem took on enormous proportions. In the midst of his water-walk, Peter succumbed to the lie that the storm's power was greater than Jesus' power, and fear overtook him.

But that's not the end of the story! Peter used his fear to encounter Jesus, crying out to Him, **"Lord, save me!"** He knew that there was only One who could save him, and he knew how to find that One.

The result? Jesus met him right where he was. He stretched out His hand and grabbed hold of him. Now I'm going to do a bit of extrapolating here, because Scripture doesn't give us the details. Notice Scripture says Peter was **beginning to sink.** He didn't sink, he just *started* to sink. Jesus **took hold of him.** It doesn't say Jesus picked him up and carried him back to the boat. He ***took hold of him.*** Perhaps grabbed him by the hand. Notice also Scripture says **they got into the boat.** It doesn't say Jesus hauled Peter back into the boat. It seems they got into the boat *together*. I am thinking that Peter put his hand in Jesus' hand, and together they walked on the water back to the boat. I am thinking that the end of this story is not Peter sinking, but Peter walking with Jesus, dependent upon Him, holding onto Him, eyes fixed on Him. That Peter used his fear to encounter the Lord in a new, deep, and dependent way, and, connected to Jesus, he walked through the storm to safety.

Developing Our Relationship With God Through Emotions

David strikes me as someone who indeed has developed a deep and tender relationship with the Lord. Although he committed adultery, murdered his loyal friend, and struggled with his rebellious children, still God calls him **a man after My own heart** (Acts 13:22, 1Sam 13:14). As I read through the Psalms, I can't help but think that his bold honesty before God was one of the keys in developing the depth of that relationship. Recorded in Second Samuel is David's last psalm:

These are the last words of David:
> **"The oracle of David son of Jesse,**
> > **the oracle of the man exalted by the Most High,**
> **the man anointed by the God of Jacob,**
> > **Israel's singer of songs:**
> **The Spirit of the LORD spoke through me;**
> > **his word was on my tongue.**
> **The God of Israel spoke,**
> > **the Rock of Israel said to me:**
> **'When one rules over men in righteousness,**
> > **when he rules in the fear of God,**
> **he is like the light of morning at sunrise**
> > **on a cloudless morning,**
> **like the brightness after rain**
> > **that brings the grass from the earth.'**
> **Is not my house right with God?**
> **Has he not made with me an everlasting covenant,**
> > **arranged and secured in every part?**
> **Will he not bring to fruition my salvation**
> > **and grant me my every desire?"**
> > > > > 2 Samuel 23:1-5 NIV

I love how David calls himself **the man anointed by the God of Jacob** and **Israel's singer of songs** (**sweet psalmist** in the NASB). David boldly describes how God has spoken to him. He is truly secure in God's love, revealing to us how God told him that he has ruled righteously and is as bright as the dawn on a cloudless day. This is truly a man who has learned how to draw near to God.

Think how difficult it is to comfort someone who denies that they have been hurt, or who pretends that they are not angry, or who does not even recognize their own pain. It's so critical that we pour it out to the Lord, dump it out – He can handle it! Hold nothing back. If we lock our pain deep inside, we barricade our hearts from His comfort. But when we are honest with ourselves, and with God, we open that door to receive His comfort.

I'd like to take you to a time in my life just before my daughter went off to college. Although God had confirmed to me many times that this college was His choice for her, as the day of her departure was approaching, I reached a point when honesty with God was so frightening that I didn't think I could possibly go there ...

I had awakened at 4 AM with a pit in my stomach, and I headed to the beach, knowing that there was something I had to acknowledge before God. It was one of those deep nasty belief systems that I wanted to pretend that I really didn't believe in. The Holy Spirit wasn't letting me remain in my state of denial, though. His Light of Truth was exposing this area of my heart, yet I really didn't want to admit ownership of it.

I abandoned my feeble attempts to pretty it up and pretend I really didn't subscribe to these horrendous thoughts. He already knew it anyway; no sense trying to cover myself in fig leaves and hide behind a bush. My anger burst out in deep wracking sobs, accusing and attacking: "You didn't protect me when I went away to school! I was raped when I went away to school! How can I trust You to protect my daughter going away to New York City!" I stood there horrified as my challenge hung in the air. I didn't even know how to start repenting.

Exhausted and spent, I waited. He was ... He was ... shockingly ... silent.

I was caught off guard. So many times in the past I had poured out my heart to Him, in anger, confusion, doubt, uncertainty, frustration, repentance, pain, terror – and as I sought Him with all my heart, He had <u>always</u> come to me; He had <u>always</u> been there; He had <u>always</u> answered me. Whether it was a glimpse of what He was doing in the tragedy, or His encouragement to stand firm and press on, or His comfort and love and reassurance that He was indeed in control and that He loved me passionately and would never leave me, He had always showed up powerfully. He rarely gave me the answer I sought or expected, but He always gave me Himself.

But not this time. My breath came in shuddering gulps as darkness pressed in and I heard ... nothing. The night was beyond still. Not even the smallest touch from His Spirit to let me know that He was listening. Nothing. I had never felt so alone.

I had no idea how to handle this. Somehow, perhaps because of the greatness of my anger and fear, I couldn't just simply walk away. I stood there in the emptiness for what seemed like ages, puzzled ... and very afraid. Had I gone too far this time? Had I said – no, shouted – the unspeakable? Maybe those verses about Him never leaving us or forsaking us didn't apply if we insulted the Creator of the Universe by questioning His trustworthiness.

Even though I could not feel His Presence in any way I was familiar with, I seemed to sense that He somehow <u>was</u> there and He was ... waiting. Waiting? Although I thought I had passed Him the ball, it felt like the ball was still in my court, and it was still my turn to make a move.

Then, somehow, I don't even know how, something welled up inside of me, and before I even knew what I was doing I declared, boldly and with no possible chance of turning back, "Lord, I choose to trust You. Even though You have not demonstrated Yourself to be trustworthy in the least in this arena" (yes, I really said that) "I <u>choose</u> to trust that You will protect my daughter."

In the thunderous silence that followed, I turned around and left. As I walked home, I had a sense that I had made a covenant with God. My words were sealed. There was no turning back. *I had chosen to trust Him, I had chosen to believe that He would protect her, and I would spend the rest of my life walking out that commitment.*

It wasn't until the next day that He answered me. I was at service at church, worshipping and praising Him with all my being, when He unexpectedly said to me, "You don't understand protection."

I caught my breath. I didn't know where He was going with this, but He was speaking so deeply in my spirit that I did not want to miss a word. The next of what He spoke was a series of impressions on my heart, His Spirit speaking to mine in Spirit-language that communicates in a few moments what it would take paragraphs to say in human words. As best as I can convey it to you, He told me something like this:

"You deeply understand what I mean when I say that in all things I am working for the good of those who love Me. People may look in on your life and declare that what you are enduring is not good, but you know that I define good in a way that is beyond human comprehension. You trust to My greater plan, and deep in your heart you grasp the truth that because You are in My hands, everything occurring in your life is for your good.

"I want you to understand protection in the same way. People may look in on your daughter's life and say that she has not been protected. Because they can only see with human eyes, they may not call this protection. But My protection is eternal and infinite, vastly more powerful than any human protection could ever be. And there will be a day when, just as you will clearly see how I was always working for your good, you will also be able to fully see My divine protection."

Divine protection! What exactly is that? I have no idea, but I do know that whatever it is, it is immeasurably better than any earthly protection I could possibly imagine. I think He gave me those words in my language, "divine protection," because He knew I would need to hold on to those words.

Looking back at that moment of unbearable silence on the beach, I see that He was waiting for me to step out in *faith. With my human eyes, I had been unable to see His protection of me. He was waiting for me to take a great leap of faith, to trust Him for what I could not see. Indeed, Scripture defines faith as **being certain of what you do not see** (Heb 11:1). I understand now that what had welled up in me was the Holy Spirit's gift of greater faith, enabling me to do what I could not do by myself: to declare a covenant of trust in Him, even in areas where I was unable to see His hand at work.*

Celeste Li
Jupiter, Florida

When we pour out our heart to Him and wait in stillness for His response, it seems He becomes a refuge for us.

Yes, my soul, find rest in God...
Trust in him at all times, you people;
pour out your hearts to him, for God is our refuge.
Psalm 62:8 NIV

The world may judge us in our pain: "That shouldn't hurt." We may even judge ourselves: "That shouldn't bother me." But the reality is that we are hurt, we are in pain. And if we deny the anger, pain, and hurt, it may fester into rage, wrath, and bitterness. Anger is not leading us to God if it is stuffed, because if we are stuffing, we are deluding ourselves, and God will not work in deception. God gives us no other choice but to admit it, and take it to Him to heal.

I find that it is not easy for me to admit my emotions – to myself or to my God – but it seems that He refuses to work in my dishonesty. I have learned that I can't find Him when I walk in denial and deception – but that He meets me in my honesty, no matter how sinful I am. I have discovered that *only He* can reveal the cause of the turmoil in my soul, and *only He* can bring me true peace and healing.

Grab your journal and ask the Lord to reveal any dark emotions churning around in your heart. Don't be afraid to be transparent before Him – He already knows the state of your heart; He is only waiting for your readiness in order to reveal.

Avoid Getting Mired in Honest Emotions

The pain of this world brings out the deepest of emotions. As I watch people process through their pain, I notice that some seem to heal and come to a new place, but others seem to get stuck. Some seem to travel on a journey through anger, unforgiveness, or grief, and arrive on the other side of the pain scarred but healed, with a new depth of relationship with God. But others seem to get mired in bitterness and resentment, never reaching a place of healing and deeper relationship with the Lord. I think that when we are in pain, and we get mired in our emotions, it may be an indication that our emotions have moved from a normal human response to a place of sin.

Psychologist Dominic Herbst is the founder of *Restoring Relationships*, a ministry that brings healing and restoration to troubled youths and hurting families. He explains that we must face our pain, and admit the depth of our pain and how it has affected our lives – but if we *stay* there, we will remain in a place of "selfish regret for our own personal loss."[1] Somehow, there is a fine line between pouring out our emotions to God and falling into the trap of selfishness, self pity, and absorption with self. Herbst explains that the secret to avoiding that trap is repentance.

But why would someone who was abused need to repent? Or someone who has cancer? Or someone whose spouse betrayed them? Or someone who lost their home in a fire, their leg in a car accident, their child to a murderer? I can hear your piercing questions already, for I have demanded answers to these questions myself.

Herbst goes on to say that we are called to repent for "not trusting Him for the wound you experienced."[2]

I am having trouble wrapping my mind around this. In the depth of my pain and sorrow and loss, God is calling me to repent for not *trusting* Him? Yes, I believe that is His call. To repent for not trusting His sovereignty, for not trusting His plan for my life and lives of those I love, for not trusting that He knows what He is doing. To repent for not trusting myself to His hands. For not trusting Him to heal. For not trusting that He is bigger than my pain, and has miraculous healing in store for me.

This is pretty heavy. Let's take it Biblically.

You are probably pretty familiar with the verse, **"In your anger do not sin; do not let the sun go down on your anger"** (Eph 4:26). As I wrestled with the emotion of anger, I was really hung up on this verse. The Bible seems to indicate that anger is not a sin, but it is a normal human emotion when we have been hurt or violated. But – I have *only one day* to be angry? Violated, crushed, betrayed, my pain more intense than I can even comprehend, and I am supposed to process all this and find healing before the sun goes down?

Well, that's what the verse seems to say. And since my anger didn't dissipate in a day, the only way that I could ensure that I wasn't sinning was to stuff the anger. To hide it deep inside of me. To pretend that I was a good Christian and I didn't have any anger that lasted past sundown.

For those of you who have tried that tactic, I don't have to tell you how poorly it works. How anger stuffed will eek out the cracks, ooze out through open doors and windows, explode out by blowing off the roof. It's one of those emotions that simply won't stay under cover. Psalm

SEVEN ~ THE LIFE OF THE HEART

39 describes how stuffed emotions are a turmoil growing to the bursting point (Ps 39:1-3).

So how do we reconcile the reality of our humanness with that verse? Dominic Herbst's discussion began to make the answer more clear to me. He went to Ephesians 4:26 in another translation and then to the Greek.

"Be angry, and do not sin:" do not let the sun go down on your wrath.

Ephesians 4:26 NKJV

The NKJV translates the first word **anger** and the second word **wrath** – *because they are two different words.*

Anger is *orge*, "anger as a state of mind."[3] But **wrath** is *thumos*, "wrath as the outburst of a vengeful mind."[4] *Thumos* is derived from the word that means tempest, thus *thumos* means "to move impetuously, particularly as the air or wind, a violent motion or passion of the mind."[5]

Anger is a natural human response to the pain that this fallen world inflicts upon us. Anger is not sin. We can use anger in a Godly way to drive us to God as we open our hearts to Him in all honesty.

Anger becomes sin when it becomes wrath that the sun goes down on. Just what does wrath entail? Let's look at that definition again. Outbursts. Violence. Explosions of rage. Tempests, cyclones, hurricanes of temper.

We can easily see how loud explosions of rage would be sin. But I don't believe that it *has to be* loud and explosive to be defined as wrath. I think that obsession with the offense is also wrath. If we are constantly talking about it, thinking about it, unable to release it. I also believe that behaviors like manipulation, subtle sarcastic digs, thinly veiled slander, and criticism disguised as prayer requests are born not out of simple human anger, but out of the wrath of black unforgiving hearts. And I want to call our attention to one more word in that definition of *thumos*: "vengeful." If we are vengeful, if we are unforgiving, then we have *thumos*, and that is sin. No sense denying it.

Now I'm going to extrapolate a bit more so that I don't let stuffers like myself off the hook. When we turn our anger inward, the tempest moves *inside of ourselves*. It is no less a tempest because it is wreaking its havoc *inside* instead of outside. I believe that anger that is stuffed is also wrath.

How fast does anger progress to wrath? For some, very quickly.

Are you with me? I'm going to challenge us a bit further on this issue of anger.

Honest Emotions: The Next Level

Let all bitterness and wrath and anger and clamor and slander be put away from you, along with all malice. Be kind to one another, tender-hearted, forgiving each other, just as God in Christ also has forgiven you.

Ephesians 4:31-32

But now you also, put them all aside: anger, wrath, malice, slander, and abusive speech from your mouth.

Colossians 3:8

So ... if anger is okay, and only wrath is a sin, why do Ephesians and Colossians command us to put aside both **anger** (*orge*) and **wrath** (*thumos*)?

Not long ago, God had something to say to me about this issue ...

I was angry. My sins in the situation were minimal. The other person's? Huge. Huge and glaring. And God wanted me to go to that person and apologize. For what? My minimal sins? And that person wasn't even admitting they did anything wrong!

"Why do I have to go first?" I complained to God.

"I'm not asking you to go first," His answer came back.

Excellent, I thought. The other person will have to apologize first.

But God continued, "I already went first. Now it's your turn."

Celeste Li
Jupiter, Florida

Yes, He has already gone first. He has forgiven me a debt I could never repay. And He expects me to release my hurtful emotions to Him and to pass on His forgiveness to others.

Indeed, anger is a natural *human* response to the pain of loss, to the frustrations of disappointment, to the wounding of rejection, to the horrors of injustice. Anger is our natural response when life isn't turning out as planned. A whole host of other emotions are also *natural human responses* to our pain: depression, hopelessness, fear, doubt, insecurity, distrust, self-pity, helplessness, resentment, jealousy, disillusionment, anxiety, to name a few.

But God calls us to a higher level. Not to deny or stuff our feelings, but to acknowledge them, to allow ourselves to experience them, to do whatever it takes to process through the pain and trauma, and then to release them to Him. For some deep heart wounds, the process may be a journey through healing classes, counseling, mentoring, or other places of recovery. The goal of this journey is to choose to forgive and release, and to love and to allow Him to heal us.

If I can't reach a place of forgiveness and love before the sun goes down, I kneel down before I go to bed and I pray, "Lord, I am sorry for my anger (or depression, or fear, or whatever). I choose to trust *You*. I am willing to be made willing to forgive and to love." I may need to pray that prayer many times over many days. He may lead me to Scriptures or places or people to help me in the process of forgiveness and healing. And, as I obey His direction and open my heart to Him, as He begins to work love and forgiveness and healing in my heart, eventually, over time, there seems to be no room for the sinful emotions any more.

Does this mean that we will never speak to the person about the pain they have caused us? We will really need to hear from the Lord on this issue. I think His answer will be different for each person and each situation. We will want to first engage in the healing process as He directs, inviting Him to work in our hearts and bring us to full forgiveness and healing. We will want to be certain that the Holy Spirit really is sending us to speak to the one who hurt us, and to be certain that it is not for our benefit or to dump our anger, but for the purpose of *restoration of the relationship*. Some people may not be spiritually mature enough to receive the information that they have hurt us. They may be in so much pain themselves that they cannot take on the additional pain of knowing that they (purposefully or inadvertently) hurt someone they care about. These people need our grace, not our dump.

Author and Christian radio show host Brant Hansen, in his book *Unoffendable*, puts it this way:

> God is "allowed" anger, yes. And other things, too, that we're not, like say — for starters — vengeance ... God is allowed to judge too. You're not. We can trust Him with judgment, because He is very different from us. He is perfect. We can trust Him with anger. His character allows this. Ours doesn't ... Yes, we get angry. Can't avoid it ...

We aren't to just pretend anger away or feel guilty for the initial emotion of anger. But we are to deal with it, with the goal of eradicating it ... I now know that anger can't live here. I can't keep it. I can't try it on, can't see how it looks. I have to ... drop that thing, much as I want to wear it awhile ... I can't handle anger. I don't have the strength of character to do it. Only God does. We can trust Him with it. Jesus gets angry, but His character is beyond question, so He's entitled.[6]

I can't take emotions like anger and try them on or wear them for awhile. Hmm ... this is a new perspective for me. Let's spend a few minutes journaling.

Sanctification of Our Hearts

It's time to leave emotions behind for now and move into deeper waters: the purification of our hearts. My *Greek Word Study* explains that although heart, *kardia*, can be used to mean "the seat of desires, feelings, affections, passions, impulses," there is yet a more profound understanding of this word. "The heart represents ... the sphere of God's influence in the human life."[7] God, by His Holy Spirit, exerts His influence *in our hearts*. When we submit our will, our desires, our beliefs to God, that submission occurs *in our hearts*. And rebellion occurs in our hearts also, for we learned in Chapter 5, *Demolishing Idols*, that when we are trapped in idolatry, we have set up idols *in our hearts* (Eze 14:3-4).

Our hearts are not hidden from God who **searches the hearts** (Rom 8:27) and **examines our hearts** (1 Th 2:4). All that is hidden in our hearts – both righteousness and unrighteousness – exerts great power, influencing our thoughts, words, beliefs, attitudes, and actions. We cannot make our hearts right in God's sight, nor can we purify our hearts – for it is God Himself who gives us a new heart:

"Moreover, I will give you a new heart and put a new spirit within you; and I will remove the heart of stone from your flesh and give you a heart of flesh. I will put My Spirit within you and cause you to walk in My statutes, and you will be careful to observe My ordinances."

Ezekiel 36:26-27

What will it take for God to remove your heart of stone? What has hardened it? Suppressed emotions, denial, unforgiveness? Recall my heart of stone in Chapter 3, hardened as I lost my identity and fell into pride and striving. Hebrews 3 warns against an evil, unbelieving heart that is hardened by the deceitfulness of sin, disobedience, and unbelief. Be still before Him, then journal what He reveals.

Submitting Our Hearts to God's Rule

The heart is the deepest deepest part of us, where free will resides. We can choose to submit our hearts to the rule of God, or to the rule of Satan. Our hearts are the abode of the Holy Spirit within us, and the seat of His control of our lives as He communicates with our spirits. As we submit more of our hearts to Him, as we give more and more of our free will over to His control, the Holy Spirit shines in our hearts in greater measure.

At the time of our salvation, our hearts are made right before God. And then we enter the process of sanctification of our hearts as the Holy Spirit works within us. As we are being conformed to the image of Christ, transformed and sanctified, the Lord is bit by bit removing our hearts of stone and giving us soft hearts that beat for Him. We allow Him to expose the sins in our hearts that are revealed by our speech, our emotions, or our behaviors. As we receive His revelation and acknowledge the sins in our hearts, He begins to fashion our hearts to please Him (Ps 32:15). And I have discovered another way He molds our hearts:

Delight yourself in the LORD;
And He will give you the desires of your heart.
Psalm 37:4

When we delight ourselves in Him, He begins to conform our hearts to His. When just being with Him becomes our greatest delight, we will spend much time in His Presence – and during these times in His Presence, He molds our hearts to look like His, and His will becomes our will. When His purposes are accomplished, He is indeed giving us the desires of our own hearts. This process is truly the working of the Holy Spirit within our hearts.

"... whoever drinks of the water that I shall give him will never thirst. But the water that I shall give him will become in him a fountain of water springing up into everlasting life ... If anyone thirsts, let him come to Me and drink. He who believes in Me, as the Scripture has said, out of his heart will flow rivers of living water." But this He spoke concerning the Spirit, whom those believing in Him would receive...
John 4:13-14, 7:37-39 NKJV

The Holy Spirit is the well of water springing up to eternal life. The Holy Spirit flows from our **heart.** The NASB says the rivers of living water flow from our **innermost being,** and the King James says from our **belly.** As we grow up in the Lord and He transforms our hearts and conforms us to the image of His Son, the Holy Spirit flows to us and in us and through us and from us in greater measure.

The enemy wages war against our hearts. We battle the enemy by guarding our hearts, protecting them, since our hearts affect all parts of our lives. How do we guard our hearts?

Do not be anxious about anything, but in everything, by prayer and petition, with thanksgiving, present your requests to God. And the peace of God, which transcends all understanding, will guard your hearts and your minds in Christ Jesus.

Philippians 4:6-7 NIV

When we submit to God, and trust in Him, He promises to grant us His peace that will guard our hearts and minds. Hearts and minds guarded with His peace protect us from going down pathways such as fear and pride and control.

Hearts and minds trusting in Him protect us from giving in to the enemy's plans.

It is essential that we seek the Holy Spirit to *lead our hearts*.

For all who are being led by the Spirit of God, these are sons of God.

Romans 8:14

Learning how to be led by the Spirit is a sign of maturity in Christ. Those who have not yet learned how to be led by the Spirit, or have not chosen to submit their heart to the Holy Spirit's leading, are yet immature in the Lord.

May the Lord direct your hearts into the love of God and into the steadfastness of Christ.

2 Thessalonians 3:5

Direct in my *Greek Word Study* means "to guide straight towards or upon something ... to guide or direct one's way or journey to a place."[8]

Indeed, our hearts are on a journey. When we invite the Lord to lead them, He will guide and direct them straight into the love of God and the steadfastness of Christ. His Spirit will lead our hearts by directing our spirit according to the truth of His Word.

How Is Your Heart Life?

When emotions surface, when temptations arise, when offenses come, we have a choice: to follow our heart, to attempt to lead it ourselves, or to guard it and submit it to God's leadership. We can follow our hearts into sin, or submit ourselves to God and place our hearts into the gentle hands of Christ. We face decisions such as these:

- We can let unforgiveness move us to anger and revenge – or we can repent and invite God to heal our pain.

- We can let disappointment move us to depression and hopelessness – or we can pour out our heart to God and receive His comfort.

- We can let stress move us to anxiety and fear – or we can cast it upon Him and take up His easy yoke.

- We can fall in love with things of the world and chase after them and become an enemy of God (Jam 4:4), – or we can do what Jesus commands and thus become His friends (Jn 15:14).

- We can set our minds on the things of the flesh and remain hostile to God (Rom 8:7) – or we can offer our bodies as living sacrifices and thus discern the will of God (Rom 12:1-2).

When Peter started to sink, Jesus asked him, **"Why did you doubt?"** Good question. Why *did* Peter doubt? Why did he take his eyes off Jesus and fall into fear? Why do we fall into such dark emotions as anger, depression, hopelessness, disillusionment, fear? Why do we succumb to temptations? Grab a pen and mark any of the statements below that pertain to you.

I think that becoming mired in these emotions or falling into temptations can occur …

- When we don't know **the breadth and length and height and depth** of God's love for us, **the love of Christ which surpasses knowledge** (Eph 3:18-19). When we begin to work to earn it – or to seek love in other places. When we have forgotten that He takes such delight in us that He rejoices over us with singing (Zeph 3:17).

- When we hold onto expectations that are not promised in Scripture. When we think that God's protection means that we will have no pain or suffering. When we don't believe Jesus when He says, **"In this world you will have trouble"** (Jn 16:33 NIV).

- When we distrust God. When we don't trust Him to take care of us and to meet all of our needs **according to his glorious riches in Christ Jesus** (Phil 4:19 NIV).

- When we are striving to earn our own righteousness, forgetting that we have **become the righteousness of God in Him** (2Cor 5:21).

- When we feel a need to control every part of our lives and the lives of those we love, not realizing that **all the peoples of the earth are regarded as nothing. He does as he pleases with the powers of heaven and the peoples of the earth. No one can hold back his hand or say to him: "What have you done?"** (Dan 4:35 NIV).

- When we look to our idols for our security, trusting in **chariots** and **horses** instead of **the name of the LORD our God** (Ps 20:7 NIV).

- When we forget that it is *the Lord* who **gives you the ability to produce wealth** (Dt 8:18), that He is the One who **fills us with skill to perform every work** (Ex 35:30-35), and that **every perfect gift is from above** (Jam 1:17).

- When we have lost our identity, forgetting **how great is the love the Father has lavished on us, that we should be called children of God! And that is what we are!** (1Jn 3:1 NIV). When we fall into pride, and forget that we are princes and princesses – not because we have slain the dragon, but because we are children of the King. When that pride brings us to start to think that we can earn God's love and acceptance.

- When we walk in self-sufficiency and independence, forgetting that **"apart from Me you can do nothing"** (Jn 15:5).

- When we forget that He owns *everything*: **The earth is the LORD's, and everything in it, the world, and all who live in it** (Ps 24:1 NIV).

- When we are having trouble surrendering to His will, forgetting that the only reason we are here is to give Him pleasure. **"You are worthy, O Lord our God, to receive glory and honor and power. For you created everything, and it is for your pleasure that they exist and were created"** (Rev 4:11 NLT).

In contrast to all these painful emotions stands God's unshakable joy and His true deep everlasting peace. A peace and joy that pervade our being only because we have been made righteous by the blood of the Lamb.

That peace and joy is always available to us, but at times we may be unable to receive it. To be released from the turmoil of difficult emotions, and to receive God's true deep peace and unshakable joy, will only come when our hearts are right with God. My *Greek Word Study* further delineates God's peace: "Those who hope for it, while continuing in their iniquity, are self-deceived."[9] When we remember the Truths we have forgotten and repent of our pride that keeps us entangled in Satan's lies, unwanted emotions will fall, and joy and peace will prevail.

I'd like to introduce you to my friend Maria. This astounding woman has eyes bright with the fire of the Lord, a heart of passion for her Savior, a precious family filled with the Holy Spirit, and blossoming ministry work every place the Lord stations her. I've asked her to wrap up this chapter by sharing the journey of sanctification her heart has traveled, from lies and pain, to truth and everlasting peace.

We were the only Hispanics in an Irish and Italian middle class neighborhood. In order to deal with the prejudice, I learned as a young child to pretend that prejudice didn't exist, and to make myself invisible and stay under the radar. I so wanted to belong, to fit in. I became good at being whatever it was I thought people wanted me to be. I learned how to perform well for the approval of my parents, my coaches, and the other authority figures in my life, and went to college on a full scholarship.

I had begun using alcohol and drugs in high school to numb the pain of not belonging, and this escalated in college to DT's and blackouts. I lost my friends, I almost lost my scholarship, and my sense of self worth was filled with shame and regret. I hit rock bottom when I awoke out of a blackout in the back of a cop car. I spent the next few weeks white-knuckle detoxing at a friend's house and going to every AA meeting I could. I was desperate. I was 21 years old sitting in meetings where I did not want to be. It didn't seem fair.

I remained clean, and set out to fill the void in my life by proving my self worth. I tried to earn, to do, to be all those things that I thought would fill me. I just kept running to the next thing, hoping this would fix it and I would be happy.

During this time I came to know Jesus as a real Person who cared about me and wanted to be in relationship with me. He was so sweet. Yet somehow I bought into the lie that I had to prove my worth to God because of my past. I thought that because I couldn't be as "spiritual" as I thought I should be, I had lost God's approval. So I slowly started going back to filling the void inside me with new people, new places, new things, etc.

I got married and started a family, but was never satisfied. I thought if we could just move into a bigger house with a bigger yard, closer to church, everything would be okay. I was still obsessed with fitting in. It wasn't long before the masks that I had perfected to the outside world were crumbling. I became depressed, angry, and emotionally unavailable. I tried to fix myself with more Bible study and fasting, but it was no help.

God started talking to me about going through Recovery again. I had gone through Recovery twenty years ago; I knew how hard the fourth and fifth steps were and I did not want to go digging all that stuff up again. Nor did I want the people at my church to know how messed up I was. But ... what were the chances that two dear friends – who lived on my remote street and would be such a powerful support for me – would be going to the same Recovery meeting that I was considering right now?

I had to decide what I wanted more: my pride and its pain, or a possible way out of my pain. I knew my coping wasn't working. I chose the way out of the pain that God was offering.

I had to admit my guilt, sarcasm, and manipulation. I had to confront my defense mechanisms of people-pleasing, rescuing others, self-pitying, denying reality, isolating, and becoming angry. I had to learn to release control and to choose humility.

Little did I know that God was using Recovery to prepare me for my husband's new job that required much travel for us. Loneliness, frequent new environments, and new people were challenges for me. But God had such wonderful things in store for me – from snow-covered mountains to endless desert, immense canyons, picturesque lakes and Pacific beaches. But the greatest blessing was the incredible privilege of going to Recovery meetings all around the country, for I found that the God who loves me here in my home state was there in that little country church meeting in Georgia, those Wednesday night office meetings in the Arizona desert, the mega church meetings in Texas.

Just as Jesus said to the paralyzed man on the mat, "Do you want to get well?" I also have a choice: to remain

*paralyzed in my pain and despair, or to get off my mat and
choose to trust God and work my program and the 12 steps.
Today I choose to trust God by refusing to believe the lie that
says I am not good enough, and replacing it with His Truth
that tells me I am complete in Him and that He will never
leave me or forsake me. I choose to trust God and reject
the lie that says I am too messed up to ever get better, and
replace it with His Truth that says, "He who began a good
work in me will be faithful to complete it" (Ph 1:6). I have
learned that I do not need the approval of others to validate
my self worth, for the truth is that I belong to Jesus, that He
loves me and He knows my name. He has carved my name
on the palms of His hands by dying on the cross for me.*

Maria
Harrisburg, Pennsylvania

Maria has journeyed a difficult road of sanctification,
which has brought her to increasingly sweet and deep
levels of intimacy with Jesus. She opened her heart to the
work of the Holy Spirit, and He has purified and healed.
Rivers of living water now flow unobstructed – in and to
and through and from her heart.

Questions Chapter 7: The Life of the Heart

Memory Verse:

**Trust in him at all times, O people;
pour out your hearts to him,
for God is our refuge.**

Psalm 62:8 NIV

1) Think how difficult it is to comfort someone who
denies that they have been hurt, or who pretends that they
are not angry, or who does not even recognize their own
pain. If we lock our pain deep inside, we barricade our

hearts from His comfort. But when we are honest with ourselves, and with God, we open that door to receive His comfort. No one passes through this life unscathed. What pain have you walled off from God?

2) Write a psalm after Psalm 13's pattern. Pour out your heart to God; then end your psalm as David did, with declarations of praise and trust.

3) From the section, *Avoid Getting Mired in Honest Emotions*, what does it mean to "not trust God for the wound you experienced"?

How will you give your heart to God to heal and lead?

4) Describe a time when Jesus called you to come to Him on the water, and you used your fear to drive you to grip His hand and depend on Him. What was the outcome of your choices?

5) Be still in the Holy Spirit's Presence and ask Him to reveal deep emotions or heart pain that He wants to deal with at this time. Then go back to the section *How Is Your Heart Life?* and look over the bullets that you marked. Ask the Lord to expose any lie that your heart believes that is keeping you mired here. Repent of believing that lie and of aligning your thoughts with the enemy. Make a covenant with the Lord to believe His truth. Look up, meditate on, and memorize the Scriptures supplied in order to partner with the Holy Spirit in uprooting that lie and replacing it with God's truth.

I have found that in order for the lie to be fully uprooted and replaced with truth, I must spend a number of weeks or even many months casting down the lie and implanting His truth in my heart. For me, some of these battles to replace lies with truth have raged for years.

Chapter 8
A Walk of Repentance

ell you've got courage, tackling a chapter entitled "Repentance." I considered giving it a prettier or more inviting title, but, then, that would have been fairly deceitful. Before we jump in, let's reflect first on another challenging word, *sanctification*.

What does it mean to be sanctified? Studying the Greek and Hebrew words and their roots, the key to understanding sanctification is to grasp the idea of being "set apart," or "consecrated."[1] Here are some definitions of sanctification from my *Greek and Hebrew Word Studies:*

- To make holy, clean, or pure.

- "To set apart from a common to sacred use."[2]

- To free from defilements and impurities.

- "Its fundamental idea is separation, consecration, devotion" to God, "sharing in God's purity and abstaining from earth's defilements."[3]

- When the object being sanctified is "filthy or common," sanctification "can only be accomplished by separation or withdrawal," such as withdrawal from "selfishness" and from "fellowship with the world."[4]

I am thinking of the sacred vessels used in the tabernacle. How they were cleansed and purified and set apart, to be used only for the Lord's service. I am thinking about us as vessels of the Holy Spirit, how much we desire to be cleansed and purified in order to be a welcoming vessel for the flow of the Holy Spirit. How we long to be set apart, to be used solely for the Lord's service. We've talked a lot about separating ourselves from worldly things in order to draw closer to the Lord. In this chapter, we're going to explore another critical pathway to sanctification: repentance.

Isn't Repentance Just a One-Time Thing?

Good question. I'm glad you asked. I've asked the same question myself. After we are saved, do we need to do any further repenting? Isn't everything simply "under the blood"? Let's explore.

We are called to repent and ask for forgiveness of our sins when we first come to the Lord (Mt 4:14, Mk 1:4-5, Lk 24:46-47, Acts 2:37-38). And it is true that all our sins, past, present, and future are forgiven at the cross when we receive Jesus as our Lord and Savior, **for there is no condemnation for those who are in Christ Jesus** (Rom 8:1). **Your sins have been forgiven you for His name's sake** (1 Jn 2:12). Our **faith is credited as righteousness** ... and blessed are we **whose lawless deeds have been forgiven, whose sins have been covered ... whose sin**

the Lord will not take into account (Rom 4:5-8). God is the One who is **able to keep you from stumbling, and to make you stand in the presence of His glory blameless with great joy** (Jude 1:24).

Yet God's cherished plan for us goes beyond that first step of salvation. It encompasses *sanctification.* After He rescues us and transfers us to the Kingdom of His Son, we embark on a lifetime of being conformed to Jesus' image:

For those whom He foreknew, He also predestined to become conformed to the image of His Son.
Romans 8:29

The process of conforming involves revelation by the Holy Spirit that something in our life is not aligned with Jesus.

- This may be an ongoing sin, a place where we know that we are in disobedience but that we have not yet addressed in our with walk with Christ.

- Or this could be an area where we have once walked in obedience, but have now fallen back into sin.

- Or it may even be a past overlooked sin that we forgot about, or never took the time to talk to God about and to ask His forgiveness.

- And sometimes, as we come closer to God, the Holy Spirit exposes as sinful a behavior or heart attitude that we did not even realize was displeasing to Him.

When the Holy Spirit has convicted us, *repentance* is the next step in the pathway to being conformed. Let's listen to this command in Revelation, as Jesus speaks to the Church at Ephesus:

"Therefore remember from where you have fallen, and repent and do the deeds you did at first; or else

**I am coming to you and will remove your lampstand
out of its place—unless you repent."**

Revelation 2:5

The writer of Hebrews recognizes how repentance
is essential to our walk, and even calls repentance an
elementary teaching:

**... we have much to say, and it is hard to explain,
since you have become dull of hearing. For though
by this time you ought to be teachers, you have
need again for someone to teach you the elementary
principles of the oracles of God, and you have come
to need milk and not solid food. For everyone who
partakes only of milk is not accustomed to the word
of righteousness, for he is an infant. But solid food
is for the mature, who because of practice have their
senses trained to discern good and evil. Therefore
leaving the elementary teaching about the Christ,
let us press on to maturity, not laying again a
foundation of repentance from dead works and faith
toward God ...**

Hebrews 5:11-6:1

When we are unable to move past elementary teachings,
we become **dull of hearing.** If we partake only of milk,
we are **not accustomed to the word of righteousness.**
We are not open to the Holy Spirit's conviction of sin and
we are not willing to align our hearts and lives in right
relationship with God and others. The NLT says it bluntly,

**And a person who is living on milk isn't very far
along in the Christian life and doesn't know much
about doing what is right ... So let us stop going
over the basics of Christianity again and again ...
Surely we don't need to start all over again with
the importance of turning away from evil deeds
[repentance] and placing our faith in God.**

Hebrews 11:13, 6:1 NLT

We can also watch the effects of repentance among the Corinthians, Christians who had wandered off track. Paul explained to them,

... now I am happy ... because your sorrow led you to repentance. For you became sorrowful as God intended ... Godly sorrow brings repentance that leads to salvation and leaves no regret, but worldly sorrow brings death.

2 Corinthians 7:9-10 NIV

Godly sorrow led the Corinthians to **repentance**. Repentance led them to **salvation**, in this context indicating sanctification, conforming to the image of Christ. The conviction of the Holy Spirit causes momentary guilt, and in humility we are driven to repent, which leads to sanctification as God forgives us through Jesus' blood and the Holy Spirit cleanses us. Darkness is cleared from our hearts and we are open to receive a greater filling of the Holy Spirit. Conviction feels cleansing and uplifting. As we accept the truth of our sin, repent, and receive His mercy and grace, we may feel lighter as the burden of our sin is lifted from us. Peace and joy result.

However, sometimes, when the Holy Spirit convicts us and we repent, instead of feeling cleansed and uplifted, we may spiral down into feelings of *condemnation*. This is an attack of the enemy. Persistent guilt and condemnation are *not* from the Holy Spirit. Shame, humiliation, condemnation, embarrassment, unforgiveness of self, and persistent guilt are *not* from God; they are from the forces of darkness. We are assured that there is no shame in Jesus:

"See, I lay a stone in Zion,
    a chosen and precious cornerstone,
and the one who trusts in him
    will never be put to shame."

1 Peter 2:6 NIV

It is crucial that we recognize within ourselves the difference between *God's conviction* and *Satan's condemnation*.

- Conviction calls us to repentance. It lifts us up, reminding us of who we are in Christ, and calls to mind the Holy Spirit's promise to be with us and strengthen us. Conviction fortifies our faith in upcoming victory, and gives us the courage and strength to press on.

- Condemnation beats us down, convincing us that we are "bad people." It drives us to fear, shame, and unworthiness. It amplifies unforgiveness of self. Condemnation breeds hopelessness and deceives us into thinking that we will never win.

One of the Holy Spirit's jobs is to guide us into all truth (Jn 16:13). He speaks truth to us, exposing our sins. This is called conviction, and His purpose here is to bring us to repentance and conform us to Christ.

However, when the Holy Spirit convicts us, if we are mired in self-hatred and self-judgment, unable to forgive ourselves and unable to receive God's grace, we will be wide open to enemy attack. We are positioned to be overwhelmed with thoughts of self-incrimination, causing us to spiral down into self-condemnation. Receiving convicting truth *without grace* can result in condemnation.

But if we have been able to forgive ourselves, to leave behind sins of worthlessness and self-judgment, then, when the Holy Spirit exposes our sins, we will be open to God's grace and forgiveness. When we repent, we will receive not Satan's condemnation, but God's sanctification. Receiving convicting truth *with grace* can result in sanctification.

Satan Attempts to Pervert Repentance

When we are in mid-process of repentance and sanctification, Satan can use unforgiveness of self to get a foothold and barrage us with thoughts and emotions of shame, condemnation, and burdensome guilt. When we recognize thoughts and feelings of shame and humiliation, we can choose to embrace them and align our minds with those thoughts, or we can choose to renounce and reject them. If we reject them and forgive ourselves, we are now open to receive God's sweet forgiveness and cleansing. Humility does not equal humiliation. Humility is necessary for repentance; Satan tries to distort *humility* into *humiliation*.

It seems that repentance must be very specific to be sincere, deep, and true. I believe that although God calls us to repent of all our sins in a general way, He also calls us to repent *specifically* of sins as the Holy Spirit brings conviction to our hearts.

Yet there is a fine balance here between Godly repentance and falling into Satan's trap of unnecessary repeated repentance. Satan remains our accuser. He will burden our mind with a list of old sins of which we have already repented. Some snares that may trap us into false guilt include ...

- If we have not forgiven ourselves.

- If we are pridefully trying to make up for our sins, instead of walking in the utter humility required to receive His undeserved and unearned forgiveness.

- If we are ensnared in shame.

- If we do not trust His forgiveness to be complete.

- If we are still entrenched in Satan's lies and unable to believe the truth of His Word, the truth of who He says He is and who He says we are. If we have lost our identity.

Don't allow Satan to rehash these sins over and over again, for he is only trying to **steal, kill, and destroy** our destiny by hamstringing us with false guilt.

I think it's time we pause and journal. Take some time to allow the Holy Spirit to help you process through what you have read in this chapter, and apply it to your walk with the Lord.

Ready for solid food? As we quit partaking of only milk, let's be careful to avoid the traps of shame and persistent guilt. Let's accept that repentance will be a way of life for those of us who are seeking to be conformed to His image. We'll move on now to solid food, and learn how sanctification will lead to intimacy with Jesus through ... (gulp) repentance.

Repentance Is a Gift

My *Greek Word Study* says that repentance "involves regret or sorrow, accompanied by a true change of heart toward God."[5] Note that repentance is a change of *heart*, not a perfect change of *behavior*. And if repentance is a change of heart, only God can accomplish it. We cannot manufacture repentance; **the kindness of God leads you to repentance** (Rom 2:4).

In His mercy God *leads us* to repentance. It will be a work of the Holy Spirit in our hearts; Second Thessalonians calls it **sanctification by the Spirit** (2Th 2:13). I think of repentance as a *gift* of His kindness, *granted* by God:

...if perhaps God may grant them repentance leading to the knowledge of the truth, and they may come to their senses and escape from the snare of the devil, having been held captive by him to do his will.

2 Timothy 2:25-26

How will this repentance leading to sanctification look in our own lives? When the Holy Spirit reveals sin in our thoughts, wills, hearts, actions, or lives ...

- We accept His conviction and confess our sins. We agree with God that we are in sin, and we choose to change.

- We set our wills to leave behind sinful behavior.

- We reject sinful thoughts when they enter our mind.

- We work to change our words.

- We renounce Satan's lies that we have been believing and choose to accept the truth of His Word.

- And we simultaneously acknowledge with all humility that our own human efforts will always fall short.

- Then we ask the *Holy Spirit* to change the depth of our heart.

- And we wait for Him to come and

   o *grant* us repentance,
   o change our hearts,
   o replace lies with truth, and
   o free us from the snare of the devil.

Go back over those bullets and circle all the verbs. Then write in your journal what you see is *your part*, and what you see is *the Holy Spirit's part*.

Often, after a time of sanctification, Holy Spirit will lead us through testings, not to discourage us, but to reveal to us the state of our heart that we are unable to see without those tests. To show us whether His intended heart work is complete in this area at this time, or to show us that the work is still in progress. We will be challenged to choose the right behavior, to walk out the truths that we now profess to believe, to speak the words as He commands. And each time we choose His way, His truth, or His path, the stronghold of Christ in us is strengthened and He shines more brilliantly.

When the Holy Spirit transforms our hearts, this change of behavior, actions, words, and thoughts will follow. But it does not always happen overnight. What defines true repentance is the *desire* of our heart. And the Holy Spirit's work of sanctification, of transformation, of bringing that repentance to completion, will be in His perfect timing.

Jesus Explains Repentance

My *Greek Word Study* on repentance goes on to say that "the first four Beatitudes may be taken as a descriptive of elements of true repentance."[6] Let's look them up.

> **"Blessed are the poor in spirit,**
>   **for theirs is the kingdom of heaven.**
> **Blessed are those who mourn,**
>   **for they shall be comforted.**
> **Blessed are the gentle,**
>   **for they shall inherit the earth.**
> **Blessed are those who hunger and thirst**
>   **for righteousness,**
>   **for they shall be satisfied."**
>
> Matthew 5:3-6

My *Greek Word Study* summarizes these Beatitudes in this way: "Poverty of spirit (the confession of one's spiritual helplessness), sorrow for sin, meekness, and hunger and thirst for righteousness are all characteristics of the soul that is turning to God from sin."[7]

The word **poor** in the Greek literally means "to crouch, like a beggar. Poor and helpless ... someone in abject poverty, utter helplessness, complete destitution." This is not someone who ekes out a living with hard labor, living hand-to-mouth, but someone who is "destitute of the necessities of life and subsisting on the alms from others."[8]

Poor in spirit. Imagine a humility so great that we are crouching, like a beggar before God, knowing our utter helplessness, knowing that there is nothing we can do, nothing we can offer, to earn His forgiveness, love, acceptance, or approval.

This leads to mourning our sins, which leads to gentleness, or meekness in the King James. *Prautes*. This is a complex word with many layers of meanings; I think of *prautes* as full and complete surrender. "We accept God's dealings with us as good and do not dispute or resist ... considering them as good in that they enhance the closeness of our relationship with Him."[9]

This surrender drives us to seek righteousness, to abandon lies and embrace truth, to align our lives in right relationship with God and man.

To summarize, Jesus describes repentance as

- Humility that enables us to recognize our utter helplessness

- Mourning our sinful state

- Surrendering to His good plan for our lives without fighting Him

- And desperately craving God to restore us to right relationship with Him and with others.

In this precious state, we will easily walk into the fifth Beatitude. When we are repenting and surrendering from a place of deep poverty of spirit, and we realize that in Jesus we have been granted His forgiveness, then with ease we can give that forgiveness to others. **"Blessed are the merciful, for they shall receive mercy"** (Mt 5:7). And as we forgive others, He forgives us (Mt 6:14-15).

And the culmination of this repentance and forgiveness? Beatitude number six,

**"Blessed are the pure in heart,
for they shall see God."**

Matthew 5:8

The Pure in Heart See God

If we really want to see Him, to know Him, to be ever-so-intimate in our relationship with Him, Jesus tells us that we must be pure in heart. His sweet gift to the pure in heart is that we see more of Him.

Yes, in Jesus we are fully righteous, pure, and holy, and in heaven when we are glorified with Him we will be untainted by the corruption of sin. But our walk on earth is a constant wrestling with the forces of darkness which are working to derail our weak flesh. Recall what we read in Hebrews:

For by one offering He has perfected forever those who are being sanctified.

Hebrews 10:14 NKJV

We are perfected forever and still being sanctified. Both at the same time. A great mystery indeed.

During our time on this earth, the greater our victory in Jesus over sin, the deeper our purification will be, and the more clearly we shall **see God.** We will understand Him with more piercing truth, our perceptions of His ways will be more accurate, and our abiding will become more profound. If we really want to **see God,** and are willing to seek out victory over sin, our walk will undoubtedly embrace repentance.

Before we discuss sanctification further, let's finish this section with the final Beatitudes:

"Blessed are the peacemakers, for they shall be called sons of God. Blessed are those who have been persecuted for the sake of righteousness, for theirs is the kingdom of heaven. Blessed are you when people insult you and persecute you, and falsely say all kinds of evil against you because of Me. Rejoice and be glad, for your reward in heaven is great; for in the same way they persecuted the prophets who were before you."

Matthew 5:9-12

I love that the repentance and sanctification that Jesus is summarizing culminates in a launch into Kingdom work: to be peacemakers, to bring the gospel of peace to the world. And Jesus ends with a word of warning: as we pursue this path of sanctification and Kingdom work, we will indeed be persecuted. **Rejoice and be glad.**

Sanctification and Repentance Intertwined

Before we proceed, let's pause and ask the Holy Spirit to purify our motives, for even seeking sanctification can be tainted with pride. Are we seeking God simply to *know* Him – or for healing or for resolution of problems? Are we seeking Him purely to *abide* in Him – or to gain control over others, to bring a wayward husband home or a fallen child back to Christ? Are we seeking purification because of a desire to *please* Him and to *bring Him glory* – or to avoid failure and to look good and wise and holy in front of family, friends, church?

> *Lord God, please give us hearts that seek merely to rest in Your Presence. Please give us hearts that completely trust in You, depend upon You, rely upon You to sustain us and to meet all our needs. Teach us to seek You just for You. Not for what You can do, but for <u>Yourself</u>. For who You are. Just to be with You, to be in Your Presence. Amen.*

Jesus' words in the Beatitudes reflect some of David's writings in Psalms. The man after God's own heart writes,

The LORD is near to the brokenhearted
And saves those who are crushed in spirit.

Psalm 34:18

When we are crushed in spirit, poor in spirit, brokenhearted over our sins, the Holy Spirit hovers near, ready to save and sanctify in His timing. In David's psalm of repentance after his sin with Bathsheba, he writes,

The sacrifices of God are a broken spirit;
A broken and a contrite heart, O God,
You will not despise.

Psalm 51:17

The Amplified translates **contrite** in Psalm 51 and **crushed in spirit** in Psalm 34 as **broken down with**

sorrow for sin and humbly and thoroughly penitent. Can you hear the echo in the Beatitudes?

David describes this deep repentance as a **sacrifice** to God. I agree – I do not find this to be an easy walk. Yet to those who have been trained by this discipline, **it yields the peaceful fruit of righteousness** (Heb 12:11).

I pray that you will come to treasure His gift of repentance and learn to beseech Him for it. God does recognize that our repentance is truly a sacrifice – and He will not despise it!

James details how repentance is the key to intimacy:

Draw near to God and He will draw near to you. Cleanse your hands, you sinners; and purify your hearts, you double-minded. Be miserable and mourn and weep; let your laughter be turned into mourning and your joy to gloom. Humble yourselves in the presence of the Lord, and He will exalt you.

James 4:8-10

How do we draw near to God? Since we are sinners, we cleanse our hands and purify our hearts. When we mourn our sins and humbly admit them, we are drawing near to Him, and that invites Him to draw near to us and lift us up.

Isaiah is clear on this point also:

**Behold, the LORD's hand is not so short
That it cannot save;
Nor is His ear so dull
That it cannot hear.
But your iniquities have made a separation
between you and your God,
And your sins have hidden His face from you
so that He does not hear.**

Isaiah 59:1-2

His hand is not too short and His ears are not hard of hearing! It is *our iniquities* that separate us from God. Our sins block our cries from reaching His ears, and thwart His good hand from reaching down to bless us. And it is our repentance that brings us close to Him.

Sanctification Is a Truth Walk

"Sanctify them in truth; Your word is truth."
John 17:17

Sanctification is a process with many layers; these layers at times seem to overlap and intertwine:

- The Holy Spirit reveals our sins and exposes the lies that have ensnared our hearts.

- The kindness of God brings us to repentance.

- We choose to daily set our hearts, minds, and lives to align with His truth.

- He transforms our hearts and delivers us from the snare of Satan.

- The power of the Holy Spirit working in our transformed hearts enables us to make Godly choices in our thoughts and our behaviors.

Psalm 15 explains it this way:

O LORD, who may abide in Your tent?
Who may dwell on Your holy hill?
He who walks with integrity,
And works righteousness,
And speaks truth in his heart.

Psalm 15:1-2

Abiding means that we speak truth in our heart. Abiding means a walk of integrity. Abiding means a work of righteousness. Taking our cue from Psalm 15, we learn that these disciplines can lead to abiding in His tent:

- *Speak truth in our heart:* We speak honestly with God about what *we know* hides in our heart, and He speaks honestly with us about what *He knows* hides in our heart. We *accept* His honest assessment of our heart, as well as His exposure of the lies that have entangled us. We cast down those lies and choose to believe His truths.

- *Walk with integrity:* Integrity means we are whole, complete, undivided, and morally sound. When our hearts are aligned with God's righteousness, and our minds, words, and actions align with our heart, we are walking with integrity.

- *Work righteousness:* We seek Him for purification, and co-labor with Him as He produces righteousness in us. We walk out our repentance by aligning our lives with Jesus' perfect way.

What will this process of sanctification look like in our own lives? To repent and be pure in heart and to see God? Something tells me it's not going to be quite so simple. More like a sacrifice.

Seeing God is a treasure so immeasurably rich that we crave more of Him. And His desire is, of course, to fill us more and more with His Spirit, to give us more of Himself. Yet I find that more of Him seems to come with a cost. I'd like to pass on to you a sanctification analogy that a friend shared with me.

Rocks in Our Jars of Clay

Imagine water being poured into a jar that contains many rocks. Of course the jar is limited in the amount of water it can hold because of the rocks. More water can be added only when the rocks are removed.

We are that jar. The water represents the Holy Spirit, entering us when we first surrender our lives to Jesus. God gives us as much of the Holy Spirit as we can handle; as much as will fit into the crevices between the rocks. Filled to the brim. He so wants to give us more, but the rocks are in the way. In the way of receiving more of His Spirit. Blocking intimacy with Him. Preventing the flow of the Holy Spirit to us and in us and through us and from us.

When I first visualized the imagery in my mind, I was ready to dump all those rocks out right away! Whatever they were, I wanted them out of there! I wanted more of Him! But ... it wasn't so easy.

The Rocks Are Our Sins

The rocks are our sins and strongholds. The parts of our character that are not aligned with God's character. The areas of our lives that are not conformed to the image of Christ. Habitual sins, addictions, sinful habits. Thought processes that are ungodly. Deep heart beliefs that are prideful or selfish. Lies that have ensnared us, taught to us by the world, by our experiences, by Satan. Unsurrendered areas of our hearts and lives. Unforgiveness, independence, pride. Rebellion, idolatry, control, lack of trust in Him. Self-contempt, hatred of self, perfectionism. Worry, anxiety, fear. Some of these rocks are small pebbles. Others are so much bigger they may be boulders.

- The smaller ones will be easier to remove than the larger ones.

- The ones that have been there for a shorter length of time will be easier to remove than the long-seated ones.

- The more superficial ones will be easier to remove than the deeper ones.

Deeper intimacy with Jesus comes with removing another rock. Now I am not talking about striving and earning; we could never *earn* more intimacy. God's love and acceptance of us is complete and infinite and eternal, no matter how many rocks are in our jar. But those rocks block us from *receiving* the outflow of His love, His infinite love that seeks to flow to us and in us and through us and from us. When the Holy Spirit convicts us of sin, our repentance is the invitation that we give to Him to begin His work. Then we work together with Him to remove another rock. Removing these rocks allows the *fullness* of the Holy Spirit into our lives.

We Work Out ... He Works In

I think that at the very core of each rock are lies that we believe. During sanctification, the Holy Spirit reveals these lies, and teaches us the deep truths of God. Together with Jesus we remove those rocks, and then we are ready to be filled with His Spirit. Let's hear how Paul prays in this way for the Ephesians:

[16] ... that He would grant you, according to the riches of His glory, to be strengthened with power through His Spirit in the inner man, [17] so that Christ may dwell in your hearts through faith; and that you, being rooted and grounded in love, [18] may be able *to comprehend with all the saints what is the breadth and length and height and depth,* [19] *and to know the love of Christ* which surpasses knowledge, that you may be filled up to all the fullness of God.

[20] Now to Him who is able to do far more abundantly beyond all that we ask or think, according to the power that works within us, [21] to Him be the glory in the church and in Christ Jesus to all generations forever and ever. Amen.

Ephesians 3:16-21, emphasis added

I think that our inner man is strengthened by the Holy Spirit to cast down lies and comprehend the truth of the depth of Christ's love for us. When we submit to the Holy Spirit and cooperate with Him, we are strengthened with the Holy Spirit's power to remove those lies that minimize God's love. And as this is accomplished, the Holy Spirit will inhabit us in greater measure, filling us up **to all the fullness of God.**

Go back now and read verse 20. He will do more than we ask or imagine – now don't miss this: **according to the power that works within us.** According to the Holy Spirit at work within us. It is His work, completely His work, but He calls us to cooperate with Him:

... work out your salvation with fear and trembling; for it is God who is at work in you, both to will and to work for His good pleasure.

Philippians 2:12-13

Work out means "to carry out a task until it is finished."[10] And, as we are working, it is actually *God* who is accomplishing everything. **Work in** is a different word than work out. **Work in** means "operative, active ... to produce an effect."[11] When God operates in us, He produces an effect and shows forth His might. As we do our part in working out our sanctification, walking it out day by day, God is at work in us, effecting something powerful in and through us, that glorifies Him.

Now can't God sanctify us without our working it out? Of course. But He won't. He won't force Himself on us. But when we come humbly to Him, offering Him everything, setting our hearts to obey Him completely and seek Him intensely, He will work mightily in us. He will reveal our sin, call us to repentance and surrender, sanctify and purify us. It may be painful, and we may encounter piercing spiritual warfare as we come to deeper surrenders. But He will be the one to work sanctification in us. *Not us. Him.*

For it is God who is at work in you, both to will and to work for His good pleasure. When He sanctifies us, He empowers us to fulfill His purpose, to act according to His good purpose, to work for His good pleasure. But more than that, He also gives us the *will* to fulfill that purpose. The great *desire* to work for His pleasure, the *passion* to live for Him and not for ourselves. These purposes that He has planned for us, the work we do that pleases Him, will not be easy. We may not naturally want to fulfill these purposes. Yet as we work out our salvation, He works deep into our hearts the desire to fulfill these purposes, no matter how painful, no matter the suffering required, no matter the depth of the hardship or trial. He will work that in us – if we are working out our sanctification.

Now why the **fear and trembling**? Because if we are rejecting sanctification, we are *fighting* against God Himself. If we are refusing to surrender, if we are evading repentance, if we are spurning His Word because we know it will convict us of sin, then we are *rebelling* against God Himself. If we are resisting being conformed to Christ's image, we are *rejecting* God Himself.

Paul illustrates this process once again in Second Corinthians. He describes people initially closed off to the convicting work of the Holy Spirit. They are refusing repentance, quenching the Holy Spirit, and hardening their minds and hearts. Paul describes this as a veil over their hearts. He goes on to explain how the veil is removed:

Whenever anyone turns to the Lord, the veil is taken away. Now the Lord is the Spirit, and where the Spirit of the Lord is, there is freedom.

2 Corinthians 3:16-17 NIV

As the Holy Spirit convicts, and we repent and *turn to the Lord*, the veil is taken away and we see Jesus more clearly. As we cast down a lie that the Holy Spirit has exposed, and choose to believe the truth of His Word, the veil is pulled aside and we see Jesus in greater measure *as He truly is*. As we repent, as we forsake lies, together with the Holy Spirit we remove another rock, God purifies us more deeply, and now we are open to receive a fresh infilling of His Spirit. **Where the Spirit of the Lord is, there is freedom.** Whatever areas we fully submit to His control, in all parts of our lives *where He is Lord,* we will be set free.

Satan's Goggles

When we are ensnared in believing a lie, the trap is often so insidious and all-encompassing that we have no idea that we are believing a lie. We have been blinded by Satan and cannot see clearly. In general, we tend to believe that all our thought processes are true. After all, who wants to believe a lie? If we *knew* that what we held to be true was a lie, we would stop believing it! What keeps us from seeing a lie for what it is? My husband calls this place of spiritual blindness, "wearing Satan's goggles."

Pause and think about this a moment. What if … we encountered a kitten, but because we are blinded by Satan, because we are wearing Satan's goggles, we actually *believe* that the kitten is a lion.

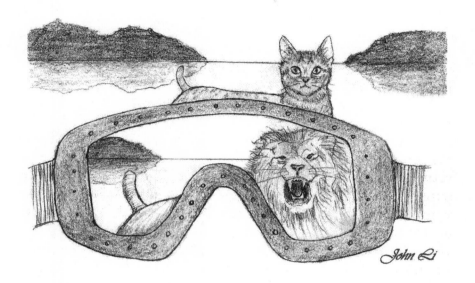

We would then react to the kitten as if he really *is* a lion. Our response would probably not be appropriate for an encounter with a kitten – and could even be damaging to the kitten.

Applying this concept to our everyday situations, we can see how being blinded may cause us to respond to people and situations in an inappropriate manner. Imagine the host of problems that might ensue. How can we remove those goggles? Removal can start when the Light of the Holy Spirit exposes the lies. Let's study some Scriptures.

"If We Say That We Have No Sin …"

Let's go to First John. John is writing to Christians, saved and indwelt by the Holy Spirit, **children of God,** who know **that He abides in us, by the Spirit whom He has given us** (1 Jn 3:2, 24). John writes,

This is the message we have heard from Him and announce to you, that God is Light, and in Him there is no darkness at all. If we say that we have fellowship with Him and yet walk in the darkness, we lie and do not practice the truth; but if we walk in the Light as He Himself is in the Light, we have fellowship with one another, and the blood of Jesus His Son cleanses us from all sin. If we say that we have no sin, we are deceiving ourselves and the truth is not in us. If we confess our sins, He is faithful and righteous to forgive us our sins and to cleanse us from all unrighteousness. If we say that we have not sinned, we make Him a liar and His word is not in us.

1 John 1:5-10

I don't know about you, but I needed to read this passage a number of times and to pray for the Holy Spirit's revelation in order to really start to grasp what God is saying here. This is what I glean:

- If we say that we have no sin, we are deceiving ourselves. We walk in darkness.

- If we walk in darkness and think that we have fellowship, intimacy, closeness, *koinonia*, with Him, then we are deceiving ourselves.

- But if we come into the Light, if we acknowledge His truth and choose to live by His truth, if we walk in the Light, *then* the blood of Jesus cleanses us from all sin. That is the sanctification process happening.

How do we come into the Light? **We confess our sins.** Interesting word, confess. In the Greek it means "to agree with ... to confess publicly, acknowledge openly ... to be in accord with someone."[12] Let's explore the details of this definition.

Confessing our sins means to *come into agreement* with God about our sin. To be in *one accord,* to be in harmony, to *acknowledge* that we have sinned. This means that we take the time to talk to God about our sin. It may not necessarily need to be a lengthy time, but a dedicated time of focus on God seems to be important. For me, I have found that giving half a nod to a sin the Holy Spirit has revealed while I am simultaneously going about my usual business is just not sufficient confession. I need to stop and take the time to be alone with God, so I can be honest about what I now see in my heart, and then I can hear what He is honestly telling me about all that *He* sees in my heart.

Now let's not gloss over those words "publicly" and "openly" in that definition. Confession doesn't mean that we need to shout our sins from the rooftops, but I find that as I am alone with God in confession, He often shows me to whom He is calling me to confess. That may be apologizing to someone when I have said something hurtful. It may be taking responsibility for my share of the blame in a relationship gone awry. It may be confessing to my prayer group or my accountability partner. These are people who will, gently and with great love, ensure that I do not minimize my sin. They will pray with me and check back with me to keep me accountable if I have slipped in this way again.

Coming Into the Light

... Light has come into the world, but men loved darkness instead of light because their deeds were evil. Everyone who does evil hates the light, and will not come into the light for fear that his deeds will be exposed. But whoever lives by the truth comes into the light ...

John 3:19-21 NIV

The thought of coming into the light, of thinking about our sins being exposed, may have caused our hearts to do a little flip-flop. Trust the Holy Spirit. He does not expose our sins to shame us or reject us, but to gently convict us, to lead us to repentance, and *to give us more of Himself.*

I want to tread very gently here, for I know that some of you may be suffering deeply as a result of *others'* sins. You may wonder, how can God be talking to me about some minor sin of mine, when someone else's major sin has raged on unchecked, without consequences, ignored by God?

I think I know how you feel, for I have struggled with this myself. Please understand that no sin, great or small, escapes God's notice. But God commands us to focus on our *own* heart, our *own* relationship with Him, and to trust Him to be a fair and righteous Judge. Someone else's sin, even against us, must have no bearing on our relationship with our Savior. We are commanded to keep our focus on Jesus, for our help comes from the Lord, not from our problems (Heb 12:2, Ps 121:1-2).

Watch what happens when we are courageous enough to come into the light:

Therefore do not be partakers with them [the sons of disobedience]**; for you were formerly darkness, but now you are Light in the Lord; walk as children of Light ... But all things become visible when they are exposed by the light, for everything that becomes visible is light. For this reason it says, "Awake, sleeper, and arise from the dead, and Christ will shine on you."**

Ephesians 5:7-8, 13-14

When we are slumbering, sluggish, in spiritual darkness, struggling to receive deep spiritual understandings and insights, we need exposure to His Light to wake us up. As Christ gives us His Light, and we are willing to come into that Light, our sins will be exposed, for all things become visible when they are exposed by light. As we acknowledge what He has revealed, and we confess and repent and receive His transformation, that area of our heart becomes Light in the Lord.

I like how the Amplified expresses it:

But when anything is exposed and reproved by the light, it is made visible and clear; and where everything is visible and clear there is light.

Ephesians 5:13 AMP

Exposed and reproved. Corrected. God's Light reveals more than our sins. His Light exposes the lies we believe that led to those sins. When those lies are exposed, we have a choice: to continue to believe those lies, or to receive His correction and choose to believe the truth of His Word.

As we enter more deeply into the Light, **everything becomes visible and clear.** *Everything.* We see God with greater clarity, we see who we are with greater accuracy, we see the world with greater transparency, and we discern darkness with greater perspicacity. We will gain clarity of who He is, receive a deeper understanding of Him, and develop a closer intimacy. Here's how John explains this:

... we are already God's children, and we can't even imagine what we will be like when Christ returns. But we do know that when he comes we will be like him, for we will see him as he really is.

1 John 3:2 NLT

When we are with Jesus in heaven, we will be like Him, because we will see Him as He really is. All lies will be purged, we will see Him in full truth, and our sanctification will be complete. And, while we are on earth, seeing Him more truly as He really is brings us deeper into sanctification:

But whenever anyone turns to the Lord, then the veil is taken away. Now, the Lord is the Spirit, and wherever the Spirit of the Lord is, he gives freedom. And all of us have had that veil removed so that we can be mirrors that brightly reflect the glory of the Lord. And as the Spirit of the Lord works within us, we become more and more like him and reflect his glory even more.

2 Corinthians 3:16-18 NLT

In summary, coming into God's Light has a fourfold result:

- God's Light exposes our sins.
- God's Light uncovers lies we believe.
- God's Light reveals the truth of who God really is.
- We become more like Him, reflecting His glory even more.

Pebble Removal

Let's go back to our analogy of rocks in the jar. What will the process of rock removal look like? I believe the first step is revelation.

Then Jesus again spoke to them, saying, "I am the Light of the world; he who follows Me will not walk in the darkness, but will have the Light of life."

John 8:12

Revelation precedes purification. Remember, spiritual growth will require that we are open to the Holy Spirit's conviction of the state of our heart. We invite Him in to work in our heart, we accept His conviction of sin and lies, we choose repentance and truth, and we pray for His transformation. This culminates in deeper intimacy.

Revelation, conviction, repentance, transformation, abiding. That is the process of conforming, the process of sanctification. How will the Holy Spirit reveal? How will His light penetrate our hearts? How will we reach closer abiding?

Certainly we will receive His revelation and enter deeper abiding as we grow in Him through the spiritual disciplines. As we study the Word, pray, and worship in church. As we immerse in Bible study and serve in ministry. As we confess our sins and connect with others for accountability. As we spend time in solitude and learn how to move from the physical to the spiritual. Through all this deep seeking of Him, He can conform us bit by bit, and together with Jesus we may remove pebble after pebble, and the water of His Holy Spirit fills us more. And that indeed is precious sanctification.

Also, as we leave sins behind, we will enter deeper abiding. Psalm 37 declares this:

Depart from evil and do good,
So you will abide forever.

Psalm 37:27

Departing from evil is removing another rock.

Rock Removal

Sometimes, however, the bigger rocks will require something more than just keeping up with our spiritual disciplines to dislodge them. The Holy Spirit may orchestrate the circumstances of our lives in such a way as to open our eyes to our sins and to increase our desire for more of Him. Peter explains it this way:

Therefore, since Christ suffered in his body, arm yourselves also with the same attitude, because he who has suffered in his body is done with sin. As a result, he does not live the rest of his earthly life for evil human desires, but rather for the will of God.
1 Peter 4:1-2 NIV

Can you see the fingerprints of God on our sufferings as the Holy Spirit moves to extract another rock?

Sometimes, the Lord doesn't remove a rock in its entirety at one time. Sometimes, the rock is so huge that He first

breaks it into pieces, then invites us to partner with Him to remove the rubble, piece after piece. The larger pieces will be harder to remove. The smaller pieces will be easier. The dust may require a lifetime to sweep it all out.

Boulder Removal

Some rocks may be deeper, larger, or more long-standing. I call these "boulders." Some boulders can be so much a part of our being that we don't even realize that they are there. We are blinded by the forces of darkness. We've got Satan's Goggles on; we think that his lies are truth. We may need to be really shaken up to recognize the existence of those boulders, to see his lies for what they really are, and to admit what a tremendous hindrance these rocks are to our relationship with Christ. As we remove rocks, as we are conformed to the image of His Son, the Holy Spirit flows to us and in us and through us and from us in greater measure.

I'd like to share a story of the Lord's boulder removal of my unforgiveness of self. I shared with you about this struggle a few chapters ago. I'm going to add some detail to that testimony here.

I had sinned and repented long ago, and I *thought* I had forgiven myself. Perhaps I had, on some level. Or perhaps it had only been a token surrender. Whatever the case, my unforgiveness-of-self boulder was so entrenched that it had become part of me. Until the Holy Spirit began to reveal ...

I had sinned. I had repented deeply. There was no restitution that could be made. Nothing.

God offered me His forgiveness. Yet somehow, I couldn't forgive myself. I tried and prayed and confessed and cried and prayed some more, I read books about forgiveness and

Scriptures on forgiveness, I asked friends to pray with me and for me, but I still couldn't make my heart forgive myself.

God was calling me, though. I could not remain in this state. I asked a friend to pray with me. As she prayed with me, my prayer welled up from deep inside my heart. In utter humility, I finally acknowledged that there was nothing, <u>nothing</u>, I could do to make up for this sin. I cried out, "Lord, all I can do is offer You the ashes of my failure, and beg for Your mercy to somehow – I don't know how – bring beauty from those ashes."

I laid this sin down at His feet. I committed to not take it up again. I covenanted with Him that I would not dwell on it, think about it, bring it up with Him, or beat myself up about it. I promised I would not use it as my identity, or even mention it unless He led me to do so. And as I prayed these prayers from deep in my heart, choking and crying, I physically felt like a massive boulder was being removed from somewhere deep inside of me. It felt as if the Holy Spirit was bringing that boulder out of the depths of my being, up through my chest, through my throat, and out onto the floor before me, where I laid it at His feet.

Feeling physically lighter after this deliverance, I left that time of prayer and entered the worship center, and became engulfed in the sweet songs of praise to our Savior. The worship leader paused between songs to read from Psalm 103: **"As far as the east is from the west, so far has He removed our transgressions from us."** *And then he prayed from Isaiah 61, "Lord, please bring beauty from our ashes…"*

Celeste Li
Jupiter, Florida

Discipline as an Opportunity for Boulder Removal

Sometimes, our boulders are driving repetitive sins that we cannot escape. If that is the case, we may need to be disciplined if we want the boulders to be removed.

"My son, do not regard lightly the discipline of the LORD, nor faint when you are reproved by Him; for those whom the LORD loves He disciplines, and He scourges every son whom He receives."

Hebrews 12:5-6

This word **discipline**, *paideia* in the Greek, comes from a root word meaning "child." *Paideia* originally meant "instruction of children; education," but my *Greek Word Study* goes on to say that it "evolved to mean chastening because all effectual instruction for the sinful children of men includes and implies chastening."[13] Chastening is a word I don't hear used much these days, so I have to admit I looked it up in Webster's. Here's what I found:

> To correct by punishment or suffering; discipline; purify. To prune of excess, pretense, or falsity; to refine. To cause to be more humble or restrained; subdue.[14]

Hmmm . . . I certainly could use more purifying, refining, humbling and restraining. Can we do that without the punishing and suffering aspect of it?

My *Greek Word Study* adds some more detail that gives a bit more clarification. It contrasts *paideia* with two other Greek words that are translated "penal infliction," and "penalty." These two contrasting words "denote penal [punitive] retribution," while *paideia* "speaks of correction, educative discipline."[15] I think these contrasting words shed some more light on the passage. While *paideia* may entail punishment or suffering, it is not administered in retaliation and revenge. Stick with me here while we unmask God's true motive, and keep in mind that **He disciplines us for our good** (Heb 12:10).

He scourges every son whom He receives. Scourges. I looked up this word really carefully. *Mastigoo* is derived from the word meaning "a whip, a scourge."[16] I think we can't wiggle out of this one.

I believe that this verse is telling us that as His sinful children, we will be instructed, disciplined, chastened with punishment and suffering, and yes, even scourged to uproot sin from our lives. It implies trials, afflictions, hardships, and anguish to remove boulders, to purify us. Speaking for myself, although I see that I can be purified on my outermost layer with Bible reading, prayer, and church attendance, that won't get to the deep roots. Devotion to these disciplines is only a superficial walk. Pain has proven necessary to get my attention, to get me out of denial and to expose the gravity of my sins. It is only through the pain of trials that I truly comprehend that my deep heart sins are the barriers that keep me from a closer relationship with Jesus. It is this pain that makes me desperate for Christ. It is this pain that drives me to seek Him for removal of those boulders, the deep sanctification process.

I did indeed want intimacy, but I have to admit that I wanted it on my own terms. I was willing to endure some kind of suffering to lead to intimacy, as long as it sort of let me off the hook. As long as it was suffering that was something I had not caused myself, something that was simply the result of living in this fallen world, something that didn't make me look bad. God, however, had a different plan.

Although the Lord had been working on the stronghold of pride in my heart for years, He now made it clear that He wanted to take the battle to another level. I had been praying for God to do whatever it would take to remove pride from me. In answer to that prayer, God offered me another season of humbling. This was not what I was expecting! During this season, He invited me to <u>choose</u> to humble myself. It seemed I was constantly wrong, and He called me to choose to admit again and again that I was wrong. It seemed I repeatedly fell into sin, and He called me to choose time after time to confess that sin. It seemed I kept making the wrong choices, and He called me to choose time and again to concede that I had made those wrong choices. He offered me a closer walk with Him, and invited me to partner with

Him in boulder removal, but it was my choice to accept or reject the humbling that His invitation would entail. It was my choice to speak out and acknowledge my failures, or to remain silent.

Somehow, I realized that He was giving me a chance to humble myself under His mighty hand (1Pt 5:6). Somehow, I grasped that if I did not, He would take the next step, for He is able to humble those who walk in pride (Dan 4:37). I had a sense that if I accepted His invitation and chose to humble myself as He led, then He would not need to humble me.

I did choose the path that He was offering to me. We labored together in some serious boulder removal. Admitting my failures began to become a bit easier. Still in mid-process, I am wondering just how many pride boulders are left in there ...

Celeste Li
Jupiter, Florida

God loves us so much, He desires His Deep to meld into our deep so desperately, that He won't stop at a superficial relationship. He will use every bit of sin and pain in this fallen world to draw us to Himself. He simply won't let us remain mired in our hidden sins and entangled in unseen lies of the enemy. And even in our chastening, His heart **yearns** for us (Jer 31:20).

I wish I could claim that Jesus has completely removed these boulders of pride, but I have to admit that Jesus and I are still in the process. I've shared this journey of humbling with you because I want you to see what it costs to receive more of His Spirit. To hear Him more clearly, to abide in Him more constantly, rest in Him more intimately.

I am encouraged to know that the world may try to shame us, but **the one who trusts in Him will never be put to shame** (Rom 9:33). The rewards of more penetrating intimacy are so precious that given the opportunity, I would indeed embark on this journey all over again — and with much less complaining this time around!

Viewing Trials as an Opportunity For Boulder Removal

Instead of viewing our trials as punishment, we can view them as invitations to grow in Christ, as unique opportunities for boulder removal. Instead of expending all our energy on *finishing* the trial, we can focus on Jesus and on developing our relationship with Him. If our purpose is simply to get to the end of the trial, we may miss the opportunity for boulder removal *during* the trial. God invites us to remain open to what He is working in our hearts *throughout* the trial.

You know that God did not invent evil. I believe that the overarching purpose of every drop of suffering that God in His sovereignty decrees for our lives is *to bring us closer to Him.* Suffering is an opportunity for intimacy. We can choose to seize that opportunity for all it's worth and leap to the next level of closeness to Him. Or we can choose to fight and kick and scream, to complain and become bitter, to shut down and wall off our hearts. We can choose, as Paul at first did, to **kick against the goads** (Acts 26:14), and thus effectively drive ourselves further from Him. We can fight against His mighty and all-loving hand. But this will only serve to increase the pain. My husband says it this way:

Pain x Resistance = Suffering

When the consequences of living in this fallen world cause pain, if we resist the work that God is doing through the pain, the pain may multiply into great suffering.

I believe that the purpose of *paideia* and *mastigoo* is to prune and purify us, to bring us to more profound fellowship with Jesus. To move us into such a deep abiding that we are not coming to Him *for answers;* we are coming to Him *for Him.* And that depth of abiding is a glorious gift indeed.

As dazzling as that gift is, we must also realize that it is not all about us. We are here to advance His Kingdom and to give Him glory. We are here to reach others for Christ. We are here as the body of Christ to encourage and help other Christians on their journey of spiritual growth and healing. We are here to give God glory, to reflect the Lord Jesus Christ who is living inside of us. Most importantly, we are here for relationship with our God. And . . . only the Father knows what particular circumstances it will take for each one of us to fulfill our unique assigned purposes.

I'd like to invite my husband to share a sweet word picture of sanctification that he painted for me the other day.

For many of us, walking through our life is like painting with a dirty paintbrush. We expect beautiful colors, but the canvas comes out brown and black and muddy. The reason is that the paintbrush is dirty; it is full of colors of our past that have not been cleaned out.

The good news is that God accepts us as we now are, and because He is timeless and sees the end from the beginning, He sees us as we will someday be.

So why bother cleaning our paintbrush? I believe it is so that others will be blessed by the beauty of the painting. The closer we come to God, the more we submit to His sanctifying and purifying process, the more vibrant and true and untainted the colors will be. With these true colors, we will reflect the Master Painter with more clarity, our light will shine in others' lives with greater brilliance, and we will be better able to love others unconditionally and to serve them selflessly. The more our brush paints true colors, the more others will see God as He really is, and not a caricature of

Him. The painting is a reflection of the Painter. Those who see the painting come to know, in part, the Painter. The more clearly the painting represents the Painter, the more the observers will see Him as He truly is.

John Li, M.D.
Jupiter, Florida

We are God's workmanship, created in Christ Jesus to do good works, which God prepared in advance for us to do.

Ephesians 2:10 NIV

I have heard it said that when people admire the invention, they are praising *the Inventor*. As John said, when people appreciate the painting, they admire the Painter. And when people are in awe of creation, they give homage to *the Creator*. When people marvel at the workmanship, they worship *the Craftsman*. As we submit to God's purification process, His workmanship in us will point others to Himself.

A Sobering Word

God's plan for our boulder removal is unique for each one of us. But what if we decline His invitation to repent and enter the sanctification process that He sets forth for us? Let's go to the Gospels to see a real life example of people who declined His invitation.

In Matthew 21, after Jesus' triumphant entry into Jerusalem, when the chief priests and Pharisees began to question Him, Jesus answered them in parables. He spoke about a landowner who rented out his vineyard to vine-growers and then sent slaves to collect the produce. The vine-growers killed the landowner's slaves, and even killed his son. Note this:

When the chief priests and the Pharisees heard His parables, they understood that He was speaking *about them.*

Matthew 21:45, emphasis added

The chief priests and Pharisees knew that this parable was *about them.* They *understood* that He was speaking about them. They had received revelation. Did they repent? No. And because they had received revelation, but hardened their hearts and refused to repent, when they asked for additional revelation, Jesus would not give it (Mt 21:27).

Similarly, I believe that if the Holy Spirit convicts us of sin, and we refuse to repent, continued revelation from Him may simply dry up.

The Difference Between Obedience and Submission

God calls us to obedience to His commands. Our obedience demonstrates our love (Jn 14:15), and is very critical in our relationship with Him. Yet I think that the key to developing a piercingly beautiful intimacy goes *beyond* obedience. Something deeper than obedience? Yes. I call it *submission.* I think this story that I heard will highlight the difference.

> *A young child was standing on the table in great excitement. His father commanded him to get down and to sit in a chair. The child did as commanded, but with a tearful torrent of words, "On the outside I may be sitting in this chair, but on the inside, I'm still standing on the table."*

Was this child obedient to his father? Yes. But was he *in submission?* Was he surrendered to the will of his father? Did his heart want whatever the father commanded, whether it was the child's desire or not? No. He made a behavioral choice to obey, but his *heart* was not in that obedience. His heart still wanted his own way.

Our relationships with our heavenly Father may look pretty similar. In obedience we may tithe to our church, go to work to support our family, get dinner on the table, put our spouses' needs first, give up our free time to take care of our baby. But our hearts may harbor resistance and resentment. In obedience we may apologize, but our hearts may be fixated on demanding that the other person apologize. In obedience to God's leading we may send our kids off to college, but the incessant worry reveals the darkness of an unsurrendered heart.

I've invited my Triumph Servant Leader Gary back because his testimony illustrates the difference between simple obedience and true submission.

I had hit the bottom. My wife had walked out on me, and I was in great financial distress. At this point, tithing seemed out of the question. Obediently tithing when I was comfortable financially was <u>completely</u> <u>different</u> than the total trust required to tithe in a time of financial distress. I concluded that tithing at this time of my life was impossible.

Yet, the more earnestly I prayed, the more God gave me signs that He was with me and was fighting for me. I knew He was calling me to trust Him for all my needs. I wrestled this through with the Lord and finally surrendered to Him. What happened next was truly miraculous.

I tithed $400 – and two days later received $4000 from the IRS! And then God <u>really</u> started to move. My struggling tree farm had a $250,000 mortgage that I couldn't afford. I had it on the market, with only three viewers in 15 months. I put it in God's hands, and the next morning I called a man that I knew had wanted my company name. I offered him the company name plus the entire farm for $250,000. He seized the opportunity, saying, "I grew up on that property, *and I wanted my kids to grow up on it. Just yesterday at 4 PM I was buying a nursery for even more money, biting off more than I could chew ... we had been under contract for four months – and the owner cancelled the contract! And at 7:45 AM today, you call me and offer me this deal!"*

Deal for him, freedom for me. I gave the tithe, despite the burdensome divorce lawyer fees – and the next day a client called me up confessing he scammed me out of $2500 – and he returned it to me!

Gary McDaniel
Triumph Servant Leader
West Palm Beach, Florida

I'm chuckling as I hear how God worked here. It does seem that He loves to bless submission, but maybe not always in such an obvious financial way. Psalm 25 teaches us that when we walk in obedience and fear of the Lord, our *soul* will abide in prosperity. Knowing Gary, I am certain that he would declare that the spiritual blessings that came forth from his walk of submission were far richer than any financial favor he received,

Gary's journey illustrates the difference between a behavioral choice of obedience, and full heart submission. Sometimes, as in Gary's case, our lack of full surrender may be exposed only when a trial strikes.

I have learned much about surrender and submission from Watchman Nee's book *Spiritual Authority*. In China in the 1900's, this Godly man was called by the Lord to bring people to surrender wholly to Him. He describes the obedience that pleases God in this way:

> The obedience of the body to the head is perfect. As soon as the head conceives an idea, the fingers move naturally, harmoniously, soundlessly ... This is the kind of obedience which satisfies God.[17]

Jesus is the head. We are members of His body. We want our obedience to Jesus to be as instantaneous as fingers moving in response to the head's thought. This kind of deep heart obedience I call *submission*. Growing closer to God requires that we move from external obedience to the much deeper heart submission. Submission means that in the depths of our heart, we truly desire whatever *God's plan* may be – whether it would have been our choice or not.

He who dwells in the shelter of the Most High
Will abide in the shadow of the Almighty.

Psalm 91:1

The Most High refers to God as Sovereign Lord. When we bow our hearts in submission to His sovereign plan, we will abide in His shadow of protection, sustenance, and grace. We cannot create this kind of submission ourselves. We can only humble our hearts and petition the Holy Spirit, asking Him to fashion our hearts to be submissive.

Chosen for Intimacy

"He who believes in Me ... out of his heart will flow rivers of living water." But this He spoke concerning the Spirit ...

John 7:38-39

We so desire the rivers of living water to flow from our heart! The boulders, rocks, and even pebbles are an obstruction to the Holy Spirit's flow. As we partner with Him and remove those rocks, we remove the hindrances to His flow. It frees Him to flow to us and in us and through us and from us.

I'd like to end this heavy chapter with a verse that has been so encouraging to me:

How blessed is the one
Whom You choose and bring near to You
To dwell in Your courts.

Psalm 65:4

If you sense that God is calling you to sanctification, you are one that He has *chosen* to bring near to Himself, to abide profoundly in Him. It is a breathtaking honor to be called on such a daringly painful journey. Deep is calling to deep. Will you answer His call?

Questions Chapter 8: A Walk of Repentance

Memory Verse:

If we say that we have fellowship with Him and yet walk in the darkness, we lie and do not practice the truth; but if we walk in the Light as He Himself is in the Light, we have fellowship with one another, and the blood of Jesus His Son cleanses us from all sin.

1 John 1:6-7

1) Read Romans 2:4. Why can we consider repentance a *gift* the Lord grants to us?

2) **Blessed are the pure in heart,**
   for they shall see God.

Matthew 5:8

What is the relationship between repentance, sanctification, and "seeing God"?

3) Read John 17:17, 1John 1:5-10, John 3:19-21, and Ephesians 5:7-8 and 13-14. Describe the connection

between lies, light, and truth. How is *truth* necessary for sanctification?

4) Look up Philippians 2:12-13 in a version that you are comfortable with. Explain this verse in your own words. What does it mean for you to work *together* with God in your sanctification process?

5) What rock is the Holy Spirit working to remove from you right now, and what methods is He using? Recall that pain x resistance = suffering. Are you willing to co-labor with Him in its removal?

Chapter 9
From Roots to Fruit

I had been praying for a long time for God to grant me humility. It didn't seem like these prayers were being answered any too quickly. I thought about the verse in Galatians that lists the fruit of the Holy Spirit, and I did not recall humility being listed as a fruit. I checked again just to be sure.

But the fruit of the Spirit is love, joy, peace, patience, kindness, goodness, faithfulness, gentleness, self-control ...

Galatians 5:22-23

Not on the list. Humility has got to be important, why wouldn't it be on that fruit list? So I asked the Lord, Why isn't humility a fruit?

His answer came back with profound simplicity, *Because it's a root.* And He began to teach me personally about roots and fruit.

"Grapes are not gathered from thorn bushes nor figs from thistles, are they? So every good tree bears good fruit, but the bad tree bears bad fruit. A good tree cannot produce bad fruit, nor can a bad tree produce good fruit."

Matthew 7:16-18

Ah, I see. If we see good fruit in our lives, we know we must have good roots. If we see bad fruit, we must have bad roots. If a good seed of humility is planted, a good tree can grow and bear good fruit. Indeed, I doubt we could exhibit love, longsuffering, goodness, or self-control without a root of humility.

But remember that these are *fruits*; we just don't wake up one morning bearing these fruits. If we desire good fruit, we must first abide in Him to prepare the soil, removing rocks and bad roots, then till the soil, plant good seed, water, nourish ... and wait – for only God makes it grow.

I think Jesus did not select this analogy of thorn bushes and grape vines haphazardly. I think He wants us to be acutely aware of the work involved in digging up bad roots, and the time element necessary to bear good fruit – from a seed to a plant to a fruit-bearing tree. There are quite a few different elements involved here. Let's explore.

Becoming Good Soil

So neither he who plants nor he who waters is anything, but only God, who makes things grow.

1 Corinthians 3:7 NIV

Only God can make the seed grow. But before we begin to think we have no responsibility, let's review the parable of the sower.

"Behold, the sower went out to sow; as he was sowing, some seed fell beside the road, and the birds came and ate it up. Other seed fell on the rocky ground where it did not have much soil; and immediately it sprang up because it had no depth of soil. And after the sun had risen, it was scorched; and because it had no root, it withered away. Other seed fell among the thorns, and the thorns came up and choked it, and it yielded no crop. Other seeds fell into the good soil, and as they grew up and increased, they yielded a crop and produced thirty, sixty, and a hundredfold."

Mark 4:3-8

We do so want to be that good soil, producing fruit a hundredfold! When His disciples asked him privately to explain the parable, Jesus taught them that the seed is the Word of God. He expounded on the different soils, and showed that we have responsibility for what kind of soil we may be. Let's listen in.

Dirt Beside the Road

When they hear, immediately Satan comes and takes away the word which has been sown in them (Mk 4:15). Satan roams this earth to **steal, kill, and destroy.** To steal away the truth that God has dropped into our heart. We can listen to the Word of God, the seed, with such superficiality that it can be snatched away from us and we remember it no more. Luke's version of the sower says that it can be **trampled** (Lk 8:5) – society, culture, the ways of the world can stampede over the message we have received and easily succeed in annihilating it from our heart.

Hearing His Word and walking away will not make us good soil. We become good soil when we treasure it in our hearts:

I have hidden your word in my heart
That I might not sin against you.

Psalm 119:11 NIV

Meditate on it, immerse in it, memorize it, store it up in your deepest heart, so that we might not sin against Him.

Rocky Ground

Initially these people receive the word with joy, and believe it for a little while, but because they have **no firm root**, they **fall away** when affliction, persecution, or temptation arises (Mk 4:17). They **withered away** because they had **no moisture** (Lk 8:6).

This is an issue of our foundation. To become good soil, we are commanded to grow up in Christ (Eph 4:15), to grow up in our salvation (1Pt 2:2), to dig down deep and lay our foundation on a rock (Lk 6:48). We need moisture to grow — we are to be cleansed by the washing with water through the word (Eph 5:26), and we are to be filled with the Holy Spirit (Eph 5:18).

Thorns

The **worries of the world,** the **deceitfulness of riches,** the **desires for other things,** and **the pleasures of this life enter in and choke the word, and it becomes unfruitful** (Mk 4:19). I don't think Jesus could have said this any more plainly.

Luke writes that these people **go on their way** (Lk 8:14). That really hits home. Instead of following Jesus, instead of pursing God's plan for their life, they choose *their own way*. Instead of looking to the Word of God to be a lamp to their feet and a light to their path (Ps 119:105), they are led astray by riches, pleasures, and worries. Busyness, stress, misplaced priorities. Wrong focus, idols, anxiety. These things choke the life within us.

Good Soil

"And those are the ones on whom seed was sown on the good soil; and they hear the word and accept it and bear fruit, thirty, sixty, and a hundredfold."

Mark 4:20

We are responsible to not only hear the word, but also to seek to accept it, understand it, and apply it to our lives. To **hear the word in an honest and good heart, and hold it fast, and bear fruit with perseverance** (Lk 8:15). This is no casual reading of the Bible! An honest heart – we discussed this in previous chapters – we are honest with God about our heart, and He is honest with us about our heart. A good heart – that is *agathos*, a heart that displays kindness in action.[1] A heart that chooses to keep this Word, retain it, hold it fast, cling to it.

James explains it this way:

Therefore, putting aside all filthiness and all that remains of wickedness, in humility receive the word implanted, which is able to save your souls. But prove yourselves doers of the word, and not merely hearers who delude themselves. For if anyone is a hearer of the word and not a doer, he is like a man who looks at his natural face in a mirror; for once he has looked at himself and gone away, he has immediately forgotten what kind of person he was. But one who looks intently at the perfect law, the law of liberty, and abides by it, not having become a forgetful hearer but an effectual doer, this man will be blessed in what he does.

James 1:21-25

In all humility, receive the Word implanted. Humility is required to deeply accept the Word, to acknowledge parts of our lives or hearts that are not aligned with the Word, to repent and come to Him for transformation. It requires humility to allow the Word to be used as a mirror, reflecting the truth of who we are, and then to do what is necessary to change. I love how James reminds us that this process is liberty, freedom, for as we admit lies and embrace truth, His Spirit will set us free from the traps of Satan.

Will the fruit burst forth immediately? Hardly. Even seeds planted in good soil must be watered and nurtured and fertilized before they will slowly drive down roots and push up sprouts, and eventually blossom and bear fruit. No wonder Jesus says that we will bear fruit **with perseverance and patience.**

I want to draw your attention to how Jesus wraps up this teaching on the sower and the seed.

"But the good soil represents those who hear and accept God's message and produce a huge harvest— thirty, sixty, or even a hundred times as much as had been planted ... Everything that is now hidden or secret will eventually be brought to light. Anyone who is willing to hear should listen and understand! And be sure to pay attention to what you hear. The more you do this, the more you will understand— and even more, besides. To those who are open to my teaching, more understanding will be given. But to those who are not listening, even what they have will be taken away from them."

Mark 4:20-25 NLT

Jesus tells us how to be good soil. Pay attention to the Word. The more we take the time to carefully listen and understand, the more revelation the Holy Spirit will give us. The more we are open to His teaching, the more the Holy Spirit will give us understanding. But if we close off our hearts to the truth of His Word, even the truths that we have previously learned will be snatched away. The birds will come and eat it up.

Uprooting Bad Roots

To make our hearts the good soil, receptive to the seed He will be planting, we will rid ourselves of rocks, as we talked about in the last chapter. A parallel analogy to removing rocks is uprooting bad roots. We'll utilize the root analogy in this chapter. Let's read Jesus' words from Mark again:

"Everything that is now hidden or secret will eventually be brought to light."

Mark 4:22 NLT

Roots are hidden under the ground; they are not apparent; we cannot see them. The *evidence* of what kind of roots we have in our hearts will be the *fruit*. God does indeed want to expose our hidden bad roots – not to shame or humiliate us, but to invite us to labor together with Him in digging them up, to make room for good seeds and good roots. Since the roots are hidden, He may draw our attention to our bad fruit, inviting us to seek His revelation to trace the fruit back to the roots, learning what deeper sins are embedded in our hearts.

If we are on the alert and our hearts are open, the Holy Spirit will allow us to see bad fruit. Unkind words, selfish thoughts, loss of temper. Irritability, anger, and impatience. Lying and deceitfulness. Acrimonious hatred, biting sarcasm, caustic speech, spiteful plans. Thoughts of self incrimination and worthlessness. Or more grave bad fruit, such as disrupted relationships, addictions, habitual sins, sexual sins. If we acknowledge that the fruit is bad and displeasing to our Heavenly Father, and if we are willing to invite Him in to dig in the garden of our heart, I believe that He will lead us on a journey of uprooting and planting, a path to greater intimacy with Him. I believe that as we continue this life-long walk with Him, we will witness Christ being formed in us (Gal 4:19), in greater and greater measure, until His work in us is completed in eternity.

Before we go on, pause and spend some time with the Lord. Re-read the bad fruit in that last paragraph, and circle any the Holy Spirit is tickling your conscience about. Then pick up your journal and write what He is speaking to you.

I've asked my friend Libby back again. One of my Triumph Servant Leaders, she is a very mature Christian who has walked close to the Lord for many decades. And at this stage in her walk, God began to draw her attention to some bad fruit. Let's listen in to how the Holy Spirit enabled her to trace it down to the bad roots.

Lately I've been reminded that I am always worrying about something. Well, there is always something to worry about, so it seems – children, grandchildren, health problems, the worries of living in a fallen world, etc. I had not made the connection before, but when I am worrying, fretting or being anxious about something, I obviously do not trust the Lord.

Psalm 37, one of my favorites, repeatedly says, "Do not fret." I've often quoted these verses, but obviously I was not living it out very well. The desire of my heart is to stop worrying, fretting or being anxious and to put my trust in the Lord Jesus Christ who is able – more than able – to handle every detail of my life. He has a plan and purpose for all He allows.

As I began earnestly seeking the Lord about this bad fruit of worry, the root problem became evident: I am not trusting God to take care of the problems. I can't be worrying and trusting at the same time. I used to say to my mother, "Why worry when you can pray?" Now I am being reminded of those words.

A good anecdote for worry is Philippians 4:6-8. I must take my worries to the Lord in prayer, and then keep my focus on those things that are true, honorable, right, pure, lovely and of good report. If I'm trusting instead of worrying, the result will be the peaceful fruit of righteous living.

*God has given me a specific word and Scripture to focus on this year. You guessed it – the word is **trust**, and the Scripture is Proverbs 3:5-6:* **Trust in the LORD with all your heart and do not lean on your own understanding. In all your ways acknowledge Him, and He will make your paths straight.**

A few months ago I was diagnosed with breast cancer. The doctor was certain it was stage one – until the pathology report of the lymph nodes came back positive for cancer cells. Now I am being put to the test – do I trust God, or lean on my own understanding and worry? I am choosing by faith to trust Him, and He has given me peace in the midst of a difficult situation. The peaceful fruit of righteousness is sweet to the soul as I put my trust in Him. Thankfully, He is not finished with me yet; I'm still a work in progress.

Libby Hammond
Triumph Servant Leader
Scipio, Indiana

The way I understand it, uprooting bad roots is the process of sanctification. **Your sins have hidden His face from you** (Isa 59:2); removing these sinful roots leads to greater intimacy with Him. The Lord graciously let Libby eat of some of her rotten fruit, because He knew her heart, her passion to please Him. He knew that when He let her taste the rotten fruit, it would send her to Him for revelation of the most hidden roots. But remember that this revelation is never to hurt or to shame – He reveals because He wants to shine His face upon us, to draw us into His dwelling place, into Himself:

> **O send out Your light and Your truth,**
> **Let them lead me;**
> **Let them bring me to Your holy hill**
> **And to Your dwelling places.**
>
> Psalm 43:3

I think that we simply cannot discover the sinfulness in our hearts by ourselves. We need His Light and His Truth to penetrate the dark corners of our hearts. Sometimes, He may shine that Light as we pray, read His Word, rest in solitude, or hear from an anointed preacher or teacher. But other times, there's work involved, and He wants us to co-labor with Him in the process. Luke's account of the grapes and thorns adds more insight:

> **"For a good tree does not bear bad fruit, nor does a bad tree bear good fruit. For every tree is known by its own fruit. For men do not gather figs from thorns, nor do they gather grapes from a bramble bush. A good man out of the good treasure of his heart brings forth good; and an evil man out of the evil treasure of his heart brings forth evil. For out of the abundance of the heart his mouth speaks."**
>
> Luke 6:43-45 NKJV

Out of the **abundance** of our hearts. Out of the **overflow** of our hearts (AMP). Out of **what the heart is full of** (NIV). The NLT says it this way: **Whatever is in your heart determines what you say.** This is indeed a heart issue. Roots refer to what is in our heart. Our speech, our thoughts, our emotions, our actions will give us a little glimpse of what is in our heart – if we are willing to seek His revelation and be open to what He exposes.

Does God take these little slip-ups of our speech seriously? He certainly does. Jesus tells us how seriously:

"Either make the tree good and its fruit good, or make the tree bad and its fruit bad; for the tree is known by its fruit. You brood of vipers, how can you, being evil, speak what is good? For the mouth speaks out of that which fills the heart. The good man brings out of his good treasure what is good; and the evil man brings out of his evil treasure what is evil. But I tell you that every careless word that people speak, they shall give an accounting for it in the day of judgment. For by your words you will be justified, and by your words you will be condemned."

Matthew 12:33-37

Because our words reflect what is in the depth of our hearts, we will give an accounting for every careless word that we speak, **for every idle word** (NKJV), **for every inoperative, nonworking word** (AMP). It is not merely the words themselves, it is the deeper issue of what is going on in our hearts that God is holding us accountable for. Hearts in right relationship with Him will overflow with right words.

Co-Laboring With Jesus in Uprooting

I would like to share a journey of root exposure in my own life to illustrate this process.

I had been irritable with my husband John when we were discussing the kids. Realizing my anger, I apologized and repented and worked to choose different emotions. In reality, that was like chopping off some thorns from a thorn bush and foolishly expecting that grapes would then grow in their place. Since I had not dealt with the roots of my anger, soon that anger was back.

When the anger resurfaced, I came before the Lord in repentance, and asked the Holy Spirit to search my heart. I wanted Him to reveal to me the cause of my anger. And He did, showing me that I had not forgiven John for making a decision about the kids without my input a few weeks prior. I was holding on to resentment and unforgiveness.

This time, I chopped off the whole branch. I chose to forgive and release. While that victory lasted a little longer, the thorns of anger and unforgiveness soon grew back. I went to the Lord again, and the Holy Spirit graciously revealed condemning judgment. I had felt John should have discussed the decision with me, and I judged him for making a decision without my input. So, I repented and chopped down the tree at the trunk. As I tore out the trunk, some of the roots came with it. But, you guessed it, soon the thorn bush was back again, even bigger and uglier than before.

With much prayer, the Holy Spirit revealed to me the deep-seated root of pride. I had felt that I was a better spouse and parent than John was. Pride had fed into my unforgiveness and my judgment of him. This time I knew that I had hit a taproot. This was indeed going to be a long process.

Celeste Li
Jupiter, Florida

If we have recognized bad fruit in our lives, we can choose the superficial route of simply lopping off the bad fruit. It will grow back, of course. And we may find the work involved in repeatedly cutting off that bad fruit to be exhausting.

But there is another path: attacking the roots. Some roots may be small tendrils; some may be larger in size. And others may be what I call a taproot. A taproot is a thick central root from which smaller roots grow. It is the source of nourishment for the smaller

John Li

roots, and it anchors the tree in the ground. In my understanding, there are two ways to attack a taproot. Working in unison with the Holy Spirit, we can whittle away at the smaller roots growing out of the taproot, and weaken it bit by bit, until the taproot is easier to pull out because there are no smaller roots helping to anchor it. Or, we can extricate the taproot first, and all the smaller roots will then wither and die because they have no source of nourishment. We will want to be sensitive to the Holy Spirit's leading in uprooting a taproot, for He may utilize different methods at different times.

How do we know if we have come up against a taproot or are still working on smaller roots, or even on a branch or trunk? There are many deep roots; I have found some to be unforgiveness, shame, selfishness, addictions, lust, greed, unbelief, independence, rebellion, and some fears. There are many even deeper taproots; some that I have encountered in my own walk are pride, control, idolatry, fears of abandonment and rejection, and distrust of God. It seems that the Holy Spirit has taken us to a taproot when we have come up against sins such as these.

Bitter Roots

How did these bad roots get there in the first place? How did we plant bad seeds? That is a really good question, and to me, the answer is not that simple. Let's go to Hebrews to take a look at this root development.

Pursue peace with all men, and the sanctification without which no one will see the Lord. See to it that no one comes short of the grace of God; that no root of bitterness springing up causes trouble, and by it many be defiled.

Hebrews 12:14-15

Bitterness in the Greek derives from the word *pikros*, "the fruits of the wild vine or bitter gourd which are so excessively bitter and acrid as to be a kind of poison."[2] That really strikes me. These deep taproots are *poisonous* to us, to our hearts, souls, emotions, minds, desires, behaviors, relationships.   How do we develop these bitter roots? Hebrews tells us: when we come short of the grace of God, when we *miss the grace of God* (NIV).

When we are too prideful to receive His grace, when we won't come to the place of humility necessary to receive His precious gifts, when we remain in a place of striving and earning His love, acceptance, approval, blessing, or forgiveness, then we may grow bitter roots.

I think perhaps He juxtaposes these two opposing things, sanctification and bitter roots, to show us that uprooting bad roots is what leads to sanctification which is what leads to seeing the Lord as He really is. *Without this sanctification no one will see the Lord.*

Although we have spent a lot of time talking about bad fruits and bad roots, understand that as we grow in Christ, we are developing good roots and are producing good fruit. For example, a root of humility may result in the good fruit of patience and self-control. A root of trust may result in the precious fruit of faithfulness and peace. A root of gratitude may produce the cherished fruit of joy. We'll explore good fruit in the next section.

Growing Good Fruit

As we are preparing the soil and uprooting bad roots, we have made room for the good seeds. It seems to me that specific bad roots need to be uprooted to make room for specific good seeds. For example, if I pray for humility, God starts exposing and removing pride first. If I am seeking Him for deeper trust, or praying for Him to grow my faith, He will be dealing with deep roots of fear. If I desire greater obedience and submission, He starts to uproot rebellion. If I ask the Holy Spirit for fear of the Lord, the roots of idolatry will be dealt with first. Bad roots must be exposed and uprooted to make room for good seed and good roots.

Planting those good seeds, nourishing those good roots, watering those sprouts will entail Scripture immersion, solitude, worship, listening, connection into the body of Christ. And remember the time element involved, for we are growing *fruit*:

Let us not become weary in doing good, for at the proper time we will reap a harvest if we do not give up.

Galatians 6:9 NIV

At the proper time. The King James says **in due season.** Patience, perseverance, and the realization that *only God makes it grow.* I'd like to hear from Mike again, for his story illustrates **due season.** You'll remember Mike from Chapter 3. Mike grew up in New York City in a household of severe abuse. He was homeless by age 14, and when he came to the Lord, Jesus miraculously rescued him from the gang he had joined. Mike became a disciple of faith and soldier of the Lord. And recently, he tasted some deliciously sweet fruit. Let's listen in.

You know some about my life and what I have gone through. I made a promise not to ever let my children go through the things I've experienced, the beatings, the abuse, being called bad names, the hatred, anger, pain, loneliness, the lack of a real father in my life and the lack of love. I made it a point that when I die, this dies with me.

God showed me how to love, to forgive, and to trust. Although I have made mistakes, God has taught me not to cause people pain and not to treat anyone with hatred. In First Corinthians Chapter 13, I learned what real love is. God filled my heart, my soul, the deepest place that is within me that I never even knew existed in me. He enabled me to love with His love.

Recently I went to Disneyland with my son, his wife, and my three grandchildren. During this time, I watched as my son cared for and loved his children. He would teach them, nurture them, guide them, answer their questions, laugh, play and let them know their Daddy loves them very much. I watched as my son played with his one-month-old daughter. He would give her a pink bear and sing her to sleep.

I had hoped that my kids would grow up better than me, but I did not see the answer to that prayer until that trip to Disney. As I sat there looking at my son and his baby, I realized that this was the answer to what had been in my heart for so many years. I realized that what God had given me, I have given to my children, and my children have given to their children: real love. I sat there and smiled as God let me know deep inside of me that He had done this, and then I felt Him smile at me.

Mike
Stuart, Florida

For Mike, it was many decades from the first uprooting of hatred, unforgiveness, and judgment to the planting of seeds of love and forgiveness, to the harvest of fruit. The sweet fruit was the parental love that Mike saw in his son. I think Mike would say that the harvest was indeed worth the work, perseverance, and waiting.

Pruning

There is another critical concept to understand as we grasp the depths of Jesus' teaching on roots and fruit: the process of pruning. Jesus taught His disciples about pruning just before His death.

"I am the true vine, and My Father is the vinedresser. Every branch in Me that does not bear fruit, He takes away; and every branch that bears fruit, He prunes it so that it may bear more fruit."
John 15:1-2

Every branch that bears fruit He *prunes* so that it may be even more fruitful. Now I don't know much about gardening, so I looked up this word "prunes" in Webster's. "To reduce especially by eliminating superfluous matter. To cut back or cut off parts of for better shape or more fruitful growth. To cut away what is unwanted or superfluous."[3]

I find this to be a very encouraging word. When we *are* bearing fruit, God will *prune* us so that we will bear even more fruit. He will remove what is unwanted in our lives, whatever is not pleasing to Him, "for better shape" – to conform us to the image of Christ.

And, He will remove what is *superfluous* in our lives. The things that He is pruning away are not necessarily bad or sinful or wrong, but they are not *His best* for us. Remember Mary and Martha? What Martha was doing was not necessarily wrong, but at that moment when Jesus showed up, what Mary was doing was far better.

If pruning sounds a bit painful to you, maybe the Lord chose this analogy for a good reason. It can be hard to let go of things that we enjoy. It can be very difficult to leave behind even ministry work where He has been using us. But if He is changing the season, He may call for a pruning to prepare us for increased fruit bearing ahead.

As Bible study teacher, Triumph Servant Leader, and marriage mentor, Bobbie is on fire for the Lord. When cancer recurred for the third time, she *already* had a deep compassion for hurting people, flourishing ministry work, and a true love of the Word. But during this season, as she continued to treasure the Word in her heart, she gained a deep understanding of the pruning process.

I was no stranger to suffering throughout my life. Yet from medical illnesses to family crises to deep heart pains, the suffering itself did not bring pruning. Suffering did slow me down, but there was limited spiritual growth. It wasn't until I immersed deeply in God's Word that the Lord convicted me and opened my heart to be "pruned" of many sins in areas of my life. Although quite painful at times, this pruning has brought me closer to God by cutting away the things that kept me from loving God and people and from surrendering to Him fully. These sins and superfluous activities also kept me from producing good fruit, and thwarted my development of a deep compassion for others.

After the pruning, and with continued deep immersion in the Word, I have seen much fruit as He has shaped me to be a servant who loves others with His love.

Bobbie Higby
Triumph Servant Leader
Church in the Gardens
Palm Beach Gardens, Florida

Bobbie told me that she had gained a lot of insight from Andrew Murray's writings:

> What is the pruning knife of this heavenly Husbandman? It is often said to be affliction. By no means in the first place ... It is the Word of God that is the knife, sharper than any two–edged sword, that pierces even to the dividing asunder of the soul and spirit, and is quick to discern the thoughts and intents of the heart. It is only when affliction leads to this discipline of the Word that it becomes a blessing; the lack of this heart-cleansing through the Word is the reason why affliction is so often unsanctified.[4]

Bobbie's words give testimony to Andrew Murray's observation: suffering without the cleansing of the Word simply does not lead to sanctification.

Are Pruning and Disciplining the Same?

Pruning is different than disciplining. In the last chapter, we talked about disciplining and scourging to open our eyes to our sins and drive us to repent and turn to God. But God *prunes* for a different reason. Pruning is *not* because of entrenched sin in our lives – pruning is to remove what is *superfluous and unwanted*. If there is something painful going on in your life right now, stop and take time with the Lord. Immerse in the Word. Ask Him if there is serious sin in your life that He is disciplining you for. Assess your relationship with Him and if you are bearing fruit. Review your walk with Him and ask Him to show you if you are becoming increasingly more Christlike in your thoughts, words, emotions, actions, and deepest parts of your heart. I believe He will show you. And if He shows you that He is not *disciplining* you, recognize that

He may be simply pruning – because His eyes have ranged to and fro across the earth and have found someone whose heart is fully committed to Him, and He wants to use that heart to bear even more fruit!

Bruce Wilkinson, founder of *Walk Thru the Bible* and author of numerous books, in *Secrets of the Vine* explains that discipline is to expose serious sin in our lives, but pruning is all about our hearts.

> Pruning goes beyond rearranging priorities to the heart of what defines us – the people we love, the possessions we cling to, our deep sense of personal rights. These are the very arenas God must rule if we are to go bear fruit … He is pruning closely to what really matters to you – not to take something good from you, but to become Lord of all you desire.[5]

Wow. Sounds a lot like God will be dealing with issues of pride and idolatry. Bruce Wilkinson goes on to say,

> Left to itself, a grape plant will always favor new growth over more grapes. The result? From a distance, luxurious growth, an impressive achievement. Up close, an underwhelming harvest.[6]

Are we willing to relinquish luxuriant growth that looks impressive? Impressive to our family, our church, our friends and peers, even ourselves? Are we willing to relinquish it in exchange for more fruit? Are we willing to submit to His process of sanctification? We can decline the Vinedresser's invitation; He will not force His plans on us.

I am thinking of what a plant looks like just after it is pruned. Sometimes a small pruning may not look too awful. But a deep pruning? Exposed, hacked, hideous – humbled. But in exchange for removing the growth that had made us look so impressive on the outside, He offers ... **more fruit.**

As I look back on my own times of pruning, I realize that His first prunings of me were quite gentle, not requiring me to look so exposed and humbled to the world. His treatment of me was so tender, for He knew that I was not quite ready for deeper pruning at first. But as He has led me to understand how He is working in my life, and the beauty that He is bringing forth, I am willing to trust myself to the Vinedresser's capable hands, wanting everything He has for me, and trusting His path and His methods. And truly, His deeper prunings, although more humbling, are no less sweet or tender.

Bruce Wilkinson also points out that "His plan for pruning is anything but random, and He works in every life uniquely — what He judges as wasteful for me might be necessary to you."[7] This cautions me to avoid judging others' pruning processes. The Vinedresser is infinitely experienced and creative, and no two branches of the Vine will look exactly the same in His hands.

To my surprise, Bruce Wilkinson cautions that as we thrive in the Lord, our pruning will *increase*. Increase? He explains, "The vine's ability to produce growth increases each year, but without intensive pruning the plant weakens and its crop diminishes. Mature branches must be pruned hard to achieve maximum yields."[8]

Mature branches must be pruned hard. Meaning that as we mature in Him, the pruning will get harder. If we don't submit to this pruning, we will weaken and our crop will diminish. Be prepared.

Pruning is all about my heart. God wants my undivided loyalty. He wants pride and self-idolatry to be driven out. He wants stubborn insistence upon my own way and inflexibility in following His leading to be expunged. He wants rebellion to be replaced with willing and joyful submission.   He wants self-reliance to be replaced by dependence upon Him and Him alone.   And He wants every drop of fear to be exposed and to flee in the face of deep trust in Him.

A Life of Uprooting and Pruning

I'd like to share with you what Paul wrote towards the end of his very fruitful life:

Not that I have already obtained all this, or have already been made perfect, but I press on to take hold of that for which Christ Jesus took hold of me.
Philippians 3:12 NIV

Yes, the Holy Spirit is revealing our hearts to us; yes He is bringing us to repentance, yes, He is uprooting bad roots bit by bit.   But He is nowhere near finished!   More transforming, more conforming, more maturity – but incomplete until we meet Him in eternity.   And yet,

...being confident of this, that he who began a good work in you will carry it on to completion until the day of Christ Jesus.
Philippians 1:6 NIV

Until the day of Christ Jesus.   He will carry on His transformation and healing and conforming all our earthly lives.   With each uprooting, with each pruning, He fills us more with His Spirit, and He brings us yet one more step closer to Him and to His image.

And what Paul writes in Second Corinthians is perhaps even more precious: God doesn't wait until He is finished to use us for His Kingdom and His glory.   Let's read it together.

But we have this treasure in jars of clay to show that this all-surpassing power is from God and not from us.

2 Corinthians 4:7 NIV

In the middle of our unfinished sanctification process, He still uses us as His hands and feet, promising,

"My grace is sufficient for you, for my power is made perfect in weakness."

2 Corinthians 12:9 NIV

He chooses to use broken vessels to bring His message of love and salvation to a bruised and hurting world – for in our brokenness, His light shines all the more brightly.

Abiding Leads to Fruit-Bearing

God doesn't *need* us in an absolute sense of the word, but He restrains Himself in order to invite us to partner with Him – to give us the great honor of co-laboring with Him as He moves, saves, heals, sanctifies. When we abide, we position ourselves to flow with Him. When we cooperate and work together with Him, it demonstrates our willingness to walk out a life of abiding. Let's look at this more concretely.

If I am struggling, for example, with a disrupted relationship, there may be an area in my life where I am not deeply connected to His Vine. First, I will seek Him to show me my heart, to reveal any bad roots that are preventing me from seeing with His eyes and loving with His heart, unconditionally and nonjudgmentally. The heart work will be necessary before any further steps; I want to be in a place – and stay in that place – of deep abiding, so that I can clearly hear Him and follow His lead.

Once He has completed the necessary heart work for this assignment, the Holy Spirit may call me to any number of next steps, such as these:

- To forgive someone even if they are not repentant.
- To repent of judging them.
- To spend time with them, develop a friendship.
- To meet them where they are.
- To give concrete help with compassion.
- To confess my sin in the situation to them and ask for their forgiveness.

If my heart is right with Him, as I extend reconciliation to this person, they are more likely to receive what I offer, and the relationship is more likely to reach healing.

There are times when I wish there wasn't so much work involved. I think I would prefer God to just do it all Himself, and allow me to sit back and watch. But it seems that He prefers not to do it all by Himself. It seems He wants to involve me.

When He does give me a part and invite me to co-labor with Him, I find these times to be vastly more challenging, clearly more humbling, yet definitely more breath-taking – thrilling and fulfilling and surprising and honoring – and I would never want to miss those opportunities. If we abide in Him, cooperate with Him, partner with Him, then the result will be Christ-honoring fruit. And realize that if He sends us into a season of fruit-bearing, we are to never leave our place of abiding, or the fruit will dry up.

"Apart From Me You Can Do Nothing"

"Abide in Me, and I in you. As the branch cannot bear fruit of itself unless it abides in the vine, so neither can you unless you abide in Me. I am the vine, you are the branches; he who abides in Me and

I in him, he bears much fruit, for apart from Me you can do nothing."

John 15:4-5

Abiding is not fruit-bearing. Fruit-bearing is the *result* of abiding, but it is important that we do not confuse the two.

Abiding is all about *relationship*. Abiding is when we are no longer seeking Him for Kingdom work assignments or for answers to our problems, but when we are seeking Him *for Him*. Abiding is intimacy, that deep *koinonia* when we share our heart with Him, and He shares His heart with us. Abiding is a branch deeply connected to, and completely dependent upon, the Vine, focusing on developing our relationship with Him and spending time with Him to nurture that connection.

Abiding is obedience and submission. A branch so connected to the Vine that it is indeed part of it. A branch whose will is so submitted to the Vine's as to have no independent desires. A branch that is not on its own agenda, but so identified with the Vine that one cannot tell when the Vine ends and the branch begins.

"If anyone loves me, he will obey my teaching. My Father will love him, and we will come to him and make our home with him."

John 14:23 NIV

Abiding is such deep connection to God that the Father, the Son, and the Holy Spirit are so welcomed in our hearts, which is their home. Abiding is willingly submitting to the Vinedresser's work in our lives, trusting to His wise and gentle hands. Abiding is such deep connection to the Vine that the sap, His Spirit, pours into us and through us. Abiding is knowing Him so deeply that we accept His perfect will for our lives without question or struggle.

No fruit bearing will be possible unless we are abiding. None. **Nothing.** We may think that we are accomplishing so much for the Kingdom, bearing so much fruit, but if we are not intimately and securely attached to Him, what we will be bringing forth will only be the result of human effort and will be burned up in the judgment (1Cor 3:10-15).

Unless the LORD builds the house,
They labor in vain who build it;
Unless the LORD guards the city,
The watchman keeps awake in vain.

Psalm 127:1

It is imperative that we maintain our tenacious connection to the Vine. Jesus says it succinctly, **"Apart from Me you can do *nothing.*"**

Transformed From Glory to Glory

God seems to work in us in seasons. Seasons of repentance, seasons of trials, seasons of healing, seasons of ministry. God seems to take me through a season of preparation, repentance and healing, prior to a season of intense ministry. Often there is overlap, but it seems when the Lord is calling me to a deep season of repentance and healing, ministry is scaled back some.

But I think that sanctification never really has a "season." It seems to me that it is a constant on-going process. His *methods* of sanctification may have seasons. At times the season may be a deep Bible study or a recovery or healing class. But during times of ministry, sanctification is not really scaled back, but changed. Instead of conviction simply through times alone with Him in the Word and listening, the Holy Spirit may also choose to expose my heart when I am out on the frontlines.

The *areas* of our sanctification may have seasons also. At times I find the Holy Spirit chipping away at the stronghold of pride, in another season the stronghold of fear, and in another season distrust or control – and then revisiting each of these strongholds repeatedly as He continues his work at deeper levels.

Recognizing the time element involved in uprooting, planting, growing, and bearing fruit, realize that God's work of sanctification is mostly slow and gradual, root by root, layer by layer. Paul describes it this way:

But we all, with unveiled face, beholding as in a mirror the glory of the Lord, are being transformed into the same image from glory to glory, just as from the Lord, the Spirit.

2 Corinthians 3:18

The Holy Spirit is transforming us from glory to glory. Each step in the sanctification process enables us to reflect Him in greater measure and bring Him greater glory. Take heart! Do not be discouraged! This is a journey overflowing with hope!

May God himself, the God of peace, sanctify you through and through. May your whole spirit, soul and body be kept blameless at the coming of our Lord Jesus Christ. The one who calls you is faithful and he will do it.

1 Thessalonians 5:23-24 NIV

How blessed are we to have been *chosen* to be brought near to Him! He reassures us that He is faithful, and **He will do it**. I like the Amplified Version of this verse:

Faithful is He Who is calling you [to Himself] and utterly trustworthy, and He will also do it [fulfill His call by hallowing and keeping you].

1 Thessalonians 5:24 AMP

At the beginning of our journey together, I invited you into a season of spending time with the Genuine – quality time in great quantity with the Genuine. A time to grow in intimacy as we learned stillness, an opportunity to reach deeper abiding as we came to more complete surrenders, and a chance to come to know Him more profoundly as we invited Him to expose our hearts and sanctify us. My prayer for you is that you are walking out in triumph of surrender. That you now recognize – from personal experience – that when you surrender more deeply, His Holy Spirit fills you more and flows to you and in you and through you and from you in greater and unhindered abundance – and that indeed is triumph.

I pray that what you have implemented in this season will become a lifestyle. That this journey of intimacy through stillness, surrender, and sanctification will not end here, but will continue as a lifetime walk of abiding.

Lisa Carr's lyrics in her *Saucer Song* proclaim, "I'm drinking from my saucer because my cup is running over."[9] My prayer for you is that as you have richly encountered the Genuine and received more of Him, you are indeed drinking from your saucer – and you would never want it any other way.

And, most importantly, I trust that as you have immersed in Him and chased after Him with all your heart, that you have discovered that He has *always* been chasing after you with all of His.

Questions Chapter 9: From Roots to Fruit

Memory Verse:

How blessed is the one
Whom You choose and bring near to You
To dwell in Your courts.

Psalm 65:4

1) Which soil are you and why?

• Dirt beside the road: Satan steals away the Word implanted in you.

• Rocky ground: You have no strong foundation to build on and no place for roots to take hold.

• Thorns: When you do read the Word, worldliness or busyness chokes it out before it can take root.

• Good soil: You receive the Word implanted with humility.

What will you do to bear fruit, **thirty, sixty, one hundred fold?**

2) Let's work on identifying bad fruit, and tracing it back to its bad roots. Consider these possibilities:

Bad Fruit   **Possible Bad Root**

Lying . . . . Pride, Fear of Rejection
Worry, anxiety, fear . . . . Distrust of God, Self-Reliance
Anger . . . . Unforgiveness, Shame
Depression . . . . .Fear of Failure, Perfectionism
Inflexibility . . . . Control, Idolatry of My Own Plan

Realize that these are just suggestions. There are many other bad roots that can be leading to the bad fruit, and often multiple roots contributing. For example, roots of lying could also be rebellion against being controlled, idolatry of reputation, fear of being shamed, fear of failure, or many other roots.

Now let's make it personal. Ask the Holy Spirit to identify a bad fruit in your life. Then earnestly seek Him, courageously asking Him to reveal the roots that are responsible for the fruit. Then ask Him for His action plan to begin the uprooting.

3) Read the difference between disciplining and pruning in the section *Are Pruning and Disciplining the Same?* Are you in a time of trial? Ask the Holy Spirit to reveal if perhaps He is disciplining you, or perhaps pruning you. (If you are not in a time of trial now, think about a time of trial in your past, and ask the Holy Spirit for revelation regarding disciplining or pruning.)

4) Define abiding in your own words. Give it a deep, rich explanation. Then go back in your journal to the questions of Chapter 1 where you first answered this question. Compare your answers to see what the Holy Spirit has taught you through this study.

His Deep has called to yours ...
and you have responded
by completing this daring study,
entering into a walk of treasured abiding.
I pray that you have come to realize
how the woman on the cover
represents each one of us,
sitting at His feet in the deepest intimacy.

Appendix 1
Soaking in His Love

I asked some of my friends, "How do you know how much God loves you?" I have printed their answers below. I encourage you to make these truths your own. Rip these pages out of this book, take one verse each week and meditate on it, memorize it, and turn it into a prayer. Ask the Holy Spirit to give you deeper revelation about each verse and to implant His Words into your heart.

"Behold, I have inscribed you on the palms of My hands."
Isaiah 49:16

For you have not received a spirit of slavery leading to fear again, but you have received a spirit of adoption as sons by which we cry out, "Abba! Father!"
Romans 8:15

The LORD is my rock and my fortress and my deliverer, my God, my rock, in whom I take refuge; my shield and the horn of my salvation, my stronghold.
Psalm 18:2

"My sheep hear My voice, and I know them, and they follow Me; and I give eternal life to them, and they will never perish; and no one will snatch them out of My hand."
John 10:27-28

If God is for us, who can be against us?
Romans 8:32 NIV

The LORD's lovingkindnesses indeed never cease, For His compassions never fail. They are new every morning; Great is Your faithfulness.
Lamentations 3:22-23

Now to Him who is able to keep you from stumbling, and to make you stand in the presence of His glory blameless with great joy.
Jude 1:24

"Have I not commanded you? Be strong and courageous! Do not tremble or be dismayed, for the LORD your God is with you wherever you go."

Joshua 1:9

The LORD your God is with you, he is mighty to save.
He will take great delight in you,
He will quiet you with his love,
He will rejoice over you with singing.

Zephaniah 3:17 NIV

Now He who establishes us with you in Christ and anointed us is God, who also sealed us and gave us the Spirit in our hearts as a pledge.

2 Corinthians 1:21-22

"Greater love has no one than this, that one lay down his life for his friends."   John 15:13

You are altogether beautiful, my love; there is no flaw in you.   Song of Songs 4:7 ESV

"For I know the plans I have for you," declares the LORD, "plans to prosper you and not to harm you, plans to give you hope and a future. Then you will call upon me and come and pray to me, and I will listen to you. You will seek me and find me when you seek me with all your heart."   Jeremiah 33:11-13 NIV

To Him who loves us and released us from our sins by His blood.   Revelation 1:5

But those who hope in the LORD
Will renew their strength.
They will soar on wings like eagles;
They will run and not grow weary,
They will walk and not be faint.   Isaiah 40:31 NIV

I can do all things through Christ who strengthens me.   Philippians 4:13 NKJV

Where can I go from Your Spirit?
Or where can I flee from Your presence?   Psalm 139:7

We wait in hope for the LORD;
He is our help and our shield.
In him our hearts rejoice,
For we trust in his holy name.
May your unfailing love rest upon us, O LORD,
Even as we put our hope in you.   Psalm 33:20-22 NIV

He will cover you with his feathers,
And under his wings you will find refuge;
His faithfulness will be your shield and rampart.
                                        Psalm 91:4 NIV

Who will separate us from the love of Christ ? Will
tribulation, or distress, or persecution, or famine,
or nakedness, or peril, or sword? ... But in all these
things we overwhelmingly conquer through Him
who loved us.   Romans 8:35, 37

"Do not call to mind the former things,
Or ponder things of the past.
Behold, I will do something new,
Now it will spring forth;
Will you not be aware of it?
I will even make a roadway in the wilderness,
Rivers in the desert."   Isaiah 43:18-19

"No longer do I call you slaves, for the slave does not
know what his master is doing; but I have called you
friends."   John 15:15

"See, I lay a stone in Zion, a chosen and precious
cornerstone, and the one who trusts in him will
never be put to shame."   1 Peter 2:6

The LORD is my light and my salvation; whom shall I
fear? The LORD is the defense of my life; whom shall
I dread?   Psalm 27:1

But God demonstrates His own love toward us, in
that while we were yet sinners, Christ died for us.

Romans 5:8

You are my hiding place;
You preserve me from trouble;
You surround me with songs of deliverance.

Psalm 32:7

For Christ's love compels us ... 2 Corinthians 5:14 NIV

In the same way the Spirit also helps our weakness;
for we do not know how to pray as we should, but
the Spirit Himself intercedes for us with groanings
too deep for words.   Romans 8:26

"Let the beloved of the LORD rest secure in him,
 For he shields him all day long,
And the one the LORD loves
Rests between his shoulders." Deuteronomy 33:12 NIV

"Do not fear, for I am with you;
Do not anxiously look about you, for I am your God.
I will strengthen you, surely I will help you,
Surely I will uphold you
With My righteous right hand."   Isaiah 41:10

"I will not leave you as orphans ..."   John 14:18

Having also believed, you were sealed in Him with
the Holy Spirit of promise ...   Ephesians 1:13

He trains my hands for battle,
So that my arms can bend a bow of bronze.

Psalm 18:34

But you are a chosen people, a royal priesthood,
a holy nation, a people belonging to God, that you
may declare the praises of him who called you out
of darkness into his wonderful light. 1 Peter 2:9 NIV

He tends his flock like a shepherd; He gathers the lambs in his arms and carries them close to his heart; He gently leads those that have young.

Isaiah 40:11

My soul, wait in silence for God only,
For my hope is from Him.
He only is my rock and my salvation,
My stronghold; I shall not be shaken.   Psalm 62:5-6

But you will receive power when the Holy Spirit comes on you.   Acts 1:8

Faithful is He Who is calling you [to Himself] and utterly trustworthy, and He will also do it [fulfill His call by hallowing and keeping you].

1 Thessalonians 5:24 AMP

"You did not choose Me but I chose you, and appointed you that you would go and bear fruit, and that your fruit would remain."   John 15:16

When he falls, he will not be hurled headlong,
Because the LORD is the One who holds his hand.

Psalm 37:24

Who is the man who fears the LORD?
He will instruct him in the way he should choose.

Psalm 25:12

As far as the east is from the west,
So far has He removed our transgressions from us.

Psalm 103:12

For I am convinced that neither death, nor life, nor angels, nor principalities, nor things present, nor things to come, nor powers, nor height, nor depth, nor any other created thing, will be able to separate us from the love of God, which is in Christ Jesus our Lord.   Romans 8:38-39

Appendix 2
Glossary of Greek and Hebrew Words

This glossary includes the Hebrew and Greek words used throughout *Triumph of Surrender*. The references for these words are in the *Endnotes*. All words are Greek unless otherwise indicated.

Adonai – (Hebrew) Name of God; Sovereign Lord, Master, Matchless Controller, possessing supreme authority, unlimited power.

agape – God's free, unconditional love, giving us what He knows is best for us, not necessarily what we desire or deserve.

agathos – good; useful and profitable; blessings that are what we need, not necessarily what we want.

akatastasia – instability, being off-balance.

diaphero – something that makes a difference, something that matters, something that is of more value.

haptomai – to connect, to bind, to exert a modifying influence, to touch for the purpose of manipulating, to lay hold of or get a grip on.

kardia – heart; seat of desires, feelings, affections, passions, impulses. The sphere of God's influence in the human life.

koinonia – fellowship; a passionate connection because two people can relate or have shared intense experiences.

mammonas – Babylonia god of materialism. Personification of riches. Root is confidence.

mastigoo – derived from word meaning a whip, a scourge.

paideia — discipline. Root is child. Originally meant instruction of children, but evolved to mean chastening because all effective instruction for children includes and implies chastening.

pikros – derives from word meaning the fruits of the wild vine or bitter gourd which are so excessively bitter and acrid as to be a kind of poison.

prautes – full and complete surrender. We accept God's dealings with us as good and do not dispute or resist, considering them as good in that they enhance the closeness of our relationship with Him.

orge – anger as a state of mind.

Qanna – (Hebrew) name of God meaning Jealous; this name means that He demands our exclusive devotion – for our good, not for His.

thumos – to move impetuously, particularly as the air or wind; a violent motion or passion of the mind.

Appendix 3
Resources

While I am not in a position to endorse or vouch for these resources, I do believe you may find them helpful.

Bibles

Maxwell, John C., *The Maxwell Leadership Bible: Lessons in Leadership from the Word of God, New International Version.* Nashville, TN: Thomas Nelson, Inc., 2007.

New Believer's Bible, New Living Translation. Carol Stream, IL: Tyndale House Publishers, 2007.

Women of Faith Study Bible, New International Version. Grand Rapids, MI: Zondervan, 2001.

Devotionals

Chambers, Oswald. *My Utmost for His Highest.* Grand Rapids, MI: Discovery House Publishers, 1992.

McCarthy, Kimberly. *The Bridegroom's Voice.* Arlington, TX: Touch Publishing, 2015.

Roberts, Frances. *Come Away My Beloved.* Ulrichsville, OH: Barbour Publishing, 2002.

Shepherd, Sheri Rose. *His Princess: Love Letters from Your King.* Colorado Springs, CO: Multinomah Books, 2004.

Young, Sarah. *Jesus Calling: Enjoying Peace in His Presence.* Nashville, TN: Thomas Nelson, Inc, 2004.

Foundations of Faith

Holladay, Tom and Warren, Kay. *Foundations: A Purpose-Driven Discipleship Resource.* Grand Rapids, MI: Zondervan, 2003.

Strobel, Lee. *The Case for Christ: A Journalist's Personal Investigation of the Evidence for Jesus.* Grand Rapids, MI: Zondervan, 1998.

Forgiveness

Cassatly, Stephanie. *Notice of Release* (not yet in print).

Hansen, Brant. *Unoffendable: How Just One Change Can Make All of Life Better.* Nashville, TN: W Publishing Group, 2015.

Herbst, Dominic. *Restoring Relationships Journal.* Lewisburg, PA: Bethesda Family Services Foundation, 2012.

Kendall, Jackie, *Free Yourself to Love,* NY, NY: FaithWords, 2009.

Kubetin, Cynthia and Mallory, James. *Shelter From the Storm: Hope for Survivors of Sexual Abuse.* Titusville, FL: Robert S. McGee Publishing, 1995.

Sande, Ken. *Resolving Everyday Conflict,* Grand Rapids, MI: Baker Books, 2011.

Greek and Hebrew Word Study Tools

Baker, Warren and Carpenter, Eugene. *The Complete Word Study Dictionary Old Testament.* Chattanooga,TN:AMG Publishers, 2003.

Strong, James. *The New Strong's Exhaustive Concordance of the Bible, Concise Dictionary of the Words in the Hebrew Bible, and in the Greek Testament.* Nashville, TN: Thomas Nelson Publishers, 1995.

Zodhiates, Spiros. *The Complete Word Study Dictionary, New Testament.* Chattanooga, TN: AMG Publishers, 1992.

Growing in Christ

Christ Fellowship Church: Gochristfellowship.com

Blackaby, Henry T. and King, Claude V. *Experiencing God: How to Live the Full Adventure of Knowing and Doing the Will of God.* Nashville, TN: Broadman & Holman Publishers, 1994.

Cloud, Dr. Henry and Townsend, Dr. John. *Boundaries: When to Say Yes, When to Say No, To Take Control of Your Life.* Grand Rapids, MI: Zondervan, 1992.

Groeschel, Craig. *Altar Ego: Becoming Who God Says You Are.* Grand Rapids, MI: Zondervan, 2013.

Maxwell, John C. *Failing Forward: Turning Mistakes into Stepping Stones for Success.* Nashville, TN: Thomas Nelson, Inc, 2000.

Maxwell, John C. *Wisdom from Women in the Bible, Giants of the Faith Speak Into Our Lives.* New York, NY: FaithWords, 2015.

Nee, Watchman. *Spiritual Authority.* New York: Christian Fellowship Publishers, Inc., 1972.

Intimacy With Jesus

Arthur, Kay. *Lord, I Want to Know You.* Colorado Springs, CO: Waterbrook Press, 2000.

Eldredge, John and Stasi. *Captivating: Unveiling the Mystery of a Woman's Soul.* Nashville, TN: Thomas Nelson, 2005.

Frost, Jack. *Experiencing the Father's Embrace.* Shippensburg, PA: Destiny Image Publishers, Inc., 2002.

Herman, Nicholas (Brother Lawrence). *Practice the Presence of*

God: The Best Rule of a Holy Life.   Fleming H. Revell Company, New York and London, 1895. Mansfield Center, CT: Martino Publishing, 2010.

Keller, Phillip. *A Shepherd Looks at Psalm 23.* Grand Rapids, MI: Zondervan, 1970.

McClung, Floyd. *The Father Heart of God.* Eugene, OR: Harvest House Publishers, 1971.

Murray, Andrew. *The Secret of God's Presence.* New Kensington, PA: Whitaker House, 1982.

Tozer, A.W. *The Knowledge of the Holy.* New York, NY: HarperCollins Publishers Inc., 1961.

Wilkinson, Bruce. *Secrets of the Vine, Breaking Through to Abundance.* Sisters, OR: Multnomah Publishers, Inc, 2001.

Prayer

Chambers, Oswald. *Prayer: A Holy Occupation.* Grand Rapids, MI: Discovery House Publishers, 1992.

Grubb, Norman. *Rees Howells, Intercessor: The Story of a Life Lived for God.* Fort Washington, PA: CLC Publications, 1952.

Maxwell, John C. *Partners in Prayer: Support and Strengthen Your Pastor and Church Leaders.* Nashville, TN: Thomas Nelson, Inc., 1996.

Omartian, Stormie. *The Power of a Praying Wife.* Eugene, OR: Harvest House Publishers, 1997.

Sheets, Dutch. *Intercessory Prayer: How God Can Use Your Prayers to Move Heaven and Earth.* Minneapolis, MN: Bethany House, 1996.

Scripture Memorization

Navigator's Scripture Memory Course, Topical Memory System. Colorado Springs, CO: Navpress, 2006.

Spiritual Warfare

Frangipane, Francis. *The Three Battlegrounds.* Cedar Rapids, IA: Arrow Publications, 1989.

Kylstra, Chester and Betsy. *Restoring the Foundations.* Hendersonville, NC, Restoring the Foundations Publications, 2001.

Shirer, Priscilla. *The Armor of God.* Nashville, TN: Lifeway Press, 2015.

Endnotes

Introduction: "Deep Calls to Deep"
[1] Francis Frangipane, *Holiness, Truth and the Presence of God,* Cedar Rapids, Iowa, Arrow Publications, 1999, pp 58-59.

Chapter 1: "My Sheep Hear My Voice"
[1] St. Augustine, *Confessions, A new translation by Henry Chadwick,* New York, Oxford University Press, Inc., 1991, p 3.

[2] Phillip Keller, *A Shepherd Looks at the Good Shepherd and His Sheep,* Grand Rapids, MI, Zondervan, 1978, pp 39-40,43-44. An amazing video of sheep responding only to their shepherd's voice can be found at www.youtube.com/watch?v=e45dVgWgV64, on 6/17/16.

[3] Keller, p 46-47.

[4] Susie Larson, *Your Beautiful Purpose, Discovering and Enjoying What God Can Do Through You,* Bloomington, MN, Bethany House Publishers, 2013, p 45.

[5] Sarah Young, *Jesus Calling,* Nashville,TN, Thomas Nelson, 2004, p x.

[6] Dr. Greg Smalley and Dr. Shawn Stoever, *The Wholehearted Marriage, Fully Engaging Your Most Important Relationship*, New York, NY, Howard Books, 2009, pp 157-159, from www.almenconi.com.

[7] www.merriam-webster.com/dictionary/burnout, on 6/17/16.

[8] www.ncbi.nlm.nih.gov/pubmedhealth/PMH0072470/, on 6/17/16.

[9] http://www.merriam-webster.com/dictionary/burnout, on 6/17/16.

[10] I probably read this from one of the books listed in the Resources, but I cannot locate the exact reference at this time.

[11] Spiros Zodhiates, *The Complete Word Study Dictionary, New Testament*, Chattanooga, TN, AMG Publishers, 1992, p 445 (no. 1308 *diaphero* = excellent).

[12] James Strong, *The New Strong's Exhaustive Concordance of the Bible, Concise Dictionary of the Words in the Greek Testament*, Nashville, TN, Thomas Nelson Publishers, 1995, p 23 (no. 1308 *diaphero* = excellent).

Chapter 2: Heaven Touches Earth
[1] *Our Daily Bread*, odb.org on 10/22/15.

[2] The Navigators, *The Spirit-Filled Follower of Jesus, Design for Discipleship 2*, Colorado Springs, CO, NavPress, 2006, p17.

[3] Joni Eareckson Tada, *When God Weeps: Why Our Sufferings Matter to the Almighty,* Grand Rapids, MI, Zondervan, 1997, pp 174-175.

[4] Strong, p 4 (no. 181 *akatastasia* = confusion, instability).

[5] John C. Maxwell, *Wisdom from Women in the Bible, Giants of the Faith Speak Into Our Lives,* New York, NY, FaithWords, 2015, pp 124, 125, 127.

[6] Zodhiates, p 1400 (no. 5182 troubled).

[7] Zodhiates, p 62 (no. 18 *agathos*). This is my extrapolation.

[8] Clint Brown, *Secret Place.* From the CD *Alone,* 2003 Tribe Records, Inc., Orlando, Florida. Lyrics from CD insert.

Chapter 3 Toppling Barriers to Intimacy

[1] Zodhiates, p 245 (no. 680 *haptomai* = harm).

[2] Chester and Betsy Kylstra, *Restoring the Foundations*, Hendersonville, NC, Restoring the Foundations Publications, 2001, p 95. Although the wording is my own, this concept of God forgiving our sins for His own sake first struck me when I read Betsy Kylstra expound on it in this book.

[3] Pastor Drew McClure, Grace Midtown Church, Atlanta, Georgia, December 6, 2015. http://gfc.tv/midtown/teachings on 12/21/15.

[4] Tenth Avenue North, *You Are More.* Released May 11, 2010, *The Light Meets the Dark,* Reunion Records. Lyrics from www.azlyrics.com on 12/6/15.

[5] Smalley, p 175.

[6] Julie Woodley, *Into My Arms,* Setauket, New York, Restoring the Heart Ministries, Inc., 2011, pp 37, 14, 25.

[7] Woodley, p 115.

[8] Adapted from Cynthia Kubetin and James Mallory, M.D., *Shelter From the Storm,* Titusville, FL, Robert S. McGee Publishing, 1995, 2004, p 168.

Chapter 4 Surrendering to His Sovereignty

[1] www.inspire21.com/stories/faithstories/CharlesBlondin on 9/21/15.

[2] www.ncbi.nlm.nih.gov/pmc/articles/PMC2810702/ on 10/26/15.

[3] John C. Maxwell, *Failing Forward: Turning Mistakes into Stepping Stones for Success,* Nashville, TN, Thomas Nelson, Inc, 2000, p 14.

[4] Francis Frangipane, *The Three Battlegrounds,* Cedar Rapids, IA, Arrow Publications, 1989, p 27.

Chapter 5 Demolishing the Idols That Obstruct Our Fellowship

[1] Quoted from Pastor Todd Mullins on 1/24/15 during his series *Contender* given to Christ Fellowship Church.

[2] Warren Baker, D.R.E. and Eugene Carpenter, Ph.D., *The Complete Word Study Dictionary Old Testament,* Chattanooga, TN, AMG Publishers, 2003, p 1000 (no. 7067 *Qanna* = jealous).

[3] Zodhiates, p 941 (no. 3126 *mammonas*).

[4] Strong, Greek, p 55 (no. 3126 *mammonas*).

[5] Baker, p 859 (no. 6090 hurtful).

[6] Baker, p 7668 (no. 7665 crushed).

[7] Zodhiates, p 873 (no. 2842 *koinonia* = fellowship).   The rest of the paragraph is my extrapolation.

[8] Young, p 108. She writes, ". . . allow My life to merge with yours." I have also read somewhere about our spirits melding with His Spirit, but I cannot locate the reference. It is probably from one of the books in the Bibliography. The rest of this paragraph leaps from those two thoughts.

Chapter 6 To Forgive As Jesus Forgives

Although the words and extrapolation are my own, the concepts in this chapter have been gleaned from the following authors:

• Ken Sande, founder of Peacemaker Ministries, authored *The Peacemaker* and *Resolving Everyday Conflict,* as well as many video series and training resources used internationally. *Resolving Everyday Conflict,* Baker Books, Grand Rapids, MI, 2011, Chapter 7, "Go and Be Reconciled: Giving Forgiveness and Arriving at a Reasonable Solution" (Grand Rapids, MI, 2011).

• Chester and Betsy Kylstra, "pioneers in inner healing," have penned a compelling chapter on forgiveness in their book, *Restoring the Foundations.*   Their ministry, *Restoring the Foundations,* brings healing and freedom to church members around the world. *Restoring the Foundations,* Chapter VI, "Forgiveness, the Key to Freedom," and Chapter XIV, "Shame-Fear-Control Stronghold" (Hendersonville, NC, 2001).

• Cynthia Kubetin is a survivor of childhood sexual abuse. She, along with James Mallory, M.D., has compiled a powerful workbook on healing from the trauma of abuse, entitled *Shelter from the Storm.* Unit 6, "Letting Go of Shame and Guilt," and Unit 10, "The Process of Forgiveness" (Titusville, FL, 1995).

• Glenda Watson has endured much personal tragedy. An author, songwriter, and live radio host she founded *Restoration Ministries* and wrote a booklet *Restoring Dignity* which captures the depth of the forgiveness process (Augusta, GA, 2002).

• Jackie Kendall, a survivor of childhood sexual abuse, is a renowned author and speaker on the topic of forgiveness. Her book that I draw from for this chapter is *Free Yourself to Love,* Chapter 4, "Held Hostage by the Size of the Offense," Chapter 5, "Held Hostage by Assaulting Memories," Chapter 7, "Held Hostage by Revenge Fantasies," and Chapter 11, "Forgiveness Tool of Growing in Faith" (New York, NY, 2009).

I highly recommend these texts for those seeking to reach full forgiveness and healing. If anyone has a right to weigh in on the topic of forgiveness, Cynthia Kubetin and Jackie Kendall, survivors of childhood sexual abuse, certainly do.

[1] Jackie Kendall, *Free Yourself to Love,* New York, NY, FaithWords, 2009, p 123.

[2] Zodhiates, p 299 (no. 863 forgive).

[3] Ken Sande, *Resolving Everyday Conflict,* Grand Rapids, MI, Baker Books, 2011, pp 88 and 94

[4] Chester and Betsy Kylstra, *Restoring the Foundations,* Hendersonville, NC, Restoring The Foundations Publications, 2001, p 85.

[5] Cynthia Kubetin and James Mallory, M.D., *Shelter From the Storm,* Titusville, FL, Robert S. McGee Publishing, 1995, p 170.

[6] Kubetin, p 163.

[7] Sande, pp 89-90.

[8] Kendall, p 81. Although all these authors expound on the importance of repeated forgiveness and release as integral to healing, the "490 Principle" is unique to Kendall.

[9] This sentence was probably adapted from one of these authors; I cannot locate the exact reference.

[10] Kylstra, p 88. Kubetin and Kendall also address accountability in their books.

[11] C.S. Lewis, *The Screwtape Letters,* New York, NY, HarperCollins Publishers, 1996, p 17. This concept derives from C.S. Lewis, who points out that we can't "manufacture charitable feelings." I believe forgiveness is one of those charitable feelings we can't "manufacture."

[12] Kendall, pp 70, 208-209. Additionally, all of these authors discuss the lengthy process of forgiveness and the requirement of a deep relationship with the Lord to complete this process.

[13] The phrasing of this sentence is probably adapted from one of these authors; I cannot locate the exact reference.

[14] Glenda Watson. I have heard this quote in her lectures and DVD's. Detailed teaching on forgiveness is contained in her booklet, *Restoring Dignity*, Augusta, GA, Restoration Ministries Intl, 2002.

[15] Woodley, p 103.

[16] Kylstra, p 96. While all of these authors discuss forgiving self, the Kylstra's comments seem most clear.

[17] Sometimes even non-Christian writings can give an astute and discerning reader a glimpse into the deep truths of God. Kahlil Gibran, *On Giving*, http://www.katsandogz.com/ongiving.html, on 4/19/16.

Chapter 7 The Life of the Heart

[1] Dominic Herbst, *Restoring Relationships Journal,* Lewisburg, PA, Bethesda Family Services Foundation, 2012, p 68. Some of the concepts in this section draw from this book and Herbst's *Restoring Relationships DVD Series*. Except where noted, the wording is my own.

[2] Herbst, p 68.

[3] Zodhiates, p 1055 (no. 3709 *orge* = anger). I first learned about *orge* and *thumos* listening to Dominic Herbst's *Restoring Relationships DVD Series*.

[4] Zodhiates, p 1055 (no. 3709, *orge* contrasted to *thumos*).

[5] Zodhiates, p 744 (no.2372 and 2366 *thumos* = wrath, tempest)

[6] Brant Hansen, *Unoffendable: How Just One Change Can Make All of Life Better,* Nashville, TN, W Publishing Group, 2015, pp 5, 21, 99. Brandt Hansen brings up Colossians 3:8 in his book. The ideas about loving and forgiving instead of getting angry permeate his book.

[7] Zodhiates, pp 819-820 (no. 2588 *kardia* = heart).

[8] Zodhiates, pp 849-850 (no. 2720 direct).

[9] Zodhiates, p 520 (no. 1515 peace without righteousness).

Chapter 8 A Walk of Repentance

[1] Baker, p 980 (no. 6942 holy).

[2] Zodhiates, p 70 (no. 40 holy).

[3] Zodhiates, p 70 (no. 40 holy).

[4] Zodhiates, p 69 (37 holy).

[5] Zodhiates, p 969 (no. 3340 repent).

[6] Zodhiates, p 970 (no. 3340 repent).

[7] Zodhiates, p 970 (no. 3340 repent).

[8] Zodhiates, p 1253 (no. 4434 poor).

[9] Zodhiates, pp 1208-1209 (no. 4236, 4239, 4240 *prautes* and derivatives).

[10] Zodhiates, p 849 (no. 2716 work out).

[11] Zodhiates, p 589 (no. 1754 work in).

[12] Zodhiates, p 1046 (no. 3671 confess).

[13] Zodhiates, p 1088 (no. 3809 *paideia* = discipline).

[14] *Merriam-Webster's Collegiate Dictionary,* 11th Edition, USA, Merriam-Webster Inc, 2003, p 209 (chasten).

[15] Zodhiates, p 1088 (no. 3809 paideia vs. punitive retribution).

[16] Zodhiates, p 948 (nos. 3146, 3147 *mastigoo* = scourges).

[17] Watchman Nee, *Spiritual Authority*, New York, Christian Fellowship Publishers, Inc., 1972, p 77.

Chapter 9 Roots to Fruit

[1] Zodhiates p 63 (no. 19 *agathos* = goodness). This is my summary of this definition.

[2] Zodhiates p 1158 (no. 4089 *pikros* = bitter).

[3] www.merriam-webster.com/dictionary/prune on 10/8/15.

[4] www.biblestudytools.com/classics/murray-mystery-true-vine/the-pruning-knife.html on 7/3/16.

[5] Bruce Wilkinson, *Secrets of the Vine, Breaking Through to Abundance,* Sisters, OR, Multnomah Publishers, Inc, 2001, pp 79-80.

[6] Wilkinson, p 59.

[7] Wilkinson, p 61.

[8] Wilkinson, p 71.

[9] africareads.wordpress.com/2010/05/31/oh-im-drinking-from-my-saucer, accessed 4/24/16. Lisa Carr is the cousin of one of my Triumph Servant Leaders, Betsy Burden. Lisa is a wonderful Godly woman who battled breast cancer, and went home to be with Jesus a few years ago.

With Heartfelt Gratitude I Thank ...

My beloved husband John and my precious children Alec and Jenna, thank you for being God's unconditional nonjudgmental love for me right here on earth. In you I have a treasure trove of riches. I am in awe of how the Lord once again assigned us work together as a family, and equipped each one of us uniquely for our role in bringing this book to fruition.

John, again your hands are all over this book, but in a slightly different way. From artwork to testimonies, from incisive editing to overall supervision, you have added the polish and brought this book to a whole different level. I could not have completed this without your love and encouragement.

Alec, I know that you sacrificed to fly in to photograph and produce this cover and to fine tune the layout. I know also that the battle being waged in the heavenly realms was not easy to face, but you persevered and stood strong in the Lord. You did not stop until the Lord released you, for indeed you were working for the Lord and not for men. I sense that the cover alone will touch many and draw them unto Him.

Jenna, I am so touched that you stopped here between New York City and Taipei to edit this book. I know of no one else who could have edited me from a literary standpoint with attention to content, flow, organization, grammar, and style – simultaneously with spiritual focus and perception. I will always treasure your sweet words of encouragement to me when you finished reading the book.

Pastors Todd and Julie Mullins, thank you for your prayers for my family and for all the families of Christ Fellowship. You lead your sheep with wisdom and compassion, you teach us the truths of His Word with creativity and fearlessness, and you provide us with a sanctuary and shelter from darkness. Julie, I am deeply honored by your insights, advice, and encouragement as your read through this book (on vacation!) and wrote the Foreword.

Pastor Tom and Donna Mullins, I am so grateful for your devotion to the Lord, for He worked through that devotion to birth Christ Fellowship Church, the place where I met Jesus and the place that I call home.

Pastor Rick Miller, you have pastored over *Triumph Over Suffering* for many years. Thank you for your compassion and encouragement for both leaders and participants, and for your wisdom and guidance during challenging circumstances and difficult decisions.

My team of mighty prayer warriors, Zully Bass, Donna Briley, Libby Hammond, Betty Johnson, Vanessa Khadij, Kathy Kino, Nina Mitzelfeld, Rosa Ortiz, Tammy Rosenthal, Kellie Sheirs, Nancy Smith, and many others who stand with me in prayer, you know that I have relied on your prayer covering for many years. Your prayers have worked to open my heart to His sanctification, have paved the way for this writing, have protected me throughout, and are right now working to prepare the hearts of those who will hold this book in their hands. We indeed know it is all God and only God, for unless the Lord builds the house, they labor in vain who build it.

My spiritual editors, Libby Hammond, Nina Mitzelfeld, Cathy Moesel, and Roxanne Nettles. Thank you for reading and re-reading, line by line, and having the courage to confront me with your questions and input. This was truly a labor of love. God has spoken through each one of you, and your prayers have enabled me to hear Him and to follow through on all He required of me. And a special thank you to Kimmy Wood for your meticulous checking of each Scripture verse.

The dazzling Wood Family, Loretta, Kristin, Daniel, and Kimmy: I will never forget the day that you arrived at my home for the cover of this book. From your deep prayers to your photogenic feet, from your humble hearts to your willingness to do *anything* necessary, you gave your all. I believe we all witnessed the Lord's Presence and work in a powerful way, and this cover simply glows with His anointing.

With deep gratitude to my precious friend *Donna Briley,* who has stood by me faithfully, prayed for me unceasingly, and worked together with me determinedly to complete the layout. You are a treasure, and I am delighted that the Lord has yoked us together in this season.

Joshua Rivaldo, the Holy Spirit brought you to this project as if on the wind, and moved you to your next assignment just as suddenly. Thank you for your intense focus as you and John teamed up to complete the illustrations. Your illustrations capture what I could not express in words.

A special thank you to *Cathy Moesel,* my mentor and cherished friend of many years. Your teaching, wisdom, guidance, encouragement, mentoring, intercession, and discernment have brought me to understand what abiding and intimacy really means. Thank you for the way that you hold me accountable without judging me, and for being available when I am in need.

Goldie Winn, Sharon Brewer, amd Elise Angiolillo, you have been the Lord's instruments as He has healed me and enabled me to forget the shame of my youth (Isa 54:4). Through the constant in-pouring of your love and encouragement, I was able to forgive myself in the Lord, and to receive His extravagant grace.

Richard Ekey, your utter Kingdom perspective is rare and inspiring, and your impact on the men is deep and eternal. If you had not founded and spearheaded the Men's Branch of *Triumph,* these books would be thwarted from reaching half of the population!

All my Triumph Servant Leaders, Linda Bloom, Betsy Burden, Priscilla Cotto, Carol Deal, Chuck and Mae Dettman, Richard Ekey, Libby Hammond, Bobbie Higby, Joan Hoffpauir, Gary McDaniel, Ed and Anneliese Rozelle, Kellie Sheirs, Nancy Smith, and Margaret Zempleni, and also my leaders-in-training Donna Briley, John and Phyllis Cintorino, Carlos Cotto, Tyshon Grimsley, Natasha Hunt, Nicolle Nie, Belinda Smith, and Juliet Wilson – as well as my many leaders over the past years – I thank my God in all my remembrance of you, always offering my prayers with joy because of our partnership in the Gospel. I pray that your eternal rewards in heaven will be rich and glorious beyond what you could ever ask or imagine.

To all who have contributed your testimonies, my readers have told me time and again how impacting your words are to them. Thank you for your transparency as you shared the depth of your hearts with others.

And to all my *Triumph alumni,* who have delved deeply into these studies, who have taken the teachings into their hearts and carried those teachings forward to places I could never reach, I have untold gratitude to all of you. Thank you for being His hands and feet.

And finally, *Mom and Dad,* although you were not directly part of bringing this book to print, thank you for laying the foundations of my faith, which paved the way for me to come to know the Lord. I know that through your fervent prayers for me I continue to draw closer to Him.

Contributors

Arica	214
Bobbie Higby	338
Cathy Moesel	36 and 178
Chuck Dettman	152
Cristina Williams	81
Gary McDaniel	20 and 316
Jade Yu	148
Jane "Goldie" Winn	40,42,43
John C.	153
John Li, M.D.	5, 96, 313
Libby Hammond	12 and 316
Maria	273
Mark and Diane	78
Michael Richter	44
Mike	88, 89, 336
Richard Ekey	245
Rosa Ortiz	165

Index: Detailed Table of Contents

Part I: Intimacy Through Stillness — 1

Chapter 1 "My Sheep Hear My Voice" — 3
Is His Deep Calling To Your Deep? — 5
Hearing Is Expected, But Not Automatic — 6
Discerning His Voice Is a Gift — 9
The Importance of Developing Discernment — 10
Training to Hear His Voice — 11
Basic Training — 12
    Become Steeped in Scriptures — 12
    Choose Your Church – and Your Companions – Wisely — 13
    Change Your Expectations — 13
    Quit Feeding Your Flesh — 14
Positioning Our Spirit Through Exposure — 15
Spending Quality Time in Great Quantity — 16
Satan's Attack on Our Relationship With God: Busyness — 18
Satan's Attack on Our Relationship With God: Burnout — 21

Chapter 2: Heaven Touches Earth — 27
Heaven Meets Earth in Corporate Worship — 28
Seeking Him in Our Time Alone With Him — 28
Thanking and Praising — 29
Meditating on God — 30
Appreciating His Creation — 31
Establishing a Secret Place of His Presence — 31
His Word — 33
Journaling — 34
Expectant Listening — 35
Stillness — 37
Music — 38
The Deep Spiritual Power of Music — 39
Our Own Music Can Usher Us Into the Holy of Holies — 43
Selecting Our Music to Enter His Presence — 46
Music's Potential to Draw Us To God — 48
Music's Potential to Lure Us Away From God — 49
Music's Potential to Drive Us Away From God — 50
Combining Avenues: Stillness in Solitude With Music — 51
Clearer Hearing: But I Want To Be Certain! — 53

Achieving Balance in Out Time With God   56
     Too Much Bible Dries Up   57
     Too Much Holy Spirit Puffs Up   57
     Perfect Balance Grows Up   58
Clarifying Balance   59
Achieving a Godly Balance Between Work and Rest   59
When Jesus Shows Up   62
"She Has Kept This for the Day of My Burial"   66

Chapter 3: Toppling Barriers to Intimacy   **71**
Question #1:
    If God is For Us, Why Does It Feel Like He's Against Me?   72
Why Doesn't God Shield Us From All the Works of the Devil?   75
The Evil One Cannot Touch Us   76
Question   #2:
    Does God Really Want To Spent Time With Me?   81
"I'm Not Valuable Enough For His Attention"   83
"Where are You?"   85
Being Pursued by God   88
How God Defines Himself   91
Why God Forgives Sins   93
Adopted by God   94
Question #3:
    If God Loves Me So Much, Why Can't I Feel That Love?   95
Trusting God's Unconditional Acceptance   101
Falling Into Satan's Identity Trap   103
A Heart of Stone   105
Soaking in His Love   105
Regaining My Identity   106
Truth #1: Who God Says We Are   107
God Gives Us Our Identity   110
Truth #2: The State of My Heart   112
Transparency Requires My Honesty About My Pain   113
Truth #3: Our Uniqueness   115
God Is Giving Us a Choice   117

Part II: Intimacy Through Surrender   **121**

Chapter 4: Surrendering To His Sovereignty   **123**
Walking Out Our Surrender   132

Adonai   133
God's Rule + His Perfect Love for Us + Our Free Will = ?   134
Defining God's Sovereignty   141
Our Response to God's Sovereignty   144
Stuck in the Agony   145
Only Grace Extricates Us From the Miry Clay   146
Surrender Requires Humility   147
Surrender Requires Trust   147
The Trap of Token Surrender   150
Deeper and Deeper Surrenders   153
Surrendering to His Plan   155
How Will You Respond to Adonai?   157
"I'll Go First."   158

Chapter 5: Demolishing Idols   **161**

His Name is Jealous   164
Identifying Mammon   166
Let's Pray   169
Idols Exposed   169
Where Is Our Trust?   171
What Do We Fear?   172
What's Constantly On Our Minds?   173
Can We Give It a Rest?   174
One More Litmus Test   175
Confusion Can Indicate Idolatry   177
Idolatry of Self   179
Idolatry Can Be a Very Insidious Sin   181
Temptation of Idolatry After Victory   181
God Hates Idolatry   183
Relying on God Instead of on Idols   185
The Challenge of Destroying Idols   187
Is Our Flesh the Enemy?   189
Koinonia   191
Hardening Our Hearts   194

Chapter 6: To Forgive as Jesus Forgives   **197**

Signs of an Unforgiving Heart   198
The Black Heart of Revenge   200
What Exactly Is Forgiveness?   201
The Process of Forgiveness   203

This Sounds Hard – Do We Really Need to Forgive?   204
Step 1: Honesty   207
Step 2: Repentance   208
Step 3: Release   209
A Debt That Can Never Be Repaid   211
Step 4: Transformation   212
Step 5: Healing   213
Positioning Ourselves to Receive the Spirit's Work   217
What Can Hinder the Forgiveness Process?   218
    Confusing Forgiveness With Trust   218
    Confusing Forgiveness With Reconciliation   219
    Confusing Forgiveness With Accountability   219
    Condemning Judgment   220
    Shame   220
    Anger With God   220
    Unrepentant Wrongdoers   221
What If We Cannot Even Choose to Forgive?   222
Layers and Layers of Forgiveness   223
How We Will Know That We Are Progressing?   227
Forgiveness of Self   229
"Jesus Plus"   231
Persistent Guilt   233
Entering the Battlefield Again and Again   235
Equipped To Be a Forgiver   237

Part III: Intimacy Through Sanctification   **239**

Chapter 7: The Life of the Heart   **241**
What Exactly Is "The Heart"?   241
Emotions Can Reveal the State of Our Heart   244
Encountering God Through Emotions   246
Emotional Turmoil Can Expose Our Heart   248
God Meets Us Where We Are Emotionally   250
Unwanted Emotions Can Drive Us Away From God – Or to Him   252
Developing Our Relationship With God Through Emotions   254
Avoid Getting Mired in Honest Emotions   259
Honest Emotions: The Next Level   262
Sanctification of Our Hearts   265
Submitting Our Hearts to God's Rule   266
How Is Your Heart Life?   269

Chapter 8: A Walk of Repentance   **277**

Isn't Repentance Just a One-Time Thing?   278
Satan Attempts To Pervert Repentance   283
Repentance Is a Gift   284
Jesus Explains Repentance   286
The Pure in Heart See God   288
Sanctification and Repentance Intertwined   289
Sanctification Is a Truth Walk   292
Rocks in Our Jars of Clay   294
The Rocks Are Our Sins   295
We Work Out ... He Works In   295
Satan's Goggles   298
"If We Say That We Have No Sin ..."   299
Coming Into the Light   301
Pebble Removal   304
Rock Removal   306
Boulder Removal   307
Discipline as an Opportunity for Boulder Removal   308
Viewing Trials as an Opportunity for Boulder Removal   312
A Sobering Word   314
The Difference Between Obedience and Submission   315
Chosen for Intimacy   318

Chapter 9: From Roots to Fruit   **321**

Becoming Good Soil   322
Dirt Beside the Road   323
Rocky Ground   324
Thorns   324
Good Soil   325
Uprooting Bad Roots   327
Co-laboring With Jesus in Uprooting   331
Bitter Roots   334
Growing Good Fruit   335
Pruning   337
Are Pruning and Discipline the Same?   339
A Life of Uprooting and Pruning   342
Abiding Leads to Fruit-Bearing   343
"Apart From Me You Can Do Nothing"   344
Transformed From Glory to Glory   346

About the Author

Celeste Li, M.D., is the author of *Triumph Over Suffering* and this sequel, *Triumph of Surrender*. Raised Catholic from childhood, Celeste surrendered her life to Jesus thirteen years ago, when she came to know Him at age 40. As she began to grow up in the Lord, chasing after Jesus with all her heart and surrendering to Him in deeper and deeper measure, she began to understand what intimacy and abiding really meant.

Celeste has been a member of Christ Fellowship Church since 2003, and is currently serving in her church's ministry for the suffering. She and John, her husband of 27 years, along with their twenty-something children Alec and Jenna, have partnered together to bring these *Triumph* books forth.

A graduate of Jefferson Medical College, Celeste's specialty is Family Practice. She worked in private practice for a few years, then in HIV and AIDS Clinic for the next twenty years. Currently, she is the Medical Director of First Care Women's Clinic, a Christian crisis pregnancy center.

Celeste's greatest passion is to guide people to experience the extravagant grace of the Father, to surrender to the passionate unconditional love of Jesus, and to learn to be led by the Holy Spirit as they mature in the Lord.

"I am the true vine, and My Father is the vinedresser ... he who abides in Me and I in him, he bears much fruit, for apart from Me you can do nothing ... My Father is glorified by this, that you bear much fruit, and so prove to be My disciples."

John 15:1,5,8